# EVERYMAN'S LIBRARY

## 546

### ORATORY

Everyman, I will go with thee, and be thy guide,
In thy most need to go by thy side

DEMOSTHENES, born in the deme of Paeania in Attica, 384 B.C. Entered public life 354 B.C. Sent as an ambassador. Took poison to avoid capture after Antipater's victory at Crannon, 322 B.C.

# DEMOSTHENES' ORATIONS

INTRODUCTION BY
JOHN WARRINGTON

LONDON J. M. DENT & SONS LTD
NEW YORK E. P. DUTTON & CO INC

# INTRODUCTION

## I

THE close of the Peloponnesian War (404 B.C.) left Sparta the predominant power in Greece. It was not until 371 that her armies were overthrown by the Theban Epaminondas at Leuctra. Thebes, however, was reluctant to impose her own hegemony; and the peace of 361, following Mantinea, declared the autonomy of all the mainland cities, an arrangement which was to have grave consequences. Thirteen years before Leuctra, in 384 B.C., Demosthenes was born. He was named after his father, a cutler and cabinet-maker of the deme Paeania. His mother was Cleobule, daughter of Gylon, who was alleged to be of Scythian descent.

It seems that the moral and intellectual qualities of Demosthenes were offset by physical weakness. Aeschines taunts him with having never taken part in sports. Moreover, there have survived, in addition to the *Lives* by Plutarch and others, several copies, evidently authentic, of a statue which was erected in the Agora some fifty years after his death. The literary sources agree in representing Demosthenes as a hard-working, water-drinking, unsociable man. The statues show "a poor, thin figure with lean arms and no muscular development. The face is care-worn and furrowed; there is no geniality, no trace of humour or good nature, as in most Greek portraits; the lower lip is contracted and retreating—a corroboration of the witnesses who tell us of his naturally defective utterance. He looks a disagreeable, painstaking, morose man; nor can we see in his face any clear marks either of the moral greatness which raised him to a foremost place among Greek patriots, or of the intellectual force which made him an orator unsurpassed in the annals of history." [1]

[1] J. P. Mahaffy, *A History of Greek Classical Literature*, vol. ii, part II (p. 92), 1895.

When Demosthenes was seven years old his father died leaving the child with a substantial fortune in the guardianship of two uncles and a family friend. On attaining his majority in 366 the young man claimed his patrimony; but the guardians proved to have been unjust stewards. He had recourse to an action at law, whereby he secured a verdict but only a small fraction of the property. The five speeches [1] composed by the plaintiff on this occasion have survived: they are the first in a series of court speeches which he delivered in person or composed for others at various dates throughout his career.

The orations of Demosthenes fall into three groups, according as they were written (a) for delivery in private lawsuits, (b) for delivery in public lawsuits, or (c) as deliberative, i.e., political, speeches before the Assembly. Those printed in this volume are, with the exception of the De Corona,[2] all of a political nature; and it is therefore with Demosthenes as statesman and deliberative orator that we are here principally concerned. The particular circumstances under which the several orations came to be delivered, as well as the political and military events which helped to frame his policy, are set out in the arguments which introduce each speech and in the Chronological Abstract of Events. We shall, then, make a general survey of the orator's policy and literary characteristics.

The speeches On the Navy Boards (354), For the Megalopolitans (353), and On the Liberty of the Rhodians (351) are described as 'Hellenic' in contrast to those which deal with the relations between Athens and the semi-barbarian state of Macedon. The policy indicated is this: the freedom, the imperial dignity, and the moral greatness of Athens must be maintained at the cost of personal sacrifice and personal danger. Democracy must be supported against despotism, Hellenism against barbarism; and in espousing this cause or

---

[1] Two against and one in reply to Aphobus (363 B.C.), and two against Onetor (362–361 B.C.).

[2] This great speech, though delivered before a jury in a public lawsuit, is often treated as political, both on account of its subject-matter and the fact that Demosthenes' refutation of the charge against Ctesiphon takes second place to the orator's review and justification of his own statesmanship and conduct in public life.

that, Athens must be guided not by grudges and the memory of bygone hates, not by lofty vision or by groundless fear, but simply by expediency.

The same motive—the salvation of Athens and through her of Greek culture and institutions—lay behind the yet greater orations delivered in face of the Macedonian threat. First, there must be no appeasement :[1] the peril must be met before it is too late. Next, trifling disputes must be laid aside, and useful alliances contracted. Finally, there must be financial reforms, and personal service must replace the hire of foreign mercenaries.

The "Hellenic speeches" are marked by a certain gravity, even diffidence, as might be expected in a young man first addressing the Assembly of his people. The style has clearly been influenced by that of Thucydides; but already there appears that profound sense of urgency, those wide horizons, which find their outlet in the full and vehement, yet dignified, oratory of the *Third Philippic* and *The Chersonese*. The greatness of Demosthenes as a statesman is that he foresaw, as a great orator and statesman of our own day foresaw, the danger; brought it in matchless language before his countrymen; indicated practical remedies and a proper policy. Yet we see him like the Persian soldier in Herodotus—πολλὰ φρονέοντα μηδενὸς κρατέειν— prescient but in fact helpless. He had to contend not only with a supine and slothful populace: he was violently opposed by able and often unscrupulous orators like Aeschines as well as by men of deeper sincerity, like Eubulus and Phocion, who advocated peace at any price. When at last, by the clarity and driving force of his argument, by the cogency of his appeal, he had roused the Athenians from their lethargy, the opportunity—if ever it had really existed—had gone for ever. All his hopes were dashed and all his fears realized by Philip's crowning victory at Chaeronea. He might have read the decree of Fate and perceived the ordained course of history; but he failed to recognize

---

[1] The one exception to this steadfast attitude appears in the speech *On the Peace* in 346. In that case, however, Demosthenes embraced a temporary expedient when the state was threatened with a general attack by the Amphyctionic League. That the orator was acting against his deeper convictions is indicated by the weakness of the speech.

that a culture, if it is to survive, must spread its roots within some framework of political unity. When he rebelled against Alexander in 336 he could not foresee that the Macedonian was no destroyer (despite the fate of Thebes) from the realms of darkness, but a torchbearer by whose arm the very words of Demosthenes himself would reach Cicero and through him influence all the prose of Europe.

Spared by the conqueror in 335, Demosthenes was forced into exile in 324. Recalled in the following year on Alexander's death, he once more tried to fan the dying embers. But the light of Greek freedom had been put out. Following Antipater's success at Crannon the Athenians were called upon to surrender the orators of the war party. Demosthenes fled to Calaurea where he took refuge in the temple of Neptune. Pursued by the Macedonian envoy Archias, he ended his life by poison. It was the sixteenth day of the month Pyanepsion in the third year of the 114th Olympiad, 322 B.C. The scene has been immortalized by Plutarch.

## II

The principal characteristics of Demosthenes as statesman and orator are his sincerity and intensity. Personal venom ($\lambda o\iota\delta o\rho\acute{\iota}a$) is absent from the political speeches, and finds its place, according to the usage of that time, only in the law-court speeches when his own character or that of his client was directly or indirectly at stake.

From the literary point of view we notice, first, a careful elaboration and conscious finish: the Greek orator was looked upon as an artist no less than the poet, the sculptor, or the potter. The rules of his art, however, were based on well-known precedents, and the greatness of Demosthenes as a prose writer consisted partly in his observation of those precedents, partly in cautious innovation.

1. He increased his vocabulary, and thereby the force of his message, by the introduction of numerous common words and exclamations which his predecessors would have regarded as mere vulgarisms. If we desire to depict by

modern examples the kind of effect which such innovations had upon the audience we may recall Churchill's 'What sort of people do they think we are?' 'Some chicken! Some neck!' Poetical expressions, metaphors, and similes are rare in Demosthenes. His diction is always simple and brief. We must, however, bear in mind that the speeches have not come down to us exactly as they were delivered: their perfection was attained only by painful revision.

2. Before his entry into political life Demosthenes observed strictly the law of *hiatus* which forbade the juxtaposition of final and initial vowels, even when separated by a pause, except in such words as ἤ and καί. Thereafter he took greater liberties with the rule, though Cicero mentions that for the most part he avoided the concourse of vowels. With regard to the rhythm of his sentences, he rejected as far as possible the collocation of more than two short syllables.

3. He had more frequent recourse than his predecessors to the so-called figures of thought—anaphora, anastrophe, systrophe, etc. His use of aposiopesis and exclamations at the end of sentences was altogether new. New also were his violent gestures upon the *bema*, and the gesticulation of his voice which is said often to have risen to a scream. But for all the contrivances of his art he never forgot, and never allowed his audience to forget, the central object of his words. For all his occasional violence he never lost his dignity and never strained his pathos. He has been considered by critics from his own day until now as the greatest orator of all time.

## III

It appears that nearly all the orations of Demosthenes (genuine or spurious) have come down to us. According to Suidas there were sixty-five, of which we still have sixty. This corpus probably represents an Alexandrian selection from older editions of which there appear to be traces in the manuscripts. There are over two hundred of these manuscripts, all derived from a single archetype. The best is

*Σ*. or S., Parisinus 2934, dating from the early tenth century. F. or M. is Marcianus 416, of the eleventh century, at Venice: from it the Aldine edition of Demosthenes was printed in 1504. The scholia which have reached us under the name of Ulpian were also published by Aldus in 1503.

1953                                        J. W.

# BIBLIOGRAPHY

WORKS. Greek text: Editio princeps, Aldus, Venice, 1504; I. Bekker (*Oratores Attici*), 1854–5; Vömel, 1843, 1845; W. Dindorf, 9 vols., 1846–51; 3rd ed., 3 vols., 1859–61; edited by F. Blass, 3 vols., 1885–9; S. H. Butcher and W. Rennie (Oxford Classical Texts), 1903–31; C. Fuhr and J. Sykutris, 1914–27; A. T. Murray, C. A. Vince, and J. H. Vince (Loeb Classical Library, with translation), 1926– (unfinished).

Greek text with English notes and commentaries: *Select Private Orations*, C. T. Penrose, 1843; *Olynthiac Orations*, D. B. Hickie, 1844; R. Whiston (Bibliotheca Classica), 1851, etc., 1859–68; *Phippics*, T. K. Arnold, 1851; E. Abbott and P. E. Matheson, 4th ed., 1897; *Philippics, Olynthiacs,* and *Embassy*, G. H. Heslop (Catena Classicorum), 1868–72, 1880; *Select Private Orations*, F. A. Paley and J. E. Sandys, 1874–5, 4th ed., 1910; *On the Crown* and *Philippics*, T. H. L. Leary, 1879; *Against Androtion* and *Timocrates*, W. Wayte, 1882, 2nd ed., 1893; *Against Canon* and *Callicles*, F. D. Swift, 1895; *Olynthiacs* and *First Philippic*, 1897; and *Second and Third Philippic, On the Peace,* and *Chersonese*, J. H. Sandys (Macmillan's Classical Series), 1900; *First and Second Olynthiac*, P. E. Whelan, 1904.

ENGLISH TRANSLATIONS. *Olynthiacs* and *Philippics* (with life), Th. Wylson, 1570; *Orations*, by several hands, under the direction of Lord Somers, 1702, 1744; *Orations of Demosthenes and Aeschines*, P. Francis, 1757–8; *Philippics*, T. Leland, 1756; *Select Speeches*, C. R. Kennedy, 1841. *Works*, C. R. Kennedy (Bohn's Classical Library); *Olynthiacs* and *Philippics*, O. Holland, 1901.

SEPARATE WORKS:

*Adversus Leptinem:* J. E. Sandys, 1890; English translation by a graduate of Cambridge, 1879, 1885.

*De Corona:* Greek text with notes: B. Drake, 1851, 6th ed. (T. Gwatkin), 1880; T. K. Arnold, 1851; G. A. and W. H. Simcox (with *Aeschines Against Ctesiphon*), 1866; A. Holmes (Catena Classicorum), 1871, 1881; M. L. d'Ooge, 1875; E. Abbot and P. E. Matheson, 1899; W. W. Goodwin, 1901. Greek text with English translation: Henry, Lord Brougham, 1840; revised edition (Lubbock's Hundred Best Books), 1893. English translations: H. Owgan, 1852; W. Brandt, 1870; Sir R. Collier, 1875; J. Biddle, 1881; C. R. Kennedy (Bohn's Shilling Series), 1888.

# Bibliography xi

*Midias:* Greek text and notes: C. A. M. Fennell, 1883; W. W. Goodwin, 1906.   English translation: C. A. M. Fennell, 1882.

*Olynthiacs:* Greek text with notes: T. K. Arnold, 1849; H. M. Wilkins, 1860; Oxford Pocket Classics, 1870; T. R. Glover (Pitt Press Series), 1897; H. Sharpley (Blackwood's Classical Tests), 1900.

*Philippics:* Greek text with notes: J. A. Davies (Pitt Press Series), 1907.   English translation (literal): Oxford translation of Classics, 1885.

BIOGRAPHICAL AND CRITICAL.   Lucian: *Demosthenis Encomium* (English translation, T. Franklin, 1781); Dionysius of Halicarnassus: *History*; Plutarch: *Life of Demosthenes* (English translation, Everyman's Library, No. 409, pp. 163–86); S. H. Butcher: *Demosthenes*, 1881; A. Schäfer: *Demosthenes und seine Zeit*, 2nd ed., 1885–7; F. Blass: *Die Attische Beredskamkeit*, vol. iii, 2nd ed., 1898; A. W. Pickard-Cambridge: *Demosthenes and the Last Days of Greek Freedom*, 1914; C. D. Adams: *Demosthenes and his Influence*, 1927; W. Jaeger: *Demosthenes, the Origin and Growth of his Policy*, 1938.

# CONTENTS

# CHRONOLOGICAL ABSTRACT OF EVENTS
# DURING THE LIFE OF DEMOSTHENES

B.C.

384 Demosthenes is born.

This was just twenty years after the termination of the Peloponnesian war. Greece was reposing under the peace of Antalcidas,
and the power of Sparta had reached its height.

383 Philip of Macedon is born.

His father, Amyntas II., has disputes with the Olynthians concerning their encroachment on his territories, and applies to
Sparta for aid.

Apollonia and Acanthus, two of the Chalcidian cities, send an embassy to Sparta for the same purpose.

Sparta declares war against Olynthus, and sends a force under
Eudamidas which takes possession of Potidæa.

382 Phœbidas, sent from Sparta to reinforce Eudamidas, stops on his
road at Thebes, and seizes the Cadmea, in which he places a
Lacedæmonian garrison. An oligarchical government is established at Thebes, at the head of which are Archias and Leontiades, devoted to Sparta. A multitude of Theban exiles fly to
Athens; among them Pelopidas.

Teleutias, brother of Agesilaus, is sent with a larger force against
Olynthus; is joined by a Theban contingent, by Amyntas, and
Derdas prince of Elymia.

The Spartans require Athens to dismiss the Theban exiles.
Athens refuses.

Teleutias defeats the Olynthians in a battle near the city, and
shuts them in their walls.

381 Teleutias is defeated by the Olynthians, and slain.

380 Agesipolis, one of the kings, is sent with reinforcements from
Sparta; takes Torone, and dies of a fever. Polybiades succeeds
to the command, and besieges Olynthus.

379 The Olynthians sue for peace, and submit to join the Peloponnesian
confederacy.

Pelopidas and his associates return to Thebes, where, having slain
Archias and Leontiades, they are joined by their countrymen,
and attack the Spartan garrison. A body of Athenian volunteers
come to their assistance, and the garrison capitulates.

The Spartans send their king Cleombrotus into Bœotia.

Chabrias, with an Athenian force, occupies the pass at Eleutheræ;
Cleombrotus enters by another road, and having dispersed a
Theban force at Platæa, takes possession of Thespiæ, where he
leaves Sphodrias, with a part of his army, and then returns to
Peloponnesus.

The Athenians, alarmed at the Spartan invasion, condemn their
generals who had aided in the recovery of the Cadmea.

378 Sphodrias marches against Athens, to surprise the Piræus; advances

B.C.

as far as the Thriasian plain, and retreats, after plundering the country.

The Athenians prepare for war with Sparta; strengthen the Piræus; increase their fleet, and make alliance with Thebes.

Chios, Byzantium, Rhodes, and Mitylene revolt from Sparta, and renew their confederacy with Athens.

Sphodrias is recalled, and Agesilaus sent with a large Peloponnesian army into Bœotia. He ravages the Theban territory, but having encountered an Athenian and Theban force, commanded by Chabrias and Gorgidas, is repulsed, and returns home, leaving Phœbidas in command at Thespiæ.

Phœbidas, after gaining partial success against Gorgidas, is defeated and slain.

377 Demosthenes loses his father, and is placed under the care of three guardians.

Agesilaus again invades Bœotia; is joined by a force of Olynthian cavalry, gains some advantage over the Thebans, and, after strengthening the oligarchical party at Thespiæ, crosses over to Megara, where he falls ill.

The Sacred Band, consisting of three hundred men, is established at Thebes.

Acoris, king of Egypt, at war with Persia, engages the services of Chabrias, who, on complaint made by Artaxerxes, is recalled by the Athenians, and Iphicrates sent to assist the satrap Pharnabazus.

376 Cleombrotus is sent into Bœotia, where he is repulsed by the Athenians and Thebans, and returns home.

A Peloponnesian fleet is sent out under the command of Pollis, to intercept the corn-ships bound for Athens. Chabrias totally defeats the fleet at Naxos.

Athens regains her ascendancy in the Ægean sea, and many of the islands return under her protection.

Timotheus sails with a fleet to Corcyra, which renews her alliance with Athens.

Jason of Pheræ establishes his power or influence over most of the towns of Thessaly.

375 Timotheus is successful against the Peloponnesians in the Ionian sea.

Pelopidas fails in an attempt to surprise Orchomenos, is attacked on his retreat by a superior force of Spartans at Tegyra. The Spartans are put to the rout, and their generals slain.

374 The Thebans send an army into Phocis, which is in alliance with Sparta. Cleombrotus crosses the Gulf of Corinth, to the assistance of the Phocians, and forces the Thebans to retreat.

The Athenians attempt to make peace with Sparta, but this is interrupted by a dispute concerning some Zacynthian exiles restored to Timotheus. A Peloponnesian fleet under Mnasippus is sent to recover Corcyra. The Athenians determine to relieve it, and despatch Timotheus with a fleet from Athens, who is forced for want of supplies to cruise about the Ægean isles and the coast of Macedonia and Thrace.

Pharnabazus and Iphicrates invade Egypt, which after partial success, they are compelled to evacuate. Iphicrates quarrels with Pharnabazus, and returns to Athens.

373 Mnasippus lands in Corcyra, and blockades the city, but is routed in a sally, and slain. His fleet retires to Leucas.

B.C.
373 Timotheus is recalled to Athens, and brought to trial, but ac-
    quitted. Iphicrates, Callistratus, and Chabrias, succeed to the
    command.

    The Athenians sail to Corcyra, and capture a Syracusan fleet sent
    to the aid of Mnasippus. Cephallenia is brought over to the
    Athenian alliance.

    The Thebans surprise Platæa, and raze the city to the ground. The
    inhabitants, allowed to depart, take refuge in Athens, and are
    admitted to the privileges of citizens.

    Thespiæ is taken, and shares the same fate.

372 Iphicrates crosses to Acarnania, and carries on the war against the
    Peloponnesians with various success; is preparing to invade
    Laconia.

371 The Athenians send ambassadors to Sparta, to conclude peace.
    The Thebans, invited to join in the embassy, send Epaminondas.

    Peace is made between the Peloponnesians and the Athenian con-
    federacy. Epaminondas refuses to concur in the treaty on
    behalf of Thebes, because she was required to acknowledge the
    independence of the Bœotian towns.

    Cleombrotus is ordered to march from Phocis into Bœotia; en-
    counters the Thebans under Epaminondas at Leuctra, is totally
    defeated and slain.

    Jason of Pheræ arrives at Leuctra after the battle. By his media-
    tion an armistice is effected, and the Lacedæmonian army
    retreats into Peloponnesus.

    A congress is held at Athens, and attended by most of the Pelo-
    ponnesian states, who resolve to maintain the independence
    declared by the peace of Antalcidas.

    The Mantineans rebuild their city, which had been dismantled by
    the Lacedæmonians.

    A democratical movement takes place in Peloponnesus.

    The Arcadians, encouraged by Epaminondas, resolve to build a
    new city, to become the seat of a federal government, to be called
    Megalopolis. Pammenes is sent with a small Theban force into
    Arcadia.

371 Tegea and Orchomenos, under the influence of Sparta and aristo-
    cratical institutions, oppose the Arcadian union. The Tegeans
    are defeated and their city taken. Sparta declares war.

    Amyntas II. dies, leaving three sons, Alexander, Perdiccas, and
    Philip. Alexander ascends the throne.

    Jason of Pheræ announces his intention of marching to Delphi
    and presiding over the Pythian games. He collects a large
    army, and excites alarm; but is murdered a short time before
    the festival. His brothers Polydorus and Polyphron succeed
    him.

    Agesilaus marches to Mantinea, ravages the country, and returns
    to Sparta.

    The Thebans prepare to invade Peloponnesus; collect troops from
    Phocis, Locris, Thessaly, and various states of northern Greece.

    Iphicrates is sent with an Athenian squadron to Macedonia, where
    he was encouraged by Amyntas to try for the recovery of Am-
    phipolis, but returns without success.

369 Pelopidas and Epaminondas lead the Theban army to Mantinea;
    are joined by the Arcadians, Eleans, and Argives, and invade
    Laconia. The Spartans are unable to oppose them in the field,

B.C.

369    but, reinforced by a small body of Peloponnesian auxiliaries, prepare to defend the capital. The Thebans, after ravaging the country, approach Sparta, are repulsed in a skirmish, and retire.

The Theban army enters Messenia, to accomplish the project of Epaminondas for the building of a new city, and the separation of that province from Laconia. The building is rapidly carried on under Theban protection. The city is called Messene, and peopled by the Messenian insurgents, with a multitude of exiles and revolted Helots. Epaminondas, leaving a garrison there, prepares for his return to Thebes.

The Lacedæmonians send an embassy to Athens, to implore her assistance, which is granted, and Iphicrates is sent with an army to Peloponnesus.

Polyphron of Pheræ, having survived Polydorus, is murdered by his nephew Alexander, who assumes the office of *Tagus*, and oppresses the Thessalian towns. The Aleuadæ of Larissa invoke the aid of Alexander, king of Macedon, who marches to their relief, and puts a garrison in Larissa and Cranon: but he is hastily recalled to Macedonia, in consequence of intrigues against him by his mother Eurydice and her paramour Ptolemy.

Iphicrates stations himself at the Isthmus of Corinth, to oppose Epaminondas, who passes by a different road, repulsing the Athenian cavalry.

368    The Thessalians apply to Thebes for aid against Alexander of Pheræ. Pelopidas is sent into Thessaly, while Epaminondas marches for the second time to invade Peloponnesus.

Dionysius of Syracuse sends a body of Celts and Iberians to the aid of Sparta.

The Spartans send an army to the Isthmus, and are joined by the Corinthians and Athenians under Chabrias. Epaminondas forces their lines, and effects a junction with his allies; after a short and unimportant campaign he makes an attempt on Corinth, is repulsed by Chabrias, and returns home.

Alexander of Macedon is murdered, and Ptolemy assumes the regency.

The Arcadians carry on the war with success in the absence of Epaminondas.

Pelopidas, having marched to Larissa, and restored tranquillity, is invited into Macedonia, to compose the disputes in the royal family. He forces Ptolemy to give security for preserving the kingdom to the heirs of Amyntas; takes hostages from him, and receives the young Philip into his charge. Philip is taken to Thebes, where he resides for several years.

The satrap Ariobarzanes makes an ineffectual attempt for the pacification of Greece.

Alexander of Pheræ raises new disturbances. Pelopidas, sent on an embassy to Thessaly, is seized by him and thrown into prison.

Alexander obtains the assistance of Athens, and defeats a body of Thebans who are sent against him, among whom Epaminondas, in temporary disgrace for the ill-success of his last campaign, was serving as a private soldier.

The Thebans destroy Orchomenos in Bœotia.

367    Iphicrates sails with an armament to the coast of Macedonia, for the purpose of recovering Amphipolis; is invited by Ptolemy and Eurydice to assist them against Pausanias, who aspired to the

B.C.

367   throne. He expels Pausanias, but is unable to reduce Amphipolis, which is supported by the Olynthians.

Epaminondas marches again into Thessaly, and effects the release of Pelopidas.

Archidamus, commanding the troops of Lacedæmon, Athens, and Corinth, with Syracusan auxiliaries, gains a great victory over the Arcadians and Argives on the borders of Laconia.

Pelopidas is sent on an embassy to Susa, and obtains the Persian king's sanction for the projects of the Thebans. On his return a congress is held at Thebes, and attended by the king's deputy, but the Greek states refuse to accept the dictation of Persia.

366   Demosthenes comes of age, and brings an action against his guardians for mal-administration of his estate, in which he obtains a verdict.

Iphicrates, with Charidemus of Oreus, sails to attack Amphipolis, but is opposed by Ptolemy and the Olynthians.

Epaminondas marches into Achaia, but without much success. Of the Achæan states Sicyon only is secured to the Theban alliance.

Themison of Eretria surprises Oropus. The Athenians send Chares to recover it, but the city is put in possession of the Thebans.

Athens makes a separate peace with the Arcadians.

365   Corinth and the Achæans make peace with Thebes.

Elis and Arcadia go to war, contending for the Triphylian towns.

Ptolemy is slain by Perdiccas III. who ascends the throne of Macedon.

The Amphipolitans negotiate with Iphicrates for the surrender of their town, and give him hostages; but he, being recalled to Athens, delivers the hostages to Charidemus, who goes off into the service of Cotys, king of Thrace, and sends back the hostages to Amphipolis.

364   Sparta assists Elis against the Arcadians, who defeat Archidamus.

The Arcadians invade Elis, and attempt to exclude the Eleans from the presidency of the Olympic games. The battle of Olympia is fought, in which the Arcadians and Argives are defeated by the troops of Elis and Achaia.

Callisthenes commands the Athenian fleet on the Macedonian coast, and makes war against Perdiccas, but agrees to an armistice. He is superseded by Timotheus, who takes Torone and Potidæa.

The Thebans are again invited into Thessaly, to give assistance against Alexander of Pheræ. Pelopidas goes with a small troop to Pharsalus, where he collects an army of Thessalians. Alexander is defeated in the battle of Cynoscephalæ, but Pelopidas is slain. Peace is made between Thebes and Alexander.

363   Dissensions arise between Mantinea and the other Arcadians. It is proposed to make peace with Elis and Sparta. The Thebans prepare for another invasion of Peloponnesus. The Mantineans ally themselves to Sparta.

Timotheus takes Pydna and Methone.

The Thebans send a fleet to Byzantium, to detach it from the Athenian alliance. Laches is sent to oppose it, but without effect.

Alexander of Pheræ sends out a squadron to infest and plunder the small Ægean islands, and lays siege to Peparethus. The

B.C.

363    Athenians having sent Leosthenes against him, he sails to Attica, takes several Athenian ships, and plunders the Piræus.

362    Epaminondas leads his army into Peloponnesus, and, joined by his Arcadian allies, assaults Sparta, but is repulsed.

The Athenians send a force of six thousand men to the assistance of the Spartans. They march to Mantinea.

Epaminondas, retreating from Laconia, marches to attack Mantinea. His cavalry are defeated by the Athenians, who sally from the town.

Agesilaus marches with his army to join the Athenians and Mantineans. Epaminondas advances to attack them, and the battle of Mantinea is fought, one of the most celebrated in Grecian history. On the one side are Bœotians, Thessalians, Eubœans, Locrians and other northern allies, together with troops of Sicyon, Argos, Arcadia, and Messenia, to the number of thirty-three thousand. On the other, Lacedæmonians, Athenians, Mantineans, and troops of Elis and Achaia; considerably less in number. After an obstinate resistance, Epaminondas breaks the centre of the enemy, but is slain in the moment of victory.

A general peace follows, but the Spartans alone refuse to acknowledge the independence of Messenia.

Timotheus, assisted by the satrap Ariobarzanes, takes Sestus, Crithote, and Elæus, in the Thracian Chersonese; and afterwards lays siege to Samos.

The satraps revolt from the king of Persia. They are promised assistance by Tachos, king of Egypt, Mausolus, king of Caria, and most of the maritime parts of the empire.

Miltocythes rebels against Cotys, king of Thrace, and engages the Athenians to assist him, by promising to cede to them the Chersonese. Cotys amuses the Athenians by negotiation, and overcomes Miltocythes.

361    Samos capitulates after a siege of eleven months.

Orontes betrays the conspirators to Artaxerxes. Datames, satrap of Cappadocia, is murdered. Tachos, preparing to make war against Persia, engages Agesilaus to command his army, and Chabrias for his admiral.

Agesilaus is sent with a thousand Spartans to Egypt, but quarrels with Tachos, and transfers his services to Nectanabis, to whom the Egyptian army revolts. Tachos flies to Persia, and Agesilaus establishes Nectanabis in the dominion of Egypt.

Artaxerxes Mnemon dies, and his son, Artaxerxes Ochus, ascends the throne of Persia.

360    Timotheus and Charidemus attack Amphipolis, which receives succour from Macedonia and Olynthus, and the Athenians are defeated.

Cotys marches into the Chersonese, and gets possession of Sestus.

Agesilaus dies on his return from Egypt.

Pammenes is sent with Theban troops to quell disturbances in Arcadia; establishes the preponderance of Megalopolis.

Artaxerxes makes an attempt to reconquer Egypt, which fails.

359    Perdiccas is slain in a battle with the Illyrians, leaving an infant son, Amyntas. Philip ascends the throne of Macedon.

At this time the Illyrians are preparing for a new invasion, the Pæonians make an irruption from the north, and there are two

B.C.

359    pretenders to the crown—Pausanias, assisted by Cotys, and Argæus, supported by the Athenians.

Philip accommodates matters with Cotys, and marches against Argæus, whom he defeats. He returns the Athenian prisoners without ransom, and makes peace with Athens. He then reduces the Pæonians to submission, and invades Illyria. Bardylis, the Illyrian prince, is defeated in a great battle, and a portion of his dominions is ceded to Macedonia.

358    Cotys, assisted by Charidemus, lays siege to Crithote and Elæus, but soon after is murdered, leaving three sons, Amadocus, Berisades, and Cersobleptes, among whom the dominions of Cotys are divided.

Charidemus takes Cersobleptes under his protection, and defeats the Athenian force.

Miltocythes, again raising disturbances, is taken prisoner by Charidemus, who sends him to Cardia, where he is put to death.

Philip lays siege to Amphipolis.

The Olynthians send an embassy to Athens, to negotiate an alliance which is prevented by the intrigues of Philip. He conciliates the Olynthians by the cession of Anthemus, and soon afterwards obtains possession of Amphipolis. He then marches to Pydna, which is surrendered to him.

Alexander of Pheræ is murdered. Tisiphonus and his brother Lycophron get the command.

357    Berisades and Amadocus combine against Cersobleptes, and are assisted by Athenodorus, the Athenian general. Cersobleptes is forced to enter into a convention, by which the kingdom is equally divided, and the Chersonese ceded to Athens, with the exception of Cardia.

The Athenians quarrel with Philip about Amphipolis. He makes an alliance with the Olynthians.

The Thebans send an army into Eubœa, from which, after much fighting, they are expelled by the Athenians.

Chares is sent to take possession of the Chersonese, which, after some opposition from Charidemus, he effects.

The Social War breaks out, in which Byzantium, Chios, Cos, and Rhodes revolt from the Athenian league. The Athenians attack Chios, and are defeated; Chabrias is slain.

The Phocians send succour to some of the Bœotian towns, attempting to revolt from Thebes. The Thebans procure an Amphictyonic decree against the Phocians for having cultivated a portion of the consecrated plain near Delphi. This was the origin of the Sacred War.

356    Philip takes Potidæa, with the assistance of the Olynthians, and gives it up to them.

Alexander is born.

Parmenio, Philip's general, gains a victory over the Illyrians.

Philip takes the mine district of the Pangæus from the Thasians, and establishes a new colony at Crenides, which he names Philippi.

The Athenians besiege Byzantium, but the siege is raised by the fleet of the allies. Chares, Timotheus, and Iphicrates command the Athenian forces, but the two latter are recalled on the complaint of Chares.

B.C.

356 The allies ravage Lemnos, Imbrus, and Samos, and levy contributions in the Ægean.

Chares, for want of supplies, lends assistance to Artabazus against
the Persian satraps.

Philomelus, the Phocian general, takes possession of Delphi, and
defeats the Locrians of Amphissa. He negotiates an alliance
with Athens and Lacedæmon, while the Locrians obtain promises of assistance from Thebes and Thessaly.

Corcyra revolts from Athens.

355 The king of Persia threatens Athens with war on account of the
aid furnished by Chares to Artabazus.

The Athenians terminate the Social War by acknowledging the
independence of the revolted states.

Timotheus and Iphicrates are brought to trial for misconduct
in the war. Timotheus is found guilty, and goes into exile.
Shortly after, he dies at Chalcis.

The Athenians send an expedition against Olynthus, without
success.

Chares takes Sestus.

Philomelus again defeats the Locrians, and being threatened with
a general war, seizes the treasures of Delphi and collects a
body of mercenaries. The Thessalians and Bœotians, having
marched into Locris, are defeated by Philomelus, who is strongly
reinforced from Peloponnesus.

Demosthenes makes the speeches against Leptines and Androtion.

354 The Thebans, largely reinforced, give battle to Philomelus in the
defiles of Parnassus. He is defeated and slain. Onomarchus
succeeds to the command, and the Thebans retire.

Philip sends Macedonian troops to assist Callias of Chalcis against
Plutarch of Eretria. The latter applies to Athens for assistance,
and is opposed by Demosthenes, who makes his first public
speech on this occasion. The Athenians determine to assist
Plutarch, and Phocion is sent with an army to Eubœa. He
defeats Callias and the Macedonians at Tamynæ, and establishes
popular government at Eretria.

The Athenians debate about making war with Persia. Demosthenes dissuades them in his speech *de Symmoriis.*

353 Onomarchus takes Thronium, and invades Bœotia. Here he takes
Orchomenus, but is defeated by the Thebans at Chæronea.

Lycophron, now sovereign of Pheræ, enters into alliance with
Onomarchus, and endeavours to oppress the independent Thessalians.

The Spartans declare war against Megalopolis, and apply for assistance to Athens. Demosthenes makes his speech *pro Megalo-
politanis,* in which he urges the Athenians to espouse the other
side. They remain neutral.

Demosthenes delivers the oration against Timocrates.

Philip takes Methone after a long siege, in which he lost an eye.

The Macedonian party prevail at Eretria, and dissolve the con-
nexion with Athens.

Mausolus, king of Caria, dies, and is succeeded by his widow
Artemisia.

The Phœnicians revolt from Artaxerxes, and enter into alliance
with Nectanabis. Cyprus soon after revolts.

352 Philip, invited by the Thessalians, marches against Lycophron,

B.C.

352　defeats Phayllus, brother of Onomarchus, and takes Pagasæ. Onomarchus marches with a large army into Thessaly, and defeats Philip in two battles, who retreats to Macedonia. Onomarchus then invades Bœotia, defeats the Thebans, and takes Coronea; but is recalled to Thessaly by intelligence that Philip had returned with large reinforcements. The decisive battle of Pagasæ is fought, in which Onomarchus is defeated and slain. Philip expels Lycophron from Pheræ, and takes the city of Magnesia. He then prepares to invade Phocis, and marches to Thermopylæ, but finds the pass guarded by an Athenian force, and retreats.

　　Phayllus, joined by a large force of auxiliaries from Sparta, Achaia, and Athens, invades Bœotia, but is defeated by the Thebans.

　　Philip sends out a fleet, plundering the Athenian coast, and ravages Lemnos, Imbrus, and Scyros. He himself marches into Thrace, where, after long being occupied in the interior extending his power over the different tribes, he turns towards the coast of the Propontis and attacks Heræum.

　　Demosthenes speaks the *Duties of the State*.

　　The oration against Aristocrates is delivered.

　　Thebes, Argos, Sicyon, and Messene send assistance to Megalopolis. The Spartans, assisted by mercenaries from Phocis, after various indecisive battles, are compelled to make peace.

　　Artaxerxes makes great preparations to recover Phœnicia and Cyprus.

351　Phayllus overruns the country of the Epicnemidian Locrians, is defeated by the Bœotians at Abæ, afterwards defeats them at Aryca, and dies; is succeeded by his nephew Phalæcus.

　　The democratical party at Rhodes solicit the aid of Athens, and are supported by Demosthenes in his speech *de Libertate Rhodiorum. First Philippic*.

　　Artemisia, queen of Caria, dies, and is succeeded by Idrieus, who, at the command of Artaxerxes, collects a large armament for the reduction of Cyprus. Phocion the Athenian is joined with Evagoras in the command of this expedition.

　　The Thessalians remonstrate with Philip for retaining Pagasæ and Magnesia.

350　Phalæcus invades Bœotia, and takes Chæronea, from which he is again driven by the Thebans, who invade and ravage Phocis.

　　Philip takes Apollonia, and threatens the Chalcidian towns. The Olynthians send to Athens to negotiate alliance.

　　Pitholaus, brother of Lycophron, recovers Pheræ, and Philip is invited to expel him. On his return from Thessaly he marches into the Chalcidian peninsula, and lays siege to Stagira.

　　Cyprus submits to Artaxerxes. Temnes, king of Sidon, assisted by Mentor at the head of Greek mercenaries, defeats the Persian satraps.

　　Demosthenes brings an action against Midias, which is afterwards compromised.

349　The Thebans receive a large subsidy from Persia, to enable them to carry on the war against Phocis.

　　The Olynthians send an embassy to Athens to implore assistance. A warm debate takes place, in which Demosthenes speaks the first Olynthiac. The Athenians vote alliance, and despatch

B.C.
349    Chares with a small force. The second and third Olynthiacs are
       delivered at short intervals after this.

       Meanwhile Stagira capitulates; Torone is taken, and most of the
       Chalcidian towns hasten to make terms with Philip. The Olyn-
       thians send another embassy, pressing for more effectual assist-
       ance. A larger armament is sent from Athens, and put under
       the command of Charidemus.

       The Olynthians, dissatisfied with Charidemus, send a third embassy,
       and entreat the aid of a native Athenian force. This is sent;
       but arrives too late.

       Artaxerxes marches in person against the Phœnicians. Temnes
       betrays Sidon, and the Phœnicians submit. Mentor is taken
       into the service of Persia.

348    Philip takes Mecyberna, the port of Olynthus, and lays siege to the
       city. After various ineffectual sallies, Olynthus is betrayed to
       Philip, who razes it to the ground.

       Phalæcus is deposed from his command by the Phocians. The
       Sacred War languishes.

       Artaxerxes sends to the Greek states to collect mercenaries for the
       invasion of Egypt. Athens and Sparta refuse assistance. The
       Thebans send Lacrates with a thousand men; the Argives
       Nicostratus with three thousand. The Asiatic Greeks furnish a
       contingent, and the king marches in person into Egypt. The
       conquest of Egypt is ultimately effected, but the exact date is
       uncertain.

347    Philip celebrates his triumph over Olynthus by a festival at Dium
       in Pieria.

       An assembly is held at Athens, to consider the expediency of
       rousing the Greeks against Philip. Æschines is sent for that
       purpose to Arcadia. The negotiations of Athens are unsuccess-
       ful.

       Philip causes it to be intimated at Athens that he is desirous of
       peace. A decree passes at Athens to send ambassadors to treat
       with him.

       The Thebans, suffering by the depredations committed on their
       territories from the hostile garrisons in Bœotia, invite Philip to
       terminate the Sacred War. The Phocians pray for aid of the
       Athenians, and offer to put them in possession of Nicæa, Thro-
       nium, and Alponus. Meanwhile Phalæcus regains his power in
       Phocia, and refuses to admit the Athenian troops.

       Parmenio besieges Halus in Thessaly.

       Demosthenes, Æschines, and eight other ambassadors, are sent to
       Pella to treat for peace. They return in the beginning of the
       following year.

346    Parmenio and Antipater are sent to Athens to negotiate the peace.
       A congress of the allies is held, and peace is concluded, on the
       terms of each party keeping his own possessions; but the
       Phocians and Cersobleptes are not named in the treaty.

       The ten Athenian ambassadors are sent to Macedonia to receive
       Philip's oath of ratification. On arriving at Pella, they find that
       Philip has marched into Thrace. There he had seized upon the
       Sacred Mount, and stripped Cersobleptes of a considerable part
       of his dominions. On his return to Pella he takes the ambassa-
       dors with him to Pheræ, and there ratifies the peace. He then
       dismisses them, hastens to Thermopylæ, takes Nicæa, Thronium,

B.C.

346 and Alponus, and being joined by the Bœotians, marches into Phocis. Archidamus with the Spartan troops, and Phalæcus with his mercenaries, retire to Peloponnesus, while the Phocian towns are either taken by storm or capitulate.

The Athenians, alarmed at this intelligence, begin to prepare for their own defence, but are reassured by a letter of Philip.

A council of Amphictyons is held at Delphi, and sentence passed on the Phocians for their sacrilege. Philip becomes a member of the council, and is chosen to preside at the Pythian games.

The lost Bœotian towns are restored to Thebes by Philip, and Nicæa given to the Thessalians.

The Amphictyonic Council send an embassy to Athens, to notify their election of Philip, and demand her recognition of it. Demosthenes delivers his Oration on the Peace, in which he dissuades the Athenians from opposing the Amphictyonic league.

345 Philip promises to assist the Messenians and Arcadians against hostilities threatened by Lacedæmon.

The Athenians send Demosthenes at the head of an embassy to Messene and Argos, to counteract the influence of Philip.

Diopithes is sent with a body of Athenian settlers to the Thracian Chersonese, who become involved in disputes with the Cardians.

Philip ravages Illyria, and takes many of the towns in that district; after which he marches into Thessaly, where the regnant family had again made head, and expels them, leaving strong garrisons in Pheræ and Magnesia. Soon afterwards he causes the whole country to be divided into tetrarchies, and governed by his own partisans.

344 Philip sends Python to Athens, to complain of the Athenian embassy to Peloponnesus. Demosthenes speaks the second Philippic.

Sostratus the pirate, having seized the island Halonnesus, is expelled by Philip. The Athenians demand its return.

Philip sends Python again to Athens, to adjust his disputes. The Athenians send Hegesippus and other envoys to make proposals for the amendment of the treaty.

The Cardians resist the attempt of Diopithes to take a portion of their territories, and apply to Philip for assistance.

343 Philip sends a letter to the Athenians, stating the terms which he is willing to consent to. Demosthenes and Hegesippus oppose them as unreasonable. The extant speech de Halonneso is supposed to be that of Hegesippus.

Phocion is sent to protect Megara against a conspiracy to betray it into the hands of the Macedonians. He secures it by fortifying Nicæa, and completing the long walls.

Philip invades Cassopia in Epirus, and annexes it to the dominions of his brother-in-law Alexander.

Demosthenes, Hegesippus, and Lycurgus are sent into Achaia and Acarnania, to form a league against Philip, to oppose his designs upon Ambracia and the western parts of Greece. They are successful, and an Athenian force is sent into Ambracia. Philip retreats from Epirus.

Aristodemus with an Athenian force makes an unsuccessful attempt upon Magnesia.

Æschines is brought to trial by Demosthenes for misconduct in the embassy, and acquitted.

B.C.

343 Philip sends assistance to the Cardians, and marches into the interior of Thrace to attack Teres. Diopithes, having collected a large body of mercenaries, endeavours to interrupt the conquests of Philip.

342 A Macedonian force is sent to Oreus in Eubœa, and establishes Philistides as governor. Clitarchus, a partisan of Philip, is secured in the government of Eretria.

Philip sends a letter to Athens, complaining of the proceedings of Diopithes as an infraction of the peace.

Philip completes the conquest of Thrace, and drives Cersobleptes from his kingdom. He then marches toward the Propontine coast.

341 Demosthenes speaks the third Philippic. Early in the year Philip besieges Selymbria.

Twenty Athenian corn-ships, intended for the relief of Selymbria, are captured by Philip. The Athenians complain, and the ships are restored.

Phocion is sent with troops to Eubœa, and expels Clitarchus and Philistides. Demosthenes is crowned by the people for having advised this expedition.

Selymbria is taken, and Philip proceeds to besiege Perinthus.

The Athenians, under the advice of Demosthenes, apply for assistance to Persia. *De Chersoneso.*

340 Philip sends his letter to the Athenians (which is still extant), in which, after reproaching them for their conduct, he virtually declares war.

He sends an army into the Chersonese.

The Persians relieve Perinthus, and Philip, leaving troops to blockade it, lays siege to Byzantium.

Demosthenes goes to Byzantium, to offer Athenian succour, which is accepted, and Chares is sent with a fleet; but the Byzantines refuse to receive him, and Phocion is sent in his stead. At the same time assistance is sent from Chios, Cos, and Rhodes, and also from other parts of Greece.

Philip is compelled to raise the siege of Perinthus and Byzantium, and his troops are driven out of the Chersonese. He breaks up his camp, and marches into Scythia.

Artaxerxes is poisoned by the satrap Bagoas, and his son Arses succeeds him.

339 Æschines goes as one of the Athenian deputies to the Amphictyonic Council. He accuses the Locrians of Amphissa, for having cultivated the sacred plain. The Delphians having attacked Cirrha are put to flight, and a resolution is passed to convoke an extraordinary meeting at Thermopylæ. At this meeting, unattended by Athens or Thebes, war is declared against the Locrians, and Cottyphus appointed to command an Amphictyonic army. He invades Locris, but without effect.

Philip, on his return from Scythia, is attacked by the Triballi, and is wounded in a hard-fought battle.

Phocion carries on successful operations against Philip in the north, but is severely wounded in an incursion into Macedonia.

Another Amphictyonic assembly is convened, at which Philip is elected general to carry into effect the decree against the Locrians.

B.C.

338 Philip marches through Thessaly, and takes possession of Elatea, which he begins to fortify.

The Athenians in alarm hold an assembly of the people, at which Demosthenes proposes to send an embassy to Thebes. This is resolved upon, and Demosthenes himself heads the embassy. Meanwhile the Athenians muster all their troops, and collect a body of ten thousand mercenaries.

An assembly is convoked at Thebes, and attended by Python on Philip's behalf; but Demosthenes prevails on the Thebans to become allies of Athens.

Philip marches against Amphissa, and defeats Chares, who had been sent to succour the Locrians. After two indecisive battles, the hostile armies meet at Chæronea. Philip is at the head of thirty-two thousand men, chiefly Macedonians and Thessalians. On the other side are the forces of Athens and Thebes, with a few auxiliaries from Peloponnesus, somewhat inferior in number. Philip gains a decisive victory.

The Athenians take energetic measures for the defence of their city. Demosthenes pronounces the funeral orations in honour of the slain. Lysicles the general is condemned to death.

Ctesiphon proposes a decree, that Demosthenes be crowned at the Dionysian festival for his services in repairing the fortifications, and his general merits as a citizen. For this a prosecution is instituted against him by Æschines.

Philip grants peace to the Athenians, and puts a Macedonian garrison into Thebes. The Bœotian towns are emancipated, and Oropus given to Athens.

Philip holds a congress of the Greeks at Corinth, and declares war against Persia. He makes a triumphant march through Peloponnesus, and obtains universal submission.

337 Attalus and Parmenio are sent with a force into Asia Minor to liberate the Greek cities.

Philip is engaged in a war with the Illyrians, after which he celebrates his marriage with Cleopatra, and is involved in domestic broils.

Arses is murdered, and Darius Codomanus raised to the throne of Persia.

336 A great festival is held at Ægæ in Macedonia, to solemnise the marriage of Philip's daughter with the king of Epirus; and attended from all parts of Greece. During the solemnity, Philip is murdered by Pausanias, one of his guards.

Demosthenes receives speedy information of Philip's death, and takes instant measures to free the Greeks from Macedonia. Ambassadors are sent to the Greek states, and a correspondence commenced with Attalus in Asia, and also with the Persian Court. A general rising is meditated in Greece, and also among the northern tribes.

Alexander hastens to Thermopylæ, joined by the Thessalians, and holds an Amphictyonic council, at which he is elected general of the Greeks. Thence he marches into Bœotia, and procures the submission of Thebes. The Athenians send ambassadors to conciliate him, and among them Demosthenes, who, after going as far as Cithæron, returns. Alexander then proceeds to Corinth, where at a general congress he is chosen to conduct the war against Persia.

B.C.

335 Alexander marches into Thrace, defeats the Triballi, crosses the
Danube, and, after receiving the submission of some barbarous
tribes, returns through Pæonia to attack the Illyrian prince
Cleitus. While he is yet in Illyria, he hears of the revolt of
Thebes.

The Thebans, having blockaded the Macedonian garrison in the
Cadmea, send to divers Greek states for assistance. Demosthenes persuades the Athenians to vote alliance, and himself
furnishes the Thebans with a supply of arms. Elis and other
cities of Peloponnesus send troops to the aid of Thebes, but they
march no further than the Isthmus, hearing of the advance of
Alexander.

Alexander besieges Thebes, which after a desperate resistance is
taken by storm, and razed to the ground.

The Athenians send a deputation to appease Alexander, who requires them to deliver up the principal leaders of the war-party,
among them, Demosthenes, Hyperides, and Lycurgus. But he
is persuaded by Demades to waive this demand.

334 Alexander crosses the Hellespont into Asia Minor.

Battle of Granicus.

Memnon intrigues with the Greek states, especially Lacedæmon, to
excite a rising against Macedonia. His death, which happens
soon after, is fatal to the Persian cause.

333 Battle of Issus.

332 Siege of Tyre.

The Lacedæmonians send an embassy to Darius.

Agis, king of Sparta, sails to Crete, and reduces the island under
the Persian dominion.

331 Alexandria in Egypt is founded.

Battle in Arbela.

Alexander enters the Persian capital.

Agis forms a confederacy in Peloponnesus.

330 Antipater marches to suppress an insurrection in Thrace. The
Lacedæmonians, commanded by Agis, rise in arms, and, joined
by the Eleans and Achaians, besiege Megalopolis. Antipater
hastens to its relief, and an obstinate battle is fought, in which
Agis is defeated and slain.

Æschines brings on the trial of Ctesiphon, and the two Orations
for the Crown are delivered. Ctesiphon is acquitted, and
Æschines retires in exile to Rhodes, where he opened a school of
rhetoric, and died many years after.

Darius is murdered.

328 Alexander sets out on his march for India.

327 Porus is overcome.

326 The army embarks on the Indus.

325 Alexander returns to Persia.

324 An order sent by Alexander is read at the Olympic games, commanding the reception of exiles by the Greek states. Demosthenes goes to Olympia to remonstrate with the Macedonian
envoy. The Athenians send an embassy to Alexander, to complain of this measure.

Messages are sent to the Greek cities, requiring them to pay
divine honours to Alexander.

Harpalus, flying from Babylon with a large treasure, arrives in
Athens. Antipater demands that he shall be given up by the

B.C.

324    Athenians, who throw him into prison, and pass a decree, on the motion of Demosthenes, to lodge his treasure in the Acropolis. A large portion of it is missing, and, on inquiry being instituted by the Areopagus, Demosthenes (among others) is charged with having received a bribe from Harpalus. He is found guilty, and sentenced to pay a fine of fifty talents.

Unable to pay this, he flies to Megara, and remains in exile.

323    Alexander dies at Babylon.

The Athenians resolve on war, and send ambassadors to stir up the Greeks. A general rising takes place, and Leosthenes the Athenian is chosen commander. Sparta remains neutral, and the Bœotians adhere to Macedonia.

Leosthenes defeats the Bœotians at Platæa, and marches to meet Antipater in Thessaly. Antipater is totally defeated, and takes refuge in Lamia, where he is blockaded.

Macedonian envoys are sent to Peloponnesus, to counteract the efforts of the Athenians. Demosthenes opposes them successfully in Argos, Corinth, and Arcadia.

Demosthenes is recalled from exile by the Athenians, and a ship sent to bring him home.

Leosthenes is killed in a sally from Lamia. Antiphilus succeeds him as general.

The siege of Lamia is raised by the advance of Leonatus, who is himself defeated and slain; but Antipater effects a junction with his army, and receives large reinforcements from Macedonia.

322    The Athenian fleet is defeated by the Macedonian.

A Macedonian force lands at Marathon and ravages Attica, but it is defeated by Phocion.

Antipater attacks the Greeks with a greatly superior army at Crannon in Thessaly, and gains a doubtful victory, which becomes decisive by the general desertion of the allies.

Antipater advances against Athens, which submits, and receives a Macedonian garrison.

The Athenians are compelled to remodel their constitution, and adopt a property qualification, which disfranchises a large number of citizens.

Demosthenes and Hyperides, with other orators of the war party, are demanded by Antipater. Demosthenes flies first to Ægina, and afterwards to Calauria, where he takes refuge in the temple of Neptune. Pursued by Archias, the Macedonian emissary, he puts an end to his life by poison.

PART I

# PART I

## THE ORATION ON THE CROWN

### ARGUMENT

THIS has justly been considered the greatest speech of the greatest
orator in the world. It derives an additional interest from the circumstance that it was the last great speech delivered in Athens. The
subject matter of it is virtually a justification of the whole public policy
and life of Demosthenes; while in point of form it is a defence of
Ctesiphon for a decree which he proposed in favour of Demosthenes
B.C. 338, not long after the battle of Chæronea.

When the news of that disastrous battle reached Athens, the people
were in the utmost consternation. Nothing less was expected than
an immediate invasion of Attica by the conqueror; and strong measures
were taken, under the advice of Hyperides, to put the city in a posture
of defence. One of the most important was the repair of the walls
and ramparts. Demosthenes at this time held the office of conservator
of walls, having been appointed by his own tribe at the end of the year
B.C. 339. The reparation, which had been commenced before, but
suspended during the late compaign, was now vigorously prosecuted.
He himself superintended the work, and expended on it three talents
of his own money, beyond what was allowed out of the public treasury.

The fears of the people were not realised. Philip, while he chastised
the Thebans, treated the Athenians with moderation and clemency;
restoring their prisoners without ransom, burying their dead upon the
field, and sending their bones to Athens. He deprived them indeed
of most of their foreign possessions, but even enlarged their domestic
territory by the addition of Oropus.

It seemed that the whole foundation upon which the credit and influence of Demosthenes had rested was overthrown. The hopes which
he had held out of successful resistance to Philip, of re-establishing
Athenian ascendancy, or maintaining the independence of Greece, were
now proved to be fallacious. The alliance of Thebes, his last great
measure for the protection of Athens, appeared to have been the
immediate cause of her defeat and disgrace. The very moderation
with which Philip had used his victory looked like a reproach to the
orator, who had so often denounced his cruelties before the Athenian
assembly, and warned them of his deadly hostility to Athens.

The Macedonian party considered that the time was come for the

B 546                              19

humiliation of their adversary. They assailed him with prosecutions. The peace which Athens concluded with Macedonia was the signal for war against Demosthenes. But his enemies were mistaken in their reckoning, when they supposed that the people would feel resentment against him as the author of their misfortunes. The Athenians took a juster and nobler view of the matter; they judged not of his counsels by the result, but by their own intrinsic merit. Demosthenes came clear and triumphant out of every prosecution; and while Lysicles the general was condemned to capital punishment for his misconduct of the war, Demosthenes received from his countrymen a signal proof of their esteem and confidence, being appointed to pronounce the funeral oration in honour of the citizens who had fallen at Chæronea.

About the same time, and not many months after the battle, Ctesiphon introduced a bill to the Council of Five Hundred, proposing to reward Demosthenes for his gifts of money to the public, and for his general integrity and good conduct as a statesman. It is not unlikely that the very object of this measure was to stop the attacks upon Demosthenes, and to give him the opportunity, in case it should be opposed, of justifying the whole course of his political life. With that view was inserted the clause eulogising his general character as a statesman. The Macedonian party naturally regarded this clause as a reflection upon themselves, and a virtual condemnation of the policy which they had for so many years espoused. They felt themselves therefore compelled to make a stand against it; and they resolved upon a course, which was open to them according to the Athenian laws, of indicting Ctesiphon as the author of an illegal measure. His bill, having been approved by the council, and then brought before the popular assembly, was passed in the shape of a decree, by which it was declared to be the will of the council and people of Athens, " that Demosthenes should be presented with a golden crown, and that a proclamation should be made in the theatre, at the great Dionysian festival, at the performance of the new tragedies, announcing that Demosthenes was rewarded by the people with a golden crown for his integrity, for the goodwill which he had invariably displayed towards all the Greeks and towards the people of Athens, and also for his magnanimity, and because he had ever both by word and deed promoted the interests of the people, and been zealous to do all the good in his power." This decree, as the opposite party conceived, was open to three objections, two of which were chiefly of a legal nature; the other, while it equally assumed a legal form, called in question the real merits of Ctesiphon's motion. An indictment, embodying all the objections, was preferred before the archon, the chief magistrate of Athens, to whose cognisance a criminal proceeding of this kind appertained. The prosecutor was Æschines, the second of Athenian orators, the deadly enemy of Demosthenes, who would not only be considered by his party as the fittest person to conduct the cause, but was stimulated to it by every motive of rivalry and revenge. The indictment, after reciting the decree, alleged that it violated the Athenian law in three points, as follows:—

First, because it was unlawful to make false allegations in any of the state documents:

Secondly, because it was unlawful to confer a crown upon any person who had an account to render of his official conduct; and Demosthenes was both a conservator of walls and a treasurer of the theoric fund:

Thirdly, because it was unlawful to proclaim the honour of a crown in the theatre at the Dionysian festival, at the performance of the new tragedies; the law being, that if the council gave a crown, it should be published in the council-hall; if the people, in the pnyx at the popular assembly.

The first of these points raised the substantial question at issue—viz. whether the decree of Ctesiphon had stated a falsehood, when it assigned the virtue and patriotism of Demosthenes as reasons for conferring public honour upon him. The other two, while they were mainly of a technical character, were strongly relied on by Æschines as affording him the means of securing a verdict.

Notice of intention to indict had probably been given at the time when the decree was passed. The bill was actually preferred on the sixth of Elaphebolion, B.C. 338, eight months after the battle of Chæronea, and a few days before the Dionysian festival, at which the honour conferred upon Demosthenes was to have been proclaimed. It had this immediate consequence, that the decree of Ctesiphon could not be carried into effect till after the trial; and thus one end, at least, was gained by Æschines and his party,—the satisfaction of having suspended their adversary's triumph. But whether they were deterred by the failure of other prosecutions against Demosthenes, or whether they judged from the temper of the people that they had but little chance of success, the indictment of Ctesiphon was suffered to lie dormant for more than seven years, and was not brought to trial till the year B.C. 330. It may seem strange that the law of Athens should have allowed a criminal prosecution to hang over a man for so long a period; but it must be borne in mind that the proceeding against Ctesiphon not only involved a charge personally affecting him, but had the further, and ostensibly the more important, object of maintaining the purity of the law itself, and preventing an unconstitutional decree from being recorded in the public archives. It is probable, however, that the case would never have been revived, but for the occurrence of political events which seemed to afford a favourable opportunity.

Within two years after his victory at Chæronea, Philip had perished by the hand of an assassin. The hopes that were excited in Greece by the news of his death were quickly dispelled by the vigorous measures of his successor. Notwithstanding the efforts of Demosthenes, it was found impossible to concert any feasible plan for a union of the Greek states against Macedonia. The rash revolt of the Thebans was punished by the extirpation of their city, which struck terror into the very heart of Greece. Athens, suspected of aiding the insurgents, hastened to appease the conqueror by humble submission; and when he insisted on the delivery up of their principal orators, including Demosthenes, it was with difficulty that he was prevailed upon to accept a less severe measure of satisfaction. The debate which took place in the Athenian assembly upon this demand of Alexander, shews that Demosthenes must still have been in high esteem at Athens. The feelings of the people, notwithstanding their fears, were against the delivery of the orators; and Phocion's counsel, urging them to surrender themselves for the public good, was not well received. Alexander in the year following (B.C. 334) passed over into Asia, and commenced his career of conquest. Meanwhile Greece had a breathing time. The states that sighed for freedom looked with anxious expectation for every intelligence from the scene of war, as if all their hopes depended on the fate of one man. The further he penetrated into Asia, the better chance there seemed to be of his being over-whelmed by the force of the Persian empire. While he was yet in the defiles of Cilicia, it was confidently asserted by Demosthenes at Athens that his army would be trampled under foot by the cavalry of Darius.  The battle of Issus belied this prophecy; yet it was still believed that the Persian monarchy had resources in itself sufficient to prevail in the war: and the length of time that Alexander was occupied in Phœnicia and Egypt, whilst Darius was collecting the strength of his empire in the east, seemed to favour these sanguine views.

About the time that Alexander was marching to fight his last and decisive battle against the Persian king in Mesopotamia, Agis, king of Sparta, put himself at the head of a confederacy, which comprised the greater part of the Peloponnesian states, and prepared to throw off the Macedonian yoke.  Taking his opportunity, whilst Antipater was engaged in suppressing a Thracian insurrection, he raised his standard in Laconia, and declared war; but, after gaining some successes and laying siege to Megalopolis, which refused to join the league, he was defeated in a hard-fought battle by Antipater, and died fighting with the valour of an ancient Spartan.  This was in the beginning of the year B.C. 330.  The confederacy was dissolved, and the voice of freedom was again changed to that of submission.

Athens had taken no part in the last movement.  The cause of her neutrality is not quite clear, though it is probably to be attributed to a want of proper concert and preparation.  Had the Athenians set their forces to assist Agis in Peloponnesus, they would have been exposed to the first attack of the enemy, and the dread of this may have restrained them from rising.  A Macedonian garrison was maintained in the Cadmea, which would gain speedy intelligence of any movement on the part of the Athenians, and the people of the Bœotian towns were friendly to Macedonia.  It is not quite clear either what part Demosthenes took upon this occasion.  Æschines represents him as boasting that he had kindled the flames of war in Peloponnesus; and both Plutarch and Dinarchus intimate that he exerted himself for that purpose: yet Æschines accuses him also of neglecting so good an opportunity for engaging Athens in the contest.  Demosthenes may in prudence have abstained from plunging the Athenians into a war, for which he saw they were ill prepared, and at the same time he may have encouraged the Peloponnesians to make an effort of which, in the event of success, his own country would equally have reaped the benefit.  So timid a policy he would not certainly have adopted eight years before; but under existing circumstances it could hardly be a reproach to him, especially when he observed the timid and temporising spirit which was gradually gaining ground among his countrymen.  Presents of Persian spoil had been sent to Athens, to decorate the Acropolis.  Phocion corresponded with Alexander as a friend; and it was generally represented by all who belonged to his party, that resistance to him was hopeless.

If such feelings prevailed to a great extent before the defeat of Agis, they must have been greatly strengthened after that event.  Macedonian arms were everywhere triumphant.  Alexander had seated himself on the throne of Darius; Antipater, his viceroy, was irresistible in Greece: Macedonian ascendency, which Demosthenes had exerted himself all his life to oppose, seemed now to be completely secure.  Athens was not what she was even at the time of Chæronea.  For sixteen years before that disastrous battle, the voice of Demosthenes had been continually resounding in the assembly, instructing, animating, improving, elevating the minds and hearts of his hearers;

exerting such an influence over them, that he may be said to have raised up, by the force of his own eloquence, a new generation of patriots. But in the eight years that followed it was very different: his voice in the cause of freedom and glory had been little heard; and besides that the people were cowed by the events which had occurred, a lethargy had fallen on their spirit, for want of some one to rouse them.

This was the time chosen by Æschines for bringing to an issue the long-suspended cause. The aspect of affairs both at home and abroad seemed favourable to the undertaking; and he summoned up all his force and resolution for the contest. It was to be not only a trial of strength between the contending parties at Athens,—the favourers of Macedonian power, and those that regretted the loss of independence, —but a final and decisive struggle between two rival statesmen, exasperated against each other by a long series of hostilities. It was manifest that Ctesiphon was but the nominal defendant; the real object of attack was Demosthenes, his whole policy and administration. The interest excited was intense, not only at Athens, but throughout all Greece; and an immense concourse of foreigners flocked from all parts to hear the two most celebrated orators in the world. A jury (of not less than five hundred) was impanelled by the archon; and before a dense and breathless audience the pleadings began.

As the speeches of both the orators are preserved to us, we have the means of comparing one with the other, and forming our opinion of their respective merits. The world in general have decided as the people of Athens did, not only upon the oratorical merits of the two rivals, but upon the principal questions at issue between them. The accuser, who thought to brand his opponent with eternal infamy, has only added to the lustre of his rival's renown. Independently of the internal evidence furnished by this and other orations of Demosthenes, which have carried to the hearts of most readers a conviction of his patriotism, we cannot fail to be strongly influenced by the judgment of the Athenians themselves, whom neither their own past misfortunes, nor the terror inspired by the late victory of Antipater, could deter from giving a verdict, by which, while they acquitted Demosthenes from all blame, they in effect declared their approbation of his measures in opposition to Macedonia.

The speech of Æschines betrays a consciousness of weakness in that part of his case where he attacks the political character of his rival. He seems to feel also that he is speaking in opposition to the general feeling of his hearers. His own character as a politician had been so dubious, his conduct so open to suspicion, that while he most bitterly assails his adversary, he is constantly under the necessity of defending himself. On the whole life, public and private, of Demosthenes, he pours a torrent of invective; to this the greater part of his speech is devoted: yet he seems to have been impelled to it rather by hate and revenge than by any calculation of advantage. On the other hand, when he deals with the legal parts of his case, commenting on those specific violations of Athenian law which Ctesiphon's measure was charged with, it is evident that his strength lay there; he handles his subject temperately, skilfully, and carefully, labouring to make every point clear to the jury, and to impress them with the conviction that to uphold the laws was the sure way to maintain constitutional government. On these points he mainly relied, hoping by this means to secure a verdict, which would give him a triumph over his enemy, and carry the general opinion over Greece, that the credit and influence of Demosthenes were extinguished.

Demosthenes, feeling his weakness as to the legal questions, dexterously throws them into the middle of his speech, and passes lightly and rapidly over them, while he devotes his greatest efforts to the vindication of his own merits as a patriot and a statesman. Refusing to comply with the insidious demand of Æschines, that he should take the questions in the same order as his accuser, he insists upon his legal right to conduct his defence as he pleases. Opening with a modest exordium, to conciliate the favour of the jury, he launches gradually into the history of his own conduct and measures: presenting first a general view of the condition of Greece when he entered public life, and of the difficulties under which the Athenians laboured in their contest with Philip; then setting forth his own views, plans, and objects, and showing that he had advised a course of action which both the circumstances of the time and the honour of the country required. He apologises for the self-praise mixed up with his speech, on the ground that he was driven to it by his opponent. Entering on the Sacred War, and the peace of B.C. 346, he labours to exculpate himself from all share in the errors then committed, imputing them chiefly to the negligence of the other ambassadors, and to the treachery of Philocrates and Æschines, who, by the false hopes which they excited at Athens, prevented the people from assisting the Phocians. Coming to the events which brought on a renewal of the war, he shows how Philip's ambitious projects and encroachments in every part of Greece made it necessary to oppose him, especially for the Athenians, who were menaced at home as well as abroad by his aggressions in Thrace, Eubœa, and Megara. He pursues these topics until he has carried with him the feelings of his hearers, which must have been strongly on his side when he dilated on the glorious issue of the campaigns in Eubœa and the Propontis, and read to them the decrees of the Byzantines, Perinthians, and Chersonesites, in honour of Athens, all which were due to the vigorous measures of his own administration. Having thus secured the goodwill and sympathy of his judges, he proceeds to discuss the legal charges against Ctesiphon. Dwelling on them but for a short time, he plunges into a personal attack upon Æschines, holding up to ridicule the meanness of his birth and parentage, and retorting on him the same coarse and opprobrious language which had been used towards himself. The bitterness of his invective is only to be excused on the ground of strong provocation, added to an assurance that his more grave charges of corruption and treason were well founded. Those charges, so often advanced before, he here repeats, denouncing more particularly the conduct of Æschines upon his mission to Delphi, B.C. 339, to which the disaster of Chæronea was attributable. The account which Æschines had given of this affair he shows to be false, and enters upon a minute examination of the proceedings which caused Philip to be appointed Amphictyonic general, and to march with an invading army, nominally against the Amphissian Locrians, really against Bœotia and Attica. A graphic description is given of the consternation at Athens on hearing that Philip had seized Elatea. The meeting of the people, the advice of Demosthenes to them, his embassy to Thebes, the success of his negotiations, and the conclusion of the alliance between Thebes and Athens are briefly recounted, Demosthenes forcibly pointing out the advantage of his measures, contending that they were not to be judged by the mere event of the battle, and that it was far more glorious for his country to be defeated in a struggle for the independence of Greece, than it would have been to keep aloof from the contest. Here he makes that noble adjuration, which has in all ages been admired, appealing to his countrymen by the deeds of their ancestors, of whom they would have acted most unworthily, had they without a struggle abandoned the post of honour bequeathed to them. He himself as a statesman would have deserved execration, had he advised such a course. The failure of their arms was not to be imputed to the minister, who had done all he could to insure their success, but rather to the commanders, or to evil fortune. As Æschines had said so much about the ill fortune which attended him, he draws a comparison between the different fortunes of himself and his rival, first, of their early life and education, next, of their career as public men. Æschines from the beginning had taken a part which put him in opposition to the true interests of Athens, which caused him to rejoice at her disasters, to quail and tremble at her successes. He never came forward to assist her by his counsels when she needed them, but only to censure others who had given their honest advice, because it had not turned out as well as was expected. It was a signal proof of his malignant disposition, that he had expatiated on the late disastrous events as if they were a subject of triumph to him, without shedding a single tear, without any faltering in his voice, without betraying the least emotion or symptom of grief. In reply to the challenge of Æschines, to say for what merit he claimed the reward of a crown, Demosthenes boldly declares, for his incorruptibility, by which he was distinguished not only from Æschines, but from the multitude of venal orators in the Grecian world. Had there been but a few more like himself in other states, Macedonia could never have risen to greatness upon their ruin. He had done all that was possible for a single man; and Athens, while she shared the misfortune of all the Greeks, had the consolation of reflecting that she had striven gallantly and bravely to avert the common calamity. Æschines had lauded the great men of a bygone age, drawing an invidious contrast between Demosthenes and them. This, says Demosthenes, was not a fair way of judging him: he should be tried by reference to his own acts, as compared with those of his contemporaries. Yet even from the former comparison he did not shrink; for he had acted on the same principles as the statesmen of olden time, striving always to maintain the honour and dignity of Athens. Attachment to his country, and earnest anxiety for her welfare, had been his constant and abiding motives of action; throughout his whole life, in the day of power, in the hour of trial and adversity, those feelings had never deserted him: that was the test of a good and honest citizen; by that he ought to be judged.

Such is, in substance, the argument of this celebrated oration, as far as relates to the main question in the cause. The effect produced by the speech upon an Athenian audience can be but faintly imagined by us who read it at this distance of time. Although Athens was not then what she had once been; although she was humbled by defeat, shorn of her honours, stripped of her empire and dependencies, without allies, without resources, without means of resistance to that iron power under which all Greece had succumbed; there was still the remembrance of the past, not yet extinguished by habitual servitude; there were still vague hopes of future deliverance, and a fire of smothered indignation burning in the hearts of the people, ready to burst into a flame at the first favourable opportunity. That such were their feelings is proved by what occurred seven years afterwards upon the death of Alexander; when Athens made one convulsive effort for freedom, ere she finally submitted to her fate. Demosthenes stood before his countrymen, representing all which remained of Athenian dignity and glory. If any man could help them, it was he. His advice had always been steady and constant; his warnings should have been earlier attended to: but even yet there might be need of him. He was their consolation for the past, their hope for the future. During the progress of his address, such thoughts rushed upon their minds with greater and greater force, till they were elevated above themselves, and all the spirit of their ancestors was for the moment regenerate within them.

They could forgive him all his egotism and self-praise. It was the praise of a life devoted to their service. Where he lauded his own acts most strongly, he identified them with the glories of his country. Whatever good results might have accrued from his measures, he ascribed the merit less to himself than to the fortune of Athens, or to the gods, of whom he was but the humble instrument in a righteous cause. His own eloquence would have been of no avail, had it not touched the true chord of Athenian feeling. Throughout his whole political career he had been supported by the judgment and convictions of the people. Thus he argued, and the people felt it was impossible for them to find him guilty, without passing sentence upon themselves, without condemning the policy which Athens had for a long series of years consistently pursued. The genius of Athens protected her from such disgrace; and by an overwhelming majority, which left the accuser no choice but to retire into exile, a verdict was given for the defendant.

I BEGIN, men of Athens, by praying to every God and Goddess, that the same goodwill, which I have ever cherished towards the commonwealth and all of you, may be requited to me on the present trial. I pray likewise—and this specially concerns yourselves, your religion, and your honour—that the Gods may put it in your minds, not to take counsel of my opponent touching the manner in which I am to be heard—that would indeed be cruel!—but of the laws and of your oath; wherein (besides the other obligations) it is prescribed that you shall hear both sides alike. This means, not only that you must pass no pre-condemnation, not only that you must extend your goodwill equally to both, but also that you must allow the parties to adopt such order and course of defence as they severally choose and prefer.

Many advantages hath Æschines over me on this trial; and two especially, men of Athens. First, my risk in the contest is not the same. It is assuredly not the same for me to forfeit your regard, as for my adversary not to succeed in his indictment. To me—but I will say nothing untowards at the outset of my address. The prosecution however is play to him. My second disadvantage is, the natural disposition of mankind to take pleasure in hearing invective and accusation, and to be annoyed by those who praise themselves. To Æschines is assigned the part which gives pleasure; that which is (I may fairly say) offensive to all, is left for me. And if, to escape from this, I make no mention of what I have done, I shall appear to be without defence against his charges, without proof of my claims to honour: whereas, if I proceed to give an account of my conduct and measures, I shall be forced to speak frequently of myself. I will endeavour then to do so with all becoming modesty: what I am driven to by the necessity of the case, will be fairly chargeable to my opponent who has instituted such a prosecution.

I think, men of the jury, you will all agree that I, as well as Ctesiphon, am a party to this proceeding, and that it is a matter of no less concern to me. It is painful and grievous to be deprived of anything, especially by the act of one's enemy; but your goodwill and affection are the heaviest loss, precisely as they are the greatest prize to gain.

Such being the matters at stake in this cause, I conjure and implore you all alike, to hear my defence to the charge in that fair manner which the laws prescribe—laws, to which their author, Solon, a man friendly to you and to popular rights, thought that validity should be given, not only by the recording of them, but by the oath of you the jurors: not that he distrusted you, as it appears to me; but, seeing that the charges and calumnies, wherein the prosecutor is powerful by being the first speaker, cannot be got over by the defendant, unless each of you jurors, observing his religious obligation, shall with like favour receive the arguments of the last speaker, and lend an equal and impartial ear to both, before he determines upon the whole case.

As I am, it appears, on this day to render an account both of my private life and my public measures, I would fain, as
*B 546

in the outset, call the Gods to my aid; and in your presence
I implore them, first, that the goodwill which I have ever
cherished towards the commonwealth and all of you may be
fully requited to me on the present trial; next, that they
may direct you to such a decision upon this indictment, as
will conduce to your common honour, and to the good conscience of each individual.

Had Æschines confined his charge to the subject of the
prosecution, I too would have proceeded at once to my justification of the decree.[1] But since he has wasted no fewer
words in the discussion of other matters, in most of them
calumniating me, I deem it both necessary and just, men of
Athens, to begin by shortly adverting to these points, that
none of you may be induced by extraneous arguments to
shut your ears against my defence to the indictment.

To all his scandalous abuse of my private life, observe my
plain and honest answer. If you know me to be such as he
alleged—for I have lived nowhere else but among you—let
not my voice be heard, however transcendent my statesmanship! Rise up this instant and condemn me! But if, in
your opinion and judgment, I am far better and of better
descent than my adversary; if (to speak without offence) I
am not inferior, I or mine, to any respectable citizens; then
give no credit to him for his other statements—it is plain
they were all equally fictions—but to me let the same goodwill, which you have uniformly exhibited upon many former
trials, be manifested now. With all your malice, Æschines,
it was very simple to suppose that I should turn from the
discussion of measures and policy to notice your scandal. I
will do no such thing: I am not so crazed. Your lies and
calumnies about my political life I will examine forthwith;
for that loose ribaldry I shall have a word hereafter, if the
jury desire to hear it.

The crimes whereof I am accused are many and grievous:
for some of them the laws enact heavy—most severe penal-

[1] The decree of the Senate procured by Ctesiphon in favour of
Demosthenes.

ties. The scheme of this present proceeding includes a combination of spiteful insolence, insult, railing, aspersion, and everything of the kind; while for the said charges and accusations, if they were true, the state has not the means of inflicting an adequate punishment, or anything like it. For it is not right to debar another of access to the people and privilege of speech; moreover, to do so by way of malice and insult—by heaven! is neither honest, nor constitutional, nor just. If the crimes which he saw me committing against the state were as heinous as he so tragically gave out, he ought to have enforced the penalties of the law against them at the time; if he saw me guilty of an impeachable offence, by impeaching and so bringing me to trial before you; if moving illegal decrees, by indicting me for them. For surely, if he can prosecute Ctesiphon on my account, he would not have forborne to indict me myself, had he thought he could convict me. In short, whatever else he saw me doing to your prejudice, whether mentioned or not mentioned in his catalogue of slander, there are laws for such things, and punishments, and trials, and judgments, with sharp and severe penalties; all of which he might have enforced against me: and had he done so—had he thus pursued the proper method with me, his charges would have been consistent with his conduct. But now he has declined the straightforward and just course, avoided all proofs of guilt at the time, and after this long interval gets up, to play his part withal, a heap of accusation, ribaldry, and scandal. Then he arraigns me, but prosecutes the defendant. His hatred of me he makes the prominent part of the whole contest; yet, without having ever met me upon that ground, he openly seeks to deprive a third party of his privileges. Now, men of Athens, besides all the other arguments that may be urged in Ctesiphon's behalf, this, methinks, may very fairly be alleged—that we should try our own quarrel by ourselves; not leave our private dispute, and look what third party we can damage. That surely were the height of injustice.

It may appear from what has been said, that all his charges are alike unjust and unfounded in truth. Yet I wish to examine them separately, and especially his calumnies about the peace and the embassy, where he attributed to me the acts of himself and Philocrates. It is necessary also, and perhaps proper, men of Athens, to remind you how affairs stood at those times, that you may consider every single measure in reference to the occasion.

When the Phocian war had broken out—not through me, for I had not then commenced public life—you were in this position: you wished the Phocians to be saved, though you saw they were not acting right; and would have been glad for the Thebans to suffer anything, with whom for a just reason you were angry; for they had not borne with moderation their good fortune at Leuctra. The whole of Peloponnesus was divided: they that hated the Lacedæmonians were not powerful enough to destroy them; and they that ruled before by Spartan influence were not masters of the states: among them, as among the rest of the Greeks, there was a sort of unsettled strife and confusion. Philip, seeing this—it was not difficult to see—lavished bribes upon the traitors in every state, embroiled and stirred them all up against each other; and so, by the errors and follies of the rest, he was strengthening himself, and growing up to the ruin of all. But when every one saw that the then overbearing, but now unfortunate, Thebans, harassed by so long a war, must of necessity have recourse to you; Philip, to prevent this, and obstruct the union of the states, offered to you peace, to them succour. What helped him then almost to surprise you in a voluntary snare? The cowardice, shall I call it? or ignorance—or both—of the other Greeks; who, whilst you were waging a long and incessant war—and that too for their common benefit, as the event has shown—assisted you neither with money nor men, nor anything else whatsoever. You, being justly and naturally offended with them, lent a willing ear to Philip.

The peace then granted was through such means brought about, not through me, as Æschines calumniously charged. The criminal and corrupt practices of these men during the treaty will be found, on fair examination, to be the cause of our present condition. The whole matter am I for truth's sake discussing and going through; for, let there appear to be ever so much criminality in these transactions, it is surely nothing to me. The first who spoke and mentioned the subject of peace was Aristodemus the actor: the seconder and mover, fellow-hireling for that purpose with the prosecutor, was Philocrates the Agnusian—your associate, Æschines, not mine, though you should burst with lying. Their supporters—from whatever motives—I pass that by for the present—were Eubulus and Cephisophon. I had nothing to do with it.

Notwithstanding these facts, which I have stated exactly according to the truth, he ventured to assert—to such a pitch of impudence had he come—that I, besides being author of the peace, had prevented the country making it in a general council with the Greeks. Why, you—I know not what name you deserve!—when you saw me robbing the state of an advantage and connection so important as you described just now, did you ever express indignation? did you come forward to publish and proclaim what you now charge me with? If indeed I had been bribed by Philip to prevent the conjunction of the Greeks, it was your business not to be silent, but to cry out, to protest, and inform the people. But you never did so—your voice was never heard to such a purpose, and no wonder; for at that time no embassy had been sent to any of the Greeks—they had all been tested long before; and not a word of truth upon the subject has Æschines spoken.

Besides, it is the country that he most traduces by his falsehoods. For, if you were at the same time calling on the Greeks to take arms, and sending your own ambassadors to treat with Philip for peace, you were performing the part

of an Eurybatus,[1] not the act of a commonwealth, or of honest
men. But it is false, it is false. For what purpose could ye
have sent for them at that period? For peace? They all
had it. For war? You were yourselves deliberating about
peace. It appears, therefore, I was not the adviser or the
author of the original peace; and none of his other calumnies
against me are shown to be true.

Observe again, after the state had concluded the peace,
what line of conduct each of us adopted. Hence you will
understand who it was that co-operated in everything with
Philip; who that acted in your behalf, and sought the advantage of the commonwealth.

I moved in the council, that our ambassadors should sail
instantly for whatever place they heard Philip was in, and
receive his oath: they would not however, notwithstanding
my resolution.[2] What was the effect of this, men of Athens?
I will explain. It was Philip's interest that the interval
before the oaths should be as long as possible; yours, that it
should be as short. Why? Because you discontinued all
your warlike preparations, not only from the day of swearing
peace, but from the day that you conceived hopes of it; a
thing which Philip was from the beginning studious to con-
trive, believing—rightly enough—that whatever of our possessions he might take before the oath of ratification, he
should hold securely; as none would break the peace on such
account. I, men of Athens, foreseeing and weighing these
consequences, moved the decree, to sail for whatever place
Philip was in, and receive his oath without delay; so that
your allies, the Thracians, might be in possession of the
places which Æschines ridiculed just now (Serrium, Myrtium,
and Ergisce) at the time of swearing the oaths; and that
Philip might not become master of Thrace by securing the

---

[1] This name, having once belonged to a notorious thief and trickster,
had passed into a byword of reproach.
[2] It is implied that the motion was carried. It then became a resolution of the Senate, on the motion of Demosthenes, and may be called
*his* resolution.

posts of vantage, nor provide himself with plenty of money and troops to facilitate his further designs. Yet this decree he neither mentions nor reads; but reproaches me, because, as Councillor, I thought proper to introduce the ambassadors. Why, what should I have done? Moved not to introduce men who were come for the purpose of conferring with you? or ordered the Manager not to assign them places at the theatre? [1] They might have had places for their two obols, if the resolution had not been moved. Was it my duty to guard the petty interests of the state, and have sold our main interests like these men? Surely not. Take and read me this decree, which the prosecutor, knowing it well, passed over. Read.

## THE DECREE [2]

" In the Archonship of Mnesiphilus, on the thirteenth of Hecatombæon, in the presidency of the Pandionian tribe, Demosthenes son of Demosthenes of Pæania moved:—

[1] Demosthenes, as member of the council, had introduced the Macedonian ambassadors, Parmenio, Antipater, and Eurylochus, and moved that they should be invited to seats of honour at the Dionysian festival. This was no more than a necessary act of civility, due to the eminent ministers whom Philip had sent to treat with the Athenians: and there could not be a more fit person to make the motion than Demosthenes, who had been one of the ten ambassadors to Philip, and (it seems) the only councillor among them. Nor did he confine himself to these formal acts, but during their stay at Athens hospitably entertained them at his own house, and on their departure accompanied them a part of the way on horseback. For these attentions he was reproached by Æschines, as if he had overacted his part, and either sought to curry favour with Philip, or to make an idle display of his wealth and importance.

[2] In this, as in most of the documents quoted in the first half of the present speech, there are found serious difficulties, which have led critics to the conviction that it is not genuine. In the first place, the name of the archon for the year B.C. 347 was not Mnesiphilus, but Themistocles. Secondly, not five, but ten ambassadors, were sent to receive the oath of Philip; and indeed the same ten who had been on the previous embassy. Thirdly, it is called a resolution of the senate and people, whereas that which Demosthenes refers to was a resolution of the senate alone. Fourthly, the ten ambassadors were sent to receive Philip's oath only, not to take the oath on behalf of their country, which had been done before. These and some other discrepancies have led to the conclusion that the decree is an interpolation.

Whereas Philip hath sent ambassadors for peace, and hath agreed upon articles of treaty, it is resolved by the Council and People of Athens, in order that the peace voted in the first assembly may be ratified, to choose forthwith from the whole body of Athenians five ambassadors; and that the persons elected do repair, without any delay, wheresoever they shall ascertain that Philip is, and as speedily as may be exchange oaths with him, according to the articles agreed on between him and the Athenian people, comprehending the allies of either party.   For ambassadors were chosen, Eubulus of Anaphlystus, Æschines of Cothocidæ, Cephisophon of Rhamnus, Democrates of Phlya, Cleon of Cothocidæ.''

Notwithstanding that I had passed this decree for the advantage of Athens, not that of Philip, our worthy ambassadors so little regarded it, as to sit down in Macedonia three whole months, until Philip returned from Thrace after entirely subjugating the country; although they might in ten days, or rather in three or four, have reached the Hellespont and saved the fortresses, by receiving his oath before he reduced them: for he would never have touched them in our presence, or we should not have sworn him; and thus he would have lost the peace, and not have obtained both, the peace and the fortresses.

Such was the first trick of Philip, the first corrupt act of these accursed miscreants, in the embassy: for which I avow that I was and am and ever will be at war and variance with them.   But mark another and still greater piece of villainy immediately after.   When Philip had sworn to the peace, having secured Thrace through these men disobeying my decree, he again bribes them not to leave Macedonia, until he had got all ready for his expedition against the Phocians. His fear was, if they reported to you his design and preparation for marching, you might sally forth, sail round with your galleys to Thermopylæ as before, and block up the strait: his desire, that, the moment you received the intelligence from them, he should have passed Thermopylæ, and you be unable to do anything. And in such terror and anxiety was Philip, lest, notwithstanding he had gained these advantages, if you voted succour before the destruction of the Phocians, his enterprise should fail; he hires this despicable fellow, no longer in common with the other ambassadors, but by himself individually, to make that statement and report to you, by which everything was lost.

I conjure and beseech you, men of Athens, throughout the trial to remember this; that, if Æschines in his charge had not travelled out of the indictment, neither would I have spoken a word irrelevant; but since he has resorted to every species both of accusation and calumny, it is necessary for me to reply briefly to each of his charges.

What then were the statements made by Æschines, through which everything was lost? That you should not be alarmed by Philip's having passed Thermopylæ—that all would be as you desired, if you kept quiet; and in two or three days you would hear, he was their friend to whom he had come as an enemy, and their enemy to whom he had come as a friend—it was not words that cemented attachments (such was his solemn phrase), but identity of interest; and it was the interest of all alike, Philip, the Phocians, and you, to be relieved from the harshness and insolence of the Thebans. His assertions were heard by some with pleasure, on account of the hatred which then subsisted against the Thebans. But what happened directly, almost immediately, afterwards? The wretched Phocians were destroyed, their cities demolished; you that kept quiet, and trusted to Æschines, were shortly bringing in your effects out of the country, while Æschines received gold; and yet more—while you got nothing but your enmity with the Thebans and Thessalians, Philip won their gratitude for what he had done. To prove what I say, read me the decree of Callisthenes, and the letter of Philip, from both of which these particulars will be clear to you. Read.

### THE DECREE [1]

"In the Archonship of Mnesiphilus, an extraordinary assembly having been convened by the Generals, with the sanction of the Presidents and the Council, on the twenty-first of Mæmacterion, Callisthenes, son of Eteonicus of Phalerum, moved:—No Athenian shall on any pretence sleep in the country, but all in the city and Piræus, except those who are stationed in the garrisons; and they shall every one keep the posts assigned to them, without absenting themselves by night or day.   Whosoever disobeys this decree shall be amenable to the penalties of treason, unless he can show that some necessity prevented him:   the judges of such necessity shall be the General of Infantry, and he of the Finance department,[2] and the Secretary of the Council.   All effects shall be conveyed out of the country as speedily as may be; those that are within a hundred and twenty furlongs into the city and Piræus, those that are beyond a hundred and twenty furlongs to Eleusis, and Phyle, and Aphidna, and Rhamnus, and Sunium.   On the motion of Callisthenes of Phalerum."

Was it with such expectations you concluded the peace? Were such the promises this hireling made you?   Come, read the letter which Philip sent after this to Athens.

[1] This decree, like the last, appears to be spurious.   Not only the name of the archon, but the date and other circumstances are incorrect. The assembly held after the news of the conquest of Phocis was not in the month here stated, but at the end of Scirrophorion (June).

[2] The duties of the generals were more numerous and varied in the time of Demosthenes than in the early period of the republic.   Formerly the ten generals were sent out all together on warlike service.   But this practice was discontinued, as the wars of Athens began to be more frequent and on a larger scale.   One, two, or three only were put in command of a single armament.   The generals had also various duties of a civil nature assigned to them, which required the presence of some of them at home.

" Philip, king of Macedonia, to the Council and People of Athens, greeting. Ye know that we have passed Thermopylæ, and reduced Phocis to submission, and put garrisons in the towns that opened their gates; those that resisted we took by storm, and rased to the ground, enslaving their inhabitants. Hearing however, that ye are preparing to assist them, I have written unto you, that ye may trouble yourselves no further in the business. For it seems to me ye are acting altogether unreasonably; having concluded peace, and nevertheless taking the field, and that too when the Phocians are not comprehended in our treaty. Wherefore, if ye abide not by your engagements, ye will gain no advantage but that of being the aggressors."

You hear how plainly, in his letter to you, he declares and asserts to his own allies—" all this I have done against the will of the Athenians, and in their despite; therefore if ye are wise, ye Thebans and Thessalians, ye will regard them as enemies, and put confidence in me;" not writing in such words, but meaning so to be understood. And by these means he carried them away with him, insomuch that they had neither foresight nor sense of the consequences, but suffered him to get everything into his power: hence the misfortunes under which those wretched people at present are. The agent and auxiliary who helped to win for him such confidence—who brought false reports here and cajoled you—he it is who now bewails the sufferings of the Thebans, and dilates upon them so pathetically, he himself being the cause both of these calamities, and those in Phocis, and all the rest which the Greeks have sustained. Truly must you, Æschines, grieve at these events, and compassionate the Thebans, when you hold property in Bœotia and farm their lands; and I rejoice at a work, whose author immediately required me to be delivered into his hands.[1]

But I have fallen upon a subject which it may be more convenient to discuss by and by. I will return then to my proofs, showing how the iniquities of these men have brought about the present state of things.

When you had been deceived by Philip through the agency of these men, who sold themselves in the embassies, and reported not a word of truth to you—when the unhappy Phocians had been deceived and their cities destroyed—what followed? The despicable Thessalians and stupid Thebans looked on Philip as a friend, a benefactor, a saviour: he was everything with them—not a syllable would they hear from any one to the contrary. You, though regarding his acts with suspicion and anger, still observed the peace; for you could have done nothing alone. The rest of the Greeks, cheated and disappointed like yourselves, gladly observed the peace, though they also had in a manner been attacked for a long time. For when Philip was marching about, subduing Illyrians and Triballians and some also of the Greeks, and gaining many considerable accessions of power, and certain citizens of the states (Æschines among them) took advantage of the peace to go there and be corrupted; all people then,

---

[1] After Thebes had been taken by Alexander, the Athenians, on the motion of Demades, sent ambassadors to congratulate him. He sent them a letter, demanding that Demosthenes, and eight others (or nine others, according to Diodorus) of the principal orators and statesmen of the anti-Macedonian party, among whom were Chares, Hyperides, and Lycurgus, should be delivered up to him. Phocion advised that they should be given up, and even urged them to surrender themselves for the good of their country. Demosthenes recited to the people the fable of Æsop, where the wolf required the sheep to give up their dogs. After some discussion Demades offered to intercede with the conqueror. He was sent on an embassy for that purpose, and by his entreaty Alexander was prevailed upon to withdraw the demand as to all but Charidemus. That Demosthenes was obnoxious to Alexander can hardly be wondered at. Æschines relates that, on Alexander's first march to Thebes, Demosthenes was sent on an embassy to him from Athens, and went as far as Cithæron, where, apprehending danger to himself, he invented an excuse for turning back. There is no doubt that both then and afterwards he had been concerting measures to shake off the yoke of Macedonia.

against whom he was making such preparations, were attacked. If they perceived it not, that is another question,
no concern of mine. I was for ever warning and protesting,
both at Athens and wheresoever I was sent. But the states
were diseased; one class in their politics and measures being
venal and corrupt, whilst the multitude of private men either
had no foresight, or were caught with the bait of present ease
and idleness; and all were under some such influence, only
they imagined each that the mischief would not approach
themselves, but that by the peril of others they might secure
their own safety when they chose. The result, I fancy, has
been, that the people, in return for their gross and unseasonable indolence, have lost their liberty: the statesmen, who
imagined they were selling everything but themselves, discovered they had sold themselves first; for, instead of
friends, as they were named during the period of bribery,
they are now called parasites, and miscreants, and the like
befitting names. Justly. For no man, O Athenians, spends
money for the traitor's benefit, or, when he has got possession
of his purchase, employs the traitor to advise him in future
proceedings: else nothing could have been more fortunate
than a traitor. But it is not so—it never could be—it is far
otherwise! When the aspirant for power has gained his
object, he is master also of those that sold it; and then—
then, I say, knowing their baseness, he loathes and mistrusts
and spurns them.

Consider only—for, though the time of the events is past,
the time for understanding them is ever present to the wise:
Lasthenes was called the friend of Philip for a while, until he
betrayed Olynthus—Timolaus for a while, until he destroyed
Thebes—Eudicus and Simus of Larissa for a while, until
they brought Thessaly under Philip's power. Since then the
world has become full of traitors, expelled, and insulted, and
suffering every possible calamity. How fared Aristratus in
Sicyon? how Perilaus in Megara? Are they not outcasts?
Hence one may evidently see, it is the vigilant defender of his

country, the strenuous opponent of such men, who secures to
you traitors and hirelings, Æschines, the opportunity of getting bribes: through the number of those that oppose your
wishes, you are in safety and in pay; for had it depended on
yourselves, you would have perished long ago.

Much more could I say about those transactions, yet
methinks too much has been said already. The fault is my
adversary's, for having spirted over me the dregs, I may say,
of his own wickedness and iniquities, of which I was obliged
to clear myself to those who are younger than the events.
You too have probably been disgusted, who knew this man's
venality before I spoke a word. He calls it friendship indeed;
and said somewhere in his speech—" the man who reproaches
me with the friendship of Alexander." I reproach you with
friendship of Alexander! Whence gotten, or how merited?
Neither Philip's friend nor Alexander's should I ever call
you; I am not so mad; unless we are to call reapers and
other hired labourers the friends of those that hire them.
That however is not so—how could it be? It is nothing of
the kind. Philip's hireling I called you once, and Alexander's
I call you now. So do all these men. If you disbelieve
me, ask them; or rather I will do it for you. Athenians! is
Æschines, think ye, the hireling, or the friend of Alexander?
You hear what they say.

I now proceed to my defence upon the indictment itself,
and to the account of my own measures, that Æschines may
hear, though he knows already, on what I found my title
both to these which have been decreed and to far greater
rewards. Take and read me the indictment itself.

### THE INDICTMENT

" In the archonship of Chærondas, on the sixth of Elaphebolion, Æschines son of Atrometus of Cothocidæ preferred
before the archon an indictment against Ctesiphon son of
Leosthenes of Anaphlystus, for an illegal measure: for that

he proposed a decree against law, to wit, that it was right to crown Demosthenes son of Demosthenes of Pæania with a golden crown, and to proclaim in the theatre at the great Dionysian festival, at the exhibition of the new tragedies, that the people crown Demosthenes son of Demosthenes of Pæania with a golden crown, on account of his virtue, and of the goodwill which he has constantly cherished towards all the Greeks as well as towards the people of Athens, and of his integrity, and because he has constantly by word and deed promoted the advantage of the people, and is zealous to do whatever good he can: all which clauses are false and illegal; the laws enacting, first, that no false allegations shall be entered in the public records; secondly, that an accountable officer [1] shall not be crowned, (but Demosthenes is a conservator of the walls, and has charge of the theoric fund); thirdly, that the crown shall not be proclaimed in the theatre at the Dionysian festival, on the new exhibition of tragedies, but if the council confer a crown, it shall be published in the council-hall of the people, in the Pnyx [2] at the assembly.

---

[1] All magistrates and public officers at Athens, whether civil or military, including the members of the two councils, were obliged, at the expiration of their term of office, to render an account to the people of the manner in which they had performed their duties. Thirty days was allowed for that purpose, and any citizen was at liberty to come forward within that period, and prefer an accusation against them. The scrutiny was not confined to pecuniary questions, but embraced an inquiry into their whole conduct and administration. It will easily however be understood, that with respect to general matters the accounting must in the first instance have been of a negative character, the magistrate having only to defend himself in case any charge was preferred; while, with respect to pecuniary transactions, he would have to give a positive account of all public monies that had been received by him, or passed through his hands. There were officers specially appointed to superintend this business: *Auditors* and *Scrutineers*, ten of each, and one for every tribe, elected by the council of five hundred. The auditors had a court under their jurisdiction, to which all charges for embezzlement, bribery, and malversation, as well as more general accusations for official misconduct, were referred by them, to be tried by a jury. The scrutineers assisted the auditors, and were subordinate to them. The importance attached by the framers of the Athenian laws to the institutions which secured the responsibility of all functionaries to the people, is apparent from this law, which Æschines made the foundation of his indictment.

[2] The place where the assemblies of the people were commonly held.

Penalty, fifty talents.  Witnesses to the summons,[1] Cephisophon son of Cephisophon of Rhamnus, Cleon son of Cleon
of Cothocidæ."

The clauses of the decree which he prosecutes are these,
men of Athens.  Now from these very clauses I think I shall
immediately make it clear to you, that my whole defence will
be just; for I shall take the charges in the same order as my
adversary, and discuss them all one by one, without a single
intentional omission.

With respect to the statement, " that I have constantly by
word and deed promoted the advantage of the people, and
am zealous to do whatever good I can," and the praising me
on such grounds, your judgment, I conceive, must depend on
my public acts; from an examination of which it will be discovered whether what Ctesiphon has alleged concerning me is
true and proper, or false.  As to his proposing to give the
crown without adding " when he has passed his accounts,"
and to proclaim the crown in the theatre, I imagine that this
also relates to my political conduct, whether I am worthy of
the crown and the public proclamation, or not.  However, I
deem it necessary to produce the laws which justified the
defendant in proposing such clauses.

Thus honestly and simply, men of Athens, have I resolved
to conduct my defence.  I now proceed to my own actual
measures.  And let no one suppose that I wander from the
indictment, if I touch upon Grecian questions and affairs: he
who attacks that clause of the decree, " that by word and
deed I have promoted your good "—he who has indicted this
for being false—he, I say, has rendered the discussion of my
whole policy pertinent and necessary to the charge.  Moreover, there being many departments of political action, I

---

[1] These were persons who accompanied the prosecutor when he summoned the defendant to appear before the magistrate.  Anciently they
were sureties also for the proper carrying on of the cause, like our
ancient pledges to prosecute.  In later times they were mere servers of
the citation or summons; but the plaint, or bill of indictment, always
had their names subscribed.

chose that which belonged to Grecian affairs: therefore I am justified in drawing my proofs from them.

The conquests which Philip had got and held before I commenced life as a statesman and orator, I shall pass over, as I think they concern not me. Those that he was baffled in from the day of my entering on such duties, I will call to your recollection, and render an account of them; premising one thing only—Philip started, men of Athens, with a great advantage. It happened that among the Greeks—not some, but all alike—there sprang up a crop of traitors and venal wretches, such as in the memory of man had never been before. These he got for his agents and supporters: the Greeks, already ill-disposed and unfriendly to each other, he brought into a still worse state, deceiving this people, making presents to that, corrupting others in every way; and he split them into many parties, when they had all one interest, to prevent his aggrandisement. While the Greeks were all in such a condition—in such ignorance of the gathering and growing mischief—you have to consider, men of Athens, what policy and measures it became the commonwealth to adopt, and of this to receive a reckoning from me; for the man who assumed that post in the administration was I.

Ought she, Æschines, to have cast off her spirit and dignity, and, in the style of Thessalians and Dolopians, helped to acquire for Philip the dominion of Greece, and extinguished the honours and rights of our ancestors? Or, if she did not this—which would indeed have been shameful—was it right that what she saw would happen if unprevented, and was for a long time, it seems, aware of, she should suffer to come to pass?

I would gladly ask the severest censurer of our acts, with what party he would have wished the commonwealth to side —with those who contributed to the disgraces and disasters of the Greeks, the party, we may say, of the Thessalians and their followers—or those who permitted it all for the hope of selfish advantage, among whom we may reckon the Arcadians, Messenians, and Argives? But many of them, or rather all, have fared worse than ourselves. If Philip after his victory had immediately marched off and kept quiet, without molesting any either of his own allies or of the Greeks in general, still they that opposed not his enterprises would have merited some blame and reproach. But when he has stripped all alike of their dignity, their authority, their liberty—nay, even of their constitutions, where he was able, —can it be doubted that you took the most glorious course in pursuance of my counsels?

But I return to the question—What should the commonwealth, Æschines, have done, when she saw Philip establishing an empire and dominion over Greece? Or what was your statesman to advise or move?—I, a statesman at Athens?— for this is most material—I who knew that from the earliest time, until the day of my own mounting the platform, our country had ever striven for precedency and honour and renown, and expended more blood and treasure for the sake of glory and the general weal than the rest of the Greeks had expended on their several interests?—who saw that Philip himself, with whom we were contending, had, in the strife for power and empire, had his eye cut out,[1] his collar-bone fractured, his hand and leg mutilated, and was ready and willing to sacrifice any part of his body that fortune chose to take, provided he could live with the remainder in honour and glory? Hardly will any one venture to say this—that it became a man bred at Pella, then an obscure and inconsiderable place, to possess such inborn magnanimity, as to aspire to the mastery of Greece and form the project in his mind, whilst you, who were Athenians, day after day in speeches and in dramas reminded of the virtue of your ancestors, should have been so naturally base, as of your own freewill and accord to surrender to Philip the liberty of Greece. No man will say this!

[1] Philip lost his eye at the siege of Methone. The other wounds were inflicted on his return from Scythia, in a battle with the Triballi, B.C. 340.

The only course then that remained was a just resistance to all his attacks upon you. Such course you took from the beginning, properly and becomingly; and I assisted by motions and counsels during the period of my political life:— I acknowledge it. But what should I have done? I put this question to you, dismissing all else: Amphipolis, Pydna, Potidæa, Halonnesus—I mention none of them: Serrium, Doriscus, the ravaging of Peparethus, and any similar wrongs which the country has suffered—I know not even of their occurrence. You indeed said, that by talking of these I had brought the people into a quarrel, although the resolutions respecting them were moved by Eubulus and Aristophon and Diopithes—not by me, you ready utterer of what suits your purpose! Neither will I speak of these now. But I ask—the man who was appropriating to himself Eubœa, and making it a fortress against Attica, and attempting Megara, and seizing Oreus, and razing Porthmus, and setting up Philistides as tyrant in Oreus, Clitarchus in Eretria, and subjugating the Hellespont, and besieging Byzantium, and destroying some of the Greek cities, restoring exiles to others, —was he by all these proceedings committing injustice, breaking the truce, violating the peace, or not? Was it meet that any of the Greeks should rise up to prevent these proceedings, or not? If not—if Greece was to present the spectacle (as it is called) of a Mysian prey,[1] whilst Athenians had life and being, then I have exceeded my duty in speaking on the subject—the commonwealth has exceeded her duty, which followed my counsels—I admit that every measure has been a misdeed, a blunder of mine. But if some one ought to have arisen to prevent these things, who but the Athenian people should it have been? Such then was the policy which I espoused. I saw him reducing all men to

---

[1] A proverbial expression applied to a people in an utterly helpless and defenceless state. It was derived, we are told, from the times of the Trojan war, when the Mysians were exposed to the enemy by the absence of their king Telephus.

subjection, and I opposed him: I continued warning and exhorting you not to make these sacrifices to Philip.

It was he that infringed the peace by taking our ships: it was not the state, Æschines. Produce the decrees themselves, and Philip's letter, and read them one after another. From an examination of them, it will be evident who is chargeable with each proceeding. Read.

### THE DECREE [1]

"In the archonship of Neocles, in the month Boedromion, an extraordinary assembly having been convened by the generals, Eubulus son of Mnesitheus of Cytherus moved: Whereas the generals have reported in the assembly, that Leodamas the admiral, and the twenty vessels despatched with him to the Hellespont for the safe-conduct of the corn, have been carried to Macedonia by Philip's general Amyntas, and are detained in custody, let the presidents and the generals take care that the council be convened, and ambassadors to Philip be chosen, who shall go and treat with him for the release of the admirals, vessels, and troops: and if Amyntas has acted in ignorance, they shall say that the people make no complaint against him; if the admiral was found wrongfully exceeding his instructions, that the Athenians will make inquiry, and punish him as his negligence deserves: if it be neither of these things, but a wilful trespass on the part of him who gave or him who received the commission, let them state this also, that the people, being apprised, may deliberate what course to take."

This decree Eubulus carried, not I. The next, Aristophon; then Hegesippus, then Aristophon again, then Philocrates, then Cephisophon, then the rest. I had no concern in the matter. Read the decree.

[1] The archon mentioned in this and the two following decrees is incorrect. Nicomachus was archon of that year.

### THE DECREE [1]

" In the archonship of Neocles, on the last day of Boedro-mion, at the desire of the council, the presidents and generals introduced their report of the proceedings of the assembly, to wit, that the people had resolved to appoint ambassadors to Philip for the recovery of the ships, and to furnish them with instructions and with the decrees of the assembly; and they appointed the following: Cephisophon son of Cleon of Ana-phlystus; Democritus son of Demophon of Anagyrus; Poly-critus son of Apemantus of Cothocidæ. In the presidency of the Hippothoontian tribe, on the motion of Aristophon of Colyttus, committee-man."

Now then, as I produce these decrees, so do you, Æschines, point out what decree of my passing makes me chargeable with the war. You cannot find one: had you any, there is nothing you would sooner have produced. Why, even Philip makes no charge against me on account of the war, though he complains of others. Read Philip's own letter.

### THE LETTER OF PHILIP

" Philip, king of Macedon, to the Council and People of Athens, greeting. Your ambassadors, Cephisophon, Demo-critus, and Polycritus, came to me and conferred about the release of the galleys which Laomedon commanded. Upon the whole, I think you must be very simple, if you imagine I do not see that those galleys were commissioned, under the pretence of conveying corn from the Hellespont to Lemnos, to relieve the Selymbrians, whom I am besieging, and who are

---

[1] We have seen that by the last decree the people had ordered a meeting of the council to be convened, to elect ambassadors to Philip. The presidents and generals, to whom that task was entrusted, convene the council accordingly, and lay before them the business for which they were called. The council proceed to execute the order of the people, and elect the ambassadors. That is, the senatorial decree containing their appointment of ambassadors, pursuant to the decree of the popular assembly.

not included in the friendly treaty subsisting between us. And these instructions were given, without leave of the Athenian people, by certain magistrates and others who are not now in office, but who are anyways desirous for the people to exchange our present amity for a renewal of war, and are far more anxious for such a consummation than to relieve the Selymbrians. They suppose it will be a source of income to themselves: however, I scarcely think it is for your advantage or mine. Wherefore I release you the vessels carried into my port; and for the future, if, instead of allowing your statesmen to adopt malignant measures, you will punish them, I too will endeavour to maintain the peace. Farewell "

Here is no mention by him of Demosthenes, or any charge against me. Why then, while he complains of the others, makes he no mention of my acts? Because he must have noticed his own aggressions, had he written aught concerning me; for on these I fixed myself—these I kept resisting. And first I proposed the embassy to Peloponnesus,[1] when into Peloponnesus he began to steal; next that to Eubœa, when on Eubœa he was laying his hands; then the expedition (no longer an embassy) to Oreus, and that to Eretria, when he established rulers in those cities. Afterwards I despatched all the armaments, by which Chersonesus was preserved, and Byzantium, and all our allies; whence to you there accrued the noblest results—praises, eulogies, honours, crowns, thanks from those you succoured; whilst the people attacked—those that trusted you then obtained deliverance, those that disregarded you have had often to remember your warnings, and to be convinced that you were not only their friends, but wise men also and prophets: for all that you predicted has come to pass.

That Philistides would have given a great deal to keep Oreus—Clitarchus a great deal to keep Eretria—Philip him-

[1] This was the embassy referred to in the third Philippic, which prevented the advance of Philip into the Peloponnese, B.C. 343.

self a great deal to have these vantage-posts against you, and
in other matters to avoid exposure, and any inquiry into his
wrongful acts in general—no man is ignorant, and least of all
you. For the ambassadors who came here then from Clitarchus and Philistides lodged with you, Æschines, and you were
their host. The commonwealth regarded them as enemies,
whose offers were neither just nor advantageous, and expelled
them; but they were your friends. None of their designs
then were accomplished;[1] you slanderer—who say of me,
that I am silent when I have got something, and bawl when
I have spent it![2] That is not your custom. You bawl
when you have something, and will never stop, unless the
jury stop you by disfranchisement to-day.[3]

When you crowned me then for those services, and Aristonicus drew up the same words that Ctesiphon here has now
drawn up, and the crown was proclaimed in the theatre—
for this now is the second proclamation in my favour—
Æschines, being present, neither opposed it, nor indicted the
mover. Take this decree now and read it.

### THE DECREE

" In the archonship of Chærondas son of Hegemon, on the
twenty-fifth of Gamelion, in the presidency of the Leontian
tribe, Aristonicus of Phrearrii moved: Whereas Demosthenes
son of Demosthenes of Pæania hath rendered many important

---

[1] The argument is—Philistides and Clitarchus were unable to accomplish their purpose, and that chiefly through my opposition. Yet
it is notorious, they would have given a large bribe to have obtained
powerful support at Athens. Then what becomes of your charge of
corruption against me?

[2] Æschines, defending himself against the reproach of having retired
from public affairs, said that his own habits were so simple, and his
desires so moderate, that he was not compelled to speak in public for
lucre's sake—Demosthenes, on the contrary, never opened his mouth
but when he was hired. Many idle stories to the same effect were
circulated against Demosthenes, besides the celebrated charge in the
affair of Harpalus.

[3] If the prosecutor failed to obtain a fifth part of the votes, besides
a fine of a thousand drachms, he incurred a partial disfranchisement,
which incapacitated him to prefer a similar charge in future.

services to the people of Athens, and to divers of her allies heretofore, and hath also on the present occasion aided them by his decrees, and liberated certain of the cities in Eubœa, and perseveres in his attachment to the people of Athens, and doth by word and deed whatever good he can for the Athenians themselves and the rest of the Greeks: It is resolved by the Council and People of Athens, to honour Demosthenes son of Demosthenes of Pæania with public praise and a golden crown, and to proclaim the crown in the theatre at the Dionysian festival at the new tragedies, and the proclamation of the crown shall be given in charge to the presiding tribe and the prize-master.[1]  On the motion of Aristonicus of Phrearrii.''

Is there one of you that knows of any disgrace falling on the state by reason of this decree, or any scorn or ridicule—consequences which this man now predicts, if I am crowned? It is when acts are recent and notorious that, if good, they obtain reward, if the contrary, punishment; and it appears that I then obtained reward, not blame or punishment.  So, up to the period of those transactions, I am acknowledged on all occasions to have promoted the interests of the state —because my speeches and motions prevailed in your councils—because my measures were executed, and procured crowns for the commonwealth and for me and all of you—because you have offered sacrifices and thanksgivings to the gods for their success.

When Philip therefore was driven out of Eubœa, with arms by you, with counsels and decrees—though some persons there should burst!—by me, he sought some new position of attack upon Athens.  Seeing that we use more foreign corn than any people, and wishing to command the passage of the corn-trade, he advanced to Thrace; the Byzantines being his allies, he first required them to join in the war against you, and when they refused, saying (truly enough)

---

[1] The person who adjudged the prizes in the various contests during the festival.

that they had not made alliance on such terms, he threw up
intrenchments before the city, planted batteries, and laid
siege to it.    What course hereupon it became you to take, I
will not ask again; it is manifest to all.    But who was it
that succoured the Byzantines, and rescued them? who prevented the alienation of the Hellespont at that crisis?   You,
men of Athens.    When I say you, I mean the commonwealth.
But who advised, framed, executed the measures of state,
devoted himself wholly and unreservedly to the public business?—I!—What benefits thence accrued to all, you need no
further to be told; you have learned by experience.    For
the war which then sprang up, besides that it brought honour
and renown, kept you in a cheaper and more plentiful supply
of all the necessaries of life than does the present peace,
which these worthies maintain to their country's prejudice in
the hope of something to come.    Perish such hope!   Never
may they share the blessings for which you men of honest
wishes pray to the gods, nor communicate their own principles to you!

Read them now the crowns of the Byzantines, and those
of the Perinthians, which they conferred upon the country
as a reward.


### THE BYZANTINE DECREE

" In the Presbytership [1] of Bosporichus, Damagetus moved
in the assembly, having obtained permission of the Council:
Whereas the people of Athens have ever in former times
been friendly to the Byzantines and their allies, and to their
kinsmen the Perinthians, and have rendered them many
signal services, and also on the present occasion, when Philip
of Macedon attempted by invasion and siege to exterminate

[1] Hieromnemon (the word in the original) appears to have been the
name of the chief magistrate at Byzantium, whose term of office furnished the date of the year, as the archon did at Athens.    The name
(which was held by the magistrates of some other Dorian states) im-
ports the performance of some priestly or religious duties.    As it sounds
harsh in English, I have ventured to translate it at the risk of cavil.

the Byzantines and Perinthians, and burned and ravaged their country, they succoured us with a hundred and twenty ships and provisions and weapons and soldiers, and rescued us from grievous perils, and preserved our hereditary constitution, our laws, and our sepulchres: it is resolved by the people of Byzantium and Perinthus to grant unto the Athenians the right of intermarriage, citizenship, purchase of land and houses, the first seat at the games, first admission to the Council and People after the sacrifices, and exemption from all public services to such as wish to reside in the city: and that three statues of sixteen cubits be erected in the harbour, representing the People of Athens crowned by the People of Byzantium and Perinthus: and deputations sent to the general assemblies of Greece, the Isthmian, Nemean, Olympian, and Pythian, to proclaim the crowns wherewith the people of Athens hath been honoured by us, that all the Greeks may know the virtue of the Athenians, and the gratitude of the Byzantines and Perinthians."

Now read the crowns given by the people of Chersonesus.

### THE DECREE OF THE CHERSONESITES

" The Chersonesites, inhabitants of Sestus, Eleus, Madytus, and Alopeconnesus, crown the Council and People of Athens with a golden crown of the value of sixty talents,[1] and build an altar to Gratitude and the Athenian People, because that People hath helped the Chersonesites to obtain the greatest of blessings, by rescuing them from the power of Philip, and restoring their country, their laws, their liberty, their sanctuaries: and in all future time they will not fail to be grateful, and do what service they can.   Decreed in general Council."

[1] According to Gronovius, Böckh, and Jacobs, we are not to suppose that a crown was given of the actual weight or value of sixty talents, but that six drachms of gold are (by a form of speech usual in some cases) called a talent.   A similar crown of a hundred talents, given by the Carthaginians to Demareta, the wife of Gelo, is mentioned by Diodorus.   (Lib. xi. 26.)

Thus the saving of Chersonesus and Byzantium, the preventing Philip's conquest of the Hellespont, and the honours
therefore bestowed on this country, were the effects of my
policy and administration; and more than this—they proved
to all mankind the generosity of Athens and the baseness of
Philip. He, the ally and friend of the Byzantines, was before
all eyes besieging them—what could be more shameful or outrageous?—You, who might justly on many grounds have
reproached them for wrongs done you in former times, instead
of bearing malice and abandoning the oppressed, appeared
as their deliverers; conduct which procured you glory, goodwill, honour from all men. That you have crowned many of
your statesmen, every one knows; but through what other
person (I mean what minister or orator), besides myself, the
commonwealth has been crowned, no one can say.

To prove now the malignity of those calumnies, which he
urged against the Euboeans and Byzantines, reminding you
of any unkindness which they had done you—prove it I shall,
not only by their falsehood, which I apprehend you know
already, but (were they ever so true) by showing the advantages of my policy—I wish to recount one or two of the
noble acts of your own state, and to do it briefly; for individuals, as well as communities, should ever strive to model
their future conduct by the noblest of their past.

Well then, men of Athens—when the Lacedæmonians had
the empire of land and sea, and held the country round
Attica by governors and garrisons, Euboea, Tanagra, all
Boeotia, Megara, Ægina, Cleonæ, the other islands; when
our state possessed neither ships nor walls; you marched out
to Haliartus,[1] and again not many days after to Corinth;
albeit the Athenians of that time had many causes of resentment against both Corinthians and Thebans for their acts in

---

[1] This was B.C. 395, at the breaking out of the war, in which Athens,
Thebes, Corinth, and Argos, combined against Lacedæmon. The
battle of Corinth, in which the Lacedæmonians defeated the allies,
took place in the year following the siege of Haliartus.

the Decelean war:[1] but they showed no resentment, none. And yet neither of these steps took they, Æschines, for benefactors, nor were they blind to the danger; but they would not for such reasons abandon people who sought their protection; for the sake of renown and glory they willingly exposed themselves to peril; just and noble was their resolve! For to all mankind the end of life is death, though one keep oneself shut up in a closet; but it becomes brave men to strive always for honour, with good hope before them, and to endure courageously whatever the Deity ordains.

Thus did your ancestors, thus the elder among yourselves. For, though the Lacedæmonians were neither friends nor benefactors, but had done many grievous injuries to our state, yet when the Thebans, victorious at Leuctra, sought their destruction, you prevented it, not fearing the power and reputation then possessed by the Thebans, nor reckoning up the merits of those whom you were about to fight for. And so you demonstrated to all the Greeks, that, however any people may offend you, you reserve your anger against them for other occasions; but should their existence or liberty be imperilled, you will not resent your wrongs or bring them into account.

And not in these instances only hath such been your temper. Again, when the Thebans were taking possession of Eubœa, you looked not quietly on—you remembered not the wrongs done you by Themison and Theodorus in the affair of Oropus,[2] but assisted even them. It was the time when the volunteer captains[3] first offered themselves to the state, of whom I was one;—but of this presently. However,

[1] The latter part of the Peloponnesian war, so called from the occupation of Decelea, a fortress in Attica, fifteen miles from Athens, B.C. 413. By means of this post the enemy got the command of the territory round Athens, and reduced the Athenians to great distress by cutting off supplies of corn and provisions.

[2] Themison and Theodorus were the rulers of Eretria, who seized upon Oropus, B.C. 366.

[3] The exertions of these voluntary trierarchs enabled the Athenians to ship off their troops in three days. The orators frequently boasted of this expedition: for example, Demosthenes in the speech against Androtion; Æschines in his speech against Ctesiphon.

it was glorious that you saved the island, but far more glorious that, when had you got their persons and their cities in your power, you fairly restored them to people who had ill-used you, and made no reckoning of your wrongs in an affair where you were trusted.

Hundreds of cases which I could mention I pass over—sea-fights, land-marches, campaigns, both in ancient times and in your own, all of which the commonwealth has undertaken for the freedom and safety of the Greeks in general. Then, having observed the commonwealth engaging in contests of such number and importance for the interests of others, what was I to urge, what course to recommend her, when the question in a manner concerned herself?—To revive grudges, I suppose, against people who wanted help, and to seek pretences for abandoning everything. And who might not justly have killed me, had I attempted even by words to tarnish any of the honours of Athens? For the thing itself, I am certain, you would never have done—had you wished, what was to hinder you?—any lack of opportunity?—had you not these men to advise it?

I must return to the next in date of my political acts; and here again consider what was most beneficial for the state. I saw, men of Athens, that your navy was decaying, and that, while the rich were getting off with small payments, citizens of moderate or small fortunes were losing their substance, and the state, by reason thereof, missing her opportunities of action. I therefore proposed a law, by which I compelled the one class (the rich) to perform their duty, and stopped the oppression of the poor; and—what was most useful to the country—I caused her preparations to be made in time. And being indicted for it, I appeared on the charge before you, and was acquitted; and the prosecutor did not get his portion [1] of the votes. But what sums, think ye, the chief men [2] of the Boards, or those in the second and third degrees,

---

[1] The fifth part, to save him from the penalty.
[2] According to Ulpian, the first three hundred among the Symmoriæ were called ἡγεμόνες. See as to this subject, vol. i. appendix v.

offered me, first, not to propose that law, secondly, when I had recorded it, to drop it on the abatement-oath? [1] Such sums, men of Athens, as I should be afraid to tell you. And no wonder they did so; for under the former laws they might divide the charge between sixteen, spending little or nothing themselves, and grinding down the needy citizens; whereas under my law every one had to pay a sum proportioned to his means, and there was a captain for two ships, where before there was a partner with fifteen others for one ship; for they were calling themselves not captains any longer, but partners. They would have given anything then to get these regulations annulled, and not be obliged to perform their duties. Read me, first, the decree for which I appeared to the indictment, then the service-rolls, that of the former law, and that under mine. Read.

### THE DECREE

" In the archonship of Polycles, on the sixteenth of Boedromion, in the presidency of the Hippothoontian tribe, Demosthenes son of Demosthenes of Pæania introduced a law for the naval service, instead of the former one under which there were the associations of joint-captains; and it was passed by the council and people. And Patrocles of Phlyus preferred an indictment against Demosthenes for an illegal measure, and, not having obtained his share of the votes, paid the penalty of five hundred drachms."

Now produce that fine roll.

[1] An oath or affidavit sworn by a party to a cause, in order to obtain some adjournment or delay. But, according to the explanation of Julius Pollux, it was applied also to the oath sworn by a person who threatened another with an indictment for an illegal measure. Any citizen was at liberty to indict the author of a decree, though passed by the popular assembly, within a twelvemonth after the passing; and it became void, if the indictment succeeded.

### THE ROLL

" Let sixteen captains be called out for every galley, as they are associated in the companies,[1] from the age of twenty-five to forty, defraying the charge equally."

Now for the roll under my law.

### THE ROLL

" Let captains be chosen according to their property by valuation, taking ten talents to a galley: if the property be valued at a higher sum, let the charge be proportionate, as far as three ships and a tender; and let it be in the same proportion for those whose property is less than ten talents, joining them in a partnership to make up ten talents." [2]

Think ye I but slightly helped the poor of Athens, or that the rich would have spent but a trifling sum to escape the doing what was right? I glory however, not only in having refused this compromise, and having been acquitted on the indictment, but because my law was beneficial, and I have proved it so by trial. For during the whole war, whilst the armaments were shipped off according to my regulations, no captain ever appealed to you against oppression, or took sanctuary at Munychia,[3] or was imprisoned by the clearing-officers;[4] no galley was lost to the state by capture abroad, or left behind from unfitness to go to sea. Under the former

[1] Literally, " according to the associations in the companies." Λόχοι here are the same as συμμορίαι, according to Wolf.

[2] The ten talents, which are made the basis of this regulation, are the rateable value of the property, which would be one-fifth of the whole for the highest class, if the valuation of B.C. 379 was in force; so that a man possessing fifty talents would have the charge of one ship, a hundred talents, of two ships, a hundred and fifty talents, of three ships; and a tender would have to be found in addition for a certain sum beyond, which is not specified. Higher the charge was not carried. Those who had less than ten talents of rateable capital clubbed together for one ship, but the rating was in a lower proportion.

[3] In a temple of Diana in the port of Munychia.

[4] Ten officers, whose business it was to expedite the equipment of the fleet, and its clearance out from port—a Board of Despatch.

laws all these things happened—because the burden was put upon the poor, and therefore difficulties frequently arose. I transferred the charge from the poor to the wealthy, and then every duty was done. For this itself too I deserve praise, that I adopted all such measures as brought glory and honour and power to the state: there is no envy, spite, or malice in any measure of mine, nothing sordid or un-worthy of Athens. The same character is apparent in my home and in my foreign policy. At home, I never preferred the favour of the wealthy to the rights of the many: abroad, I valued not the presents or the friendship of Philip above the general interests of Greece.

I conceive it remains for me to speak of the proclamation and the accounts: for, that I acted for the best—that I have throughout been your friend and zealous in your service—is proved abundantly, methinks, by what I have said already. The most important part of my policy and administration I pass by, considering that I have in regular course to reply to the charge of illegality; and besides—though I am silent as to the rest of my political acts—the knowledge you all have will serve me equally well.

As to the arguments which he jumbled together about the counter-written laws, I hardly suppose you comprehend them—I myself could not understand the greater part. However I shall argue a just case in a straightforward way. So far from saying that I am not accountable, as the pro-secutor just now falsely asserted, I acknowledge that I am all my life accountable for what as your statesman I have under-taken or advised; but for what I have voluntarily given to the people out of my own private fortune, I deny that I am any day accountable—do you hear, Æschines?—nor is any other man, let him even be one of the nine archons.[1] For what law is so full of injustice and inhumanity as to enact, that one who has given of his private means, and done an act

---

[1] The archons were also liable to an examination by the council previous to admission to their office.

of generosity and munificence, instead of having thanks, shall be brought before malignants, appointed to be the auditors of his liberality? None. If he says there is, let him produce it, and I will be content and hold my tongue. But there is none, men of Athens. The prosecutor in his malice, because I gave some of my own money when I superintended the theatre fund, says—" the Council praised him before he had rendered his account." Not for any matters of which I had an account to render, but for what I spent of my own, you malignant!

" Oh, but you were a Conservator of Walls!" says he. Yes; and for that reason was I justly praised, because I gave the sums expended and did not charge them. A charge requires auditing and examiners; a donation merits thanks and praise: therefore the defendant made this motion in my favour.

That this is a settled principle in your hearts as well as in the laws, I can show by many proofs easily. First, Nausicles has often been crowned by you for what he expended out of his own funds whilst he was general. Secondly, Diotimus was crowned for his present of shields; and Charidemus too. Again, Neoptolemus here, superintendent of divers works, has been honoured for his donations. It would indeed be cruel, if a man holding an office should either, by reason of his office, be precluded from giving his own money to the state, or have, instead of receiving thanks, to render an account of what he gave. To prove the truth of my statements, take and read me the original decrees made in favour of these men.

## A DECREE [1]

" Archon, Demonicus of Phlyus. On the twenty-sixth of Boedromion, with the sanction of the council and people,

[1] The event referred to in this decree seems to have taken place during the Social War, B.C. 355, when the Chians, Rhodians, and Byzantines made a descent upon Lemnos and Imbrus. In that year Callistratus was archon. Nausicles is frequently mentioned by Æschines and Demosthenes in terms of praise. He commanded an Athenian force in the Sacred War, B.C. 352.

Callias of Phrearrii moved: That the council and people resolve to crown Nausicles, general of foot, for that, there being
two thousand Athenian troops of the line in Imbrus, for the
defence of the Athenian residents in that island, and Philo of
the finance department being by reason of storms unable to
sail and pay the troops, he advanced money of his own, and
did not ask the people for it again; and that the crown be
proclaimed at the Dionysian festival, at the new tragedies."

### ANOTHER DECREE

" Callias of Phrearrii moved, the presidents declaring it to
be with the sanction of the council: Whereas Charidemus,
general of foot, having been sent to Salamis, he and Diotimus,
general of horse, after certain of the troops had in the
skirmish by the river been disarmed by the enemy, did at
their own expense arm the young men with eight hundred
shields: It hath been resolved by the council and people to
crown Charidemus and Diotimus with a golden crown, and
to proclaim it at the great Panathenaic festival, during the
gymnastic contest, and at the Dionysian festival, at the
exhibition of the new tragedies: the proclamation to be
given in charge to the judges,[1] the presidents, and the prize-
masters."

Each of these men, Æschines, was accountable for the office
which he held, but not accountable for the matters in respect
of which he was crowned. No more then am I; for surely
I have the same rights, under the same circumstances, as
other men. Have I given money? I am praised for that,
not being accountable for what I gave. Did I hold office?
Yes; and I have rendered an account of my official acts, not
of my bounties. Oh, but I was guilty of malpractices in

---

[1] Such is the name which I give to the six junior archons, to avoid
the uncouth title of Thesmothetes. It does not indeed (any more than
Thesmothetes itself) convey a perfect idea of the official duties which
they had to discharge; yet it is by no means inappropriate, seeing that
the most important part of them were of a judicial character.

office! And you, present when the auditors brought me up,[1]
accused me not?

To show you that he himself bears testimony to my having
been crowned for what I had no account to render of, take
and read the whole decree drawn up in my favour. By the
portions of the bill which he never indicted it will appear
that his prosecution is vexatious. Read.

## THE DECREE [2]

" In the archonship of Euthycles, on the twenty-second of
Pyanepsion, in the presidency of the Œneian tribe, Ctesiphon
son of Leosthenes of Anaphlystus moved: Whereas Demosthenes son of Demosthenes of Pæania, having been superintendent of the repair of the walls, and having expended on
the works three additional talents out of his own money, hath
given that sum to the people; and whereas, having been
appointed treasurer of the theoric fund, he hath given to
the theoric officers of the tribes a hundred minas towards
the sacrifices, the council and people of Athens have resolved
to honour Demosthenes son of Demosthenes of Pæania with
public praise, for the goodness and generosity which he has
shown throughout on every occasion towards the people of
Athens, and to crown him with a golden crown, and to proclaim the crown in the theatre, at the Dionysian festival, at
the performance of the new tragedies: the proclamation to
be given in charge to the prize-master."

These were my donations; none of which have you indicted: the rewards which the council says I deserve for

---

[1] Demosthenes had passed the scrutiny of the Logistæ, and had no
charge preferred against him at the close of his official year. This
however, in point of law, was no answer to his opponent's argument;
for the legality of Ctesiphon's measure was to be tried by reference
to the time when he introduced it, at which time Demosthenes had
not cleared himself of his official responsibility.

[2] The name of the archon is again wrong here, and the decree is not
in all manuscripts. The terms of it do not agree with the recital in
the indictment, though it is the same in substance.

them are what you arraign.  To receive the gifts then you confess to be legal; the requital of them you indict for illegality.  In the name of heaven! what sort of person can a monster of wickedness and malignity be, if not such a person as this?

Concerning the proclamation in the theatre, I pass over the fact, that thousands of thousands have been proclaimed, and I myself have been crowned often before.  But by the Gods! are you so perverse and stupid, Æschines, as not to be able to reflect, that the party crowned has the same glory from the crown wherever it be published, and that the proclamation is made in the theatre for the benefit of those who confer the crown?  For the hearers are all encouraged to render service to the state, and praise the parties who show their gratitude more than the party crowned.  Therefore has our commonwealth enacted this law.  Take and read me the law itself.

### THE LAW

" Whensoever any of the townships bestow crowns, proclamations thereof shall be made by them in their several townships, unless where any are crowned by the people of Athens or the council; and it shall be lawful for them to be proclaimed in the theatre at the Dionysian festival."

Do you hear, Æschines, the law distinctly saying—" unless where any are voted by the people or the council; such may be proclaimed? "  Why then, wretched man, do you play the pettifogger?  Why manufacture arguments?  Why don't you take hellebore [1] for your malady?  Are you not ashamed to bring on a cause for spite, and not for any offence?—to alter some laws, and to garble others, the whole of which should in

[1] Hellebore was used by the ancients to purge the brain, and cure people of insanity; and because it grew abundantly in the island of Anticyra, " to send a person to Anticyra," was as good as saying he was mad.

justice be read to persons sworn to decide according to the laws? And you that act thus describe the qualities which belong to a friend of the people, as if you had ordered a statue according to contract, and received it without having what the contract required; or as if friends of the people were known by words, and not by acts and measures! And you bawl out, regardless of decency, a sort of cart-language,[1] applicable to yourself and your race, not to me.

Again, men of Athens—I conceive abuse to differ from accusation in this, that accusation has to do with offences for which the laws provide penalties, abuse with the scandal which enemies speak against each other according to their humour. And I believe our ancestors built these courts, not that we should assemble you here and bring forth the secrets of private life for mutual reproach, but to give us the means of convicting persons guilty of crimes against the state. Æschines knew this as well as I, and yet he chose to rail rather than to accuse.

Even in this way he must take as much as he gives; but before I enter upon such matters, let me ask him one question—Should one call you the state's enemy, or mine, Æschines? Mine, of course. Yet, where you might, for any offence which I committed, have obtained satisfaction for the people according to the laws, you neglected it—at the audit, on the indictments and other trials; but where I in my own person am safe on every account, by the laws, by time, by prescription,[2] by many previous judgments on every point, by my never having been convicted of a public offence—and where the country must share, more or less, in the repute of measures which were her own—here it is you have encountered me. See if you are not the people's enemy, while you pretend to be mine!

---

[1] Billingsgate, as the Londoners would say. It was the custom of the Athenian women, in divers solemn processions, especially at the Eleusinian mysteries, when they were conveyed in open waggons or carts, to amuse themselves by jeering and joking one another, without the slightest regard to modesty or propriety of language.

[2] " By the Statute of Limitations, as we should say."

Since therefore the righteous and true verdict is made clear to all; but I must, it seems—though not naturally fond of railing, yet on account of the calumnies uttered by my opponent—in reply to so many falsehoods, just mention some leading particulars concerning him, and show who he is, and from whom descended, that so readily begins using hard words—and what language he carps at, after uttering such as any decent man would have shuddered to pronounce— Why, if my accuser had been Æacus, or Rhadamanthus, or Minos, instead of a prater, a hack of the market, a pestilent scribbler, I don't think he would have spoken such things, or found such offensive terms, shouting, as in a tragedy, " O Earth! O Sun! O Virtue! " and the like; and again appealing to Intelligence and Education, by which the honourable is distinguished from the base:—all this you undoubtedly heard from his lips. Accursed one! What have you or yours to do with virtue? How should you discern what is honourable or otherwise? How were you ever qualified? What right have you to talk about education? Those who really possess it would never say as much of themselves, but rather blush if another did: those who are destitute like you, but make pretensions to it from stupidity, annoy the hearers by their talk, without getting the reputation which they desire.

I am at no loss for materials concerning you and your family, but am in doubt what to mention first—whether how your father Tromes, being servant to Elpias, who kept a reading-school in the temple of Theseus, wore a weight of fetters and a collar;[1] or how your mother, by her morning spousals in the cottage by Hero Calamites,[2] reared up you,

---

[1] According to Reiske, a round board with a hole in the middle, put on the necks of thievish slaves, to prevent them from reaching their hands to their mouths. Or it may be the stocks; as in the Knights of Aristophanes.

[2] A Hero of that name is the common interpretation. Schaefer, however, referring to the oration of Demosthenes on the Embassy, thinks that Heros was the name of a physician, who received the title of Calamites, because he set fractured bones with splinters of reeds.

the beautiful statue, the eminent third-rate actor !—But all know these things without my telling—Or how the galley-piper Phormio, the slave of Dion of Phrearrii, removed her from that honourable employment. But, by Jupiter and the gods! I fear, in saying what is proper about you, I may be thought to have chosen topics unbecoming to myself. All this therefore I shall pass by, and commence with the acts of his own life; for indeed he came not of common parents, but of such as are execrated by the people. Very lately—lately do I say?—it is but yesterday that he has become both an Athenian and an orator—adding two syllables, he converted his father from Tromes to Atrometus, and dignified his mother by the name of Glaucothea, who (as every one knows) was called Empusa;[1] having got that title (it is plain) from her doing and submitting to anything—how else could she have got it? However, you are so ungrateful and wicked by nature, that after being raised through the people from servitude to freedom, from beggary to affluence, instead of returning their kindness, you work against them as a hireling politician.

Of the speeches, which it may possibly be contended he has made for the good of the country, I will say nothing: of the acts which he was clearly proved to have done for the enemy, I will remind you.

What man present but knows of the outcast Antiphon, who came into the city under promise to Philip that he would burn your arsenal? I found him concealed in Piræus, and brought him before the Assembly; when this mischief-maker, shouting and clamouring that it was monstrous in a free state that I should ill-treat unfortunate citizens, and enter houses without warrant, procured his release. And had not the Council of Areopagus, discovering the fact, and perceiving your ill-timed error, made search after the man, seized and brought him before you, a fellow like that would

[1] This denoted a frightful spectre or hobgoblin. According to Aristophanes (Frogs, 293), it could change itself into various shapes.

have been rescued, would have slipped through the hands of
justice, and been sent out of the way by his declaimer.  As
it was, you put him to torture and to death, as you ought this
man also.  The Council of Areopagus were informed what
Æschines had done, and therefore, though you had elected
him for your advocate on the question of the Delian temple,[1]
in the same ignorance by which you have sacrificed many of
the public interests, as you referred the matter to the council,
and gave them full powers, they immediately removed him
for his treason, and appointed Hyperides to plead; for which
purpose they took their ballots from the altar,[2] and not a
single ballot was given for this wretch.  To prove the truth
of my statements, call me the witnesses.

### WITNESSES

" We, Callias of Sunium, Zenon of Phlyus, Cleon of Phalerum, Demonicus of Marathon, testify for Demosthenes in the
name of all, that, the people having formerly elected Æschines
for their advocate before the Amphictyons on the question of
the Delian temple, we in council determined that Hyperides
was more worthy to plead on behalf of the state, and Hyperides was commissioned."

Thus, by removing this man when he was about to plead,
and appointing another, the council pronounced him a traitor
and an enemy.

Such is one of this boy's political acts, similar—is it not?

[1] The Athenians claimed the superintendence of the temple of Delos,
which the Delians disputed with them.  The question was referred to
the decision of the Amphictyonic Council at Thermopylæ, and each of
the two states sent a deputy to plead their cause.  Some fragments
remain of a speech made by Hyperides on this occasion, entitled
Deliacus.

[2] This was the most solemn method of voting.  An example is mentioned by Herodotus (VIII. 123), on a memorable occasion, when the
Greek generals met at the Isthmus after the battle of Salamis, to declare what two men had done the greatest service in the war.  They
voted standing at the altar of Neptune; and while each awarded the
first place to himself, the great majority concurred in allowing the
second place to Themistocles.  Another example may be seen in the
speech of Demosthenes against Macartatus, 1054.

—to what he charges me with. Now let me remind you of another. When Philip sent Python of Byzantium, together with an embassy from all his own allies, with the intention of putting our commonwealth to shame, and proving her in the wrong, then—when Python swaggered and poured a flood of abuse upon him—I neither yielded nor gave way; I rose and answered him, and betrayed not the rights of the commonwealth. So plainly did I convict Philip of injustice, that his very allies rose up and acknowledged it; while Æschines fought his battle, and bore witness, aye, false witness, against his own country.

Nor was this enough. Again, some time afterwards, he was found meeting Anaxinus the spy at Thraso's house.[1] A man, I say, who had a private meeting and conference with an emissary of the foe, must himself have been a spy by nature and an enemy to his country. To prove these statements, call me the witnesses.

### WITNESSES

" Teledemus son of Cleon, Hyperides son of Callæschrus, Nicomachus son of Diophantus, testify for Demosthenes, as they swore before the generals, that Æschines son of Atrometus of Cothocidæ did, to their knowledge, meet by night in Thraso's house, and confer with Anaxinus, who was adjudged to be a spy of Philip. These depositions were returned before Nicias,[2] on the third of Hecatombæon."

A vast deal besides that I could say about him I omit. For thus (methinks) it is. I could produce many more such

---

[1] Anaxinus was an Orite. The transaction is supposed to have occurred B.C. 342. Æschines, in his speech (85), asserts that the whole affair was a contrivance of Demosthenes, to prevent an impeachment with which he had threatened him; and he reproached Demosthenes with having put a man to the rack, at whose house in Oreus he had lodged and received hospitality.

[2] It is uncertain whether this Nicias is the name of a spurious archon, or the secretary of the council, or an error for Nicomachus, who was archon B.C. 341.

cases, where Æschines was discovered at that period assisting
the enemy and harassing me. But these things are not trea-
sured up by you for careful remembrance or proper resentment. You have, through evil custom, given large licence to
any one that chooses to supplant and calumniate your honest
counsellors, exchanging the interest of the state for the pleasure and gratification of hearing abuse; and so it is easier and
safer always to be a hireling serving your enemies than a
statesman attached to you.

That he should co-operate openly with Philip before the
war, was shocking—O heaven and earth! could it be otherwise?—against his country! Yet allow him if you please,
allow him this. But when the ships had openly been made
prize, Chersonesus was ravaged, the man was marching against
Attica, matters were no longer doubtful, war had begun—
nothing that he ever did for you can this malicious iambic-
mouther show—not a resolution has Æschines, great or small,
concerning the interests of the state. If he asserts it, let
him prove it now whilst my waterglass is running.[1] But
there is none. He is reduced to an alternative;—either he
had no fault to find with my measures, and therefore moved
none against them; or he sought the good of the enemy, and
therefore would not propose any better.

Did he abstain from speaking as well as moving, when any
mischief was to be done to you? Why, no one else could

---

[1] The Athenians, to prevent the parties from saying more than was
necessary, timed them by a glass, in which water trickled through
a narrow tube, like sand in one of our minute-glasses. The measure of
water is not always the same, and varied according to the importance
of the cause. Mention is made of a certain quantity of water being
allowed in certain causes; but this gives us no idea of the length of
time, as we do not know the construction of the glass. Our best evidence of this is the length of the speeches which have come down to
us. Each party was commonly allowed to have two speeches, the
defendant having the last reply; and the second speech might be half
as long as the first. If either got a friend to plead for him, he gave
up so much of his own time as the friend's speech would occupy.
The admeasurement of the water was seen to by the superintending
magistrate. An officer of the court stood by the glass, and stopped it
whenever a witness was called, or a law or other document was read
to the jury.

speak a word. Other things, it appears, the country could endure, and he could accomplish without detection: but one last act he achieved, O Athenians, which crowned all he had done before; on which he lavished that multitude of words, recounting the decrees against the Amphissian Locrians, in hopes of distorting the truth. But the thing admits it not. No! never will you wash yourself clean from your performances there—talk as long as you will!

In your presence, men of Athens, I invoke all the gods and goddesses to whom the Attic territory belongs, and Pythian Apollo the Father-god [1] of our state; and I implore them all! As I shall declare the truth to you, as I declared it in your assembly at the time, the very moment I saw this wretch putting his hand to the work—for I perceived, instantly perceived it—so may they grant me favour and protection! If from malice or personal rivalry I bring a false charge against my opponent, may they cut me off from every blessing!

But wherefore this imprecation, this solemn assurance? Because, though I have documents lying in the public archives, from which I shall clearly prove my assertions, though I know you remember the facts, I fear this man may be considered unequal to the mischiefs which he has wrought; as before happened, when he caused the destruction of the unhappy Phocians by his false reports to you.

The Amphissian war, I say—which brought Philip to Elatea, which caused him to be chosen general of the Amphictyons, which ruined everything in Greece—was this man's contrivance. He is the single author of all our heaviest calamities. I protested at the time, and cried out in the assembly—" You are bringing a war, Æschines, into Attica, an Amphictyonic war "—but his packed party would not let me be heard; the rest wondered, and supposed that I was bringing an idle charge against him out of personal enmity. However, the real character of those transactions, the purpose

---

[1] So called, as being the father of Ion, the ancient king of Athens. See the Ion of Euripides.

for which they were got up, the manner in which they were accomplished, hear ye now, men of Athens, as ye were prevented then. You will see that the thing was well concerted, and it will help you much to get a knowledge of public affairs, and what craftiness there was in Philip you will observe.

Philip could neither finish nor get rid of the war with Athens, unless he made the Thebans and Thessalians her enemies. Though your generals fought against him without fortune or skill, yet from the war itself and the cruisers he suffered infinite damage. He could neither export any of the produce of his country, nor import what he needed. He was not then superior to you at sea, nor able to reach Attica, unless the Thessalians followed him and the Thebans gave him a passage; so that, while he overcame in war the generals whom you sent out—such as they were—I say nothing about that—he found himself distressed by the difference of your local position and means. Should he urge either Thessalians or Thebans to march in his own quarrel against you, none, he thought, would attend to him: but should he, under the pretence of taking up their common cause, be elected general, he trusted partly by deceit and partly by persuasion to gain his ends more easily. He sets to work therefore—observe how cleverly—to get the Amphictyons into a war, and create a disturbance in the congress. For this he thought they would immediately want him. Now, if any of the presbyters commissioned by himself or any of his allies brought it forward he imagined that both Thebans and Thessalians would suspect the thing, and would all be on their guard; whereas, if the agent were an Athenian and commissioned by you his opponents, it would easily pass unnoticed. And thus it turned out.

How did he effect his purpose? He hires the prosecutor. No one (I believe) was aware of the thing or attending to it, and so—just as these things are usually done at Athens—Æschines was proposed for Pylæan deputy, three or four held up their hands for him, and his election was declared. When clothed with the dignity of the state he arrived among the Amphictyons, dismissing and disregarding all besides, he hastened to execute what he was hired for. He makes up a pretty speech and story, showing how the Cirrhæan plain came to be consecrated; reciting this to the presbyters, men unused to speeches and unsuspicious of any consequences, he procures a vote from them to walk round the district, which the Amphissians maintained they had a right to cultivate, but which he charged to be parcel of the sacred plain. The Locrians were not then instituting any suit against us, or any such proceedings as Æschines now falsely alleges.[1] This will show you—It was impossible (I fancy) for the Locrians to carry on process against our commonwealth without a citation. Who summoned us then? In whose archonship? Say who knows—point him out. You cannot. Your pretence was flimsy and false.

When the Amphictyons at the instance of this man walked over the plain, the Locrians fell upon them and well-nigh speared them all; some of the presbyters they carried off captive. Complaints having followed, and war being stirred up against the Amphissians, at first Cottyphus led an army composed entirely of Amphictyons; but as some never came, and those that came did nothing, measures were taken against the ensuing congress by an instructed gang, the old traitors of Thessaly and other states, to get the command for Philip. And they had found a fair pretext: for it was necessary, they said, either to subsidise themselves and maintain a mercenary force and fine all recusants, or to elect him. What need of many words? He was thereupon chosen general; and immediately afterwards collecting an army, and marching professedly against Cirrha, he bids a long farewell to the Cirrhæans and Locrians, and seizes Elatea. Had not the

---

[1] Æschines had stated in his speech (70), that the Amphissian Locrians proposed to fine the Athenians fifty talents, for an inscription which they had put on a golden shield in the temple, commemorating the alliance of the Thebans with Persia. This he alleged to have been the cause of his own proceeding against them.

Tebans, upon seeing this, immediately changed their minds and sided with us, the whole thing would have fallen like a torrent upon our country. As it was, they for the instant stopped him; chiefly, O Athenians, by the kindness of some divinity to Athens, but secondly, as far as it could depend on a single man, through me. Give me those decrees, and the dates of the several transactions, that you may know what mischiefs this pestilent creature has stirred up with impunity. Read me the decrees.

### THE DECREE OF THE AMPHICTYONS

" In the priesthood of Clinagoras, at the spring congress, it hath been resolved by the deputies and councillors of the Amphictyons, and by the assembly of the Amphictyons, seeing that the Amphissians trespass upon the sacred plain and sow and depasture it with cattle, that the deputies and councillors do enter thereupon and define the boundaries with pillars, and enjoin the Amphissions not to trespass for the future."

### ANOTHER DECREE

" In the priesthood of Clinagoras,[1] at the spring congress, it hath been resolved by the deputies and councillors of the Amphictyons and by the assembly of the Amphictyons, seeing that the people of Amphissa have partitioned among themselves the sacred plain and cultivate and feed cattle upon the same, and on being interrupted have come in arms, and with force resisted the general council of the Greeks, and have wounded some of them: that Cottyphus the Arcadian,[2] who hath been elected general of the Amphictyons, be sent ambassador to Philip of Macedon, and do request him to come to the aid of Apollo and the Amphictyons, that he may not

[1] The name of the priest seems to mark the year, as that of the archon at Athens.

[2] Æschines calls Cottyphus a Pharsalian.

suffer the god to be insulted by the impious Amphissians; and do announce that the Greeks who are members of the Amphictyonic Council appoint him general with absolute powers."

Now read the dates of these transactions. They correspond with the time when Æschines was deputy. Read.

### DATES

" Mnesithides [1] archon, on the sixteenth of the month Anthesterion."

Now give me the letter which, when the Thebans would not hearken to Philip, he sends to his allies in Peloponnesus, that you may plainly see even from this how the true motives of his enterprise, his designs against Greece and the Thebans and yourselves, were concealed by him, whilst he affected to be taking measures for the common good under a decree of the Amphictyons. The man who furnished him with these handles and pretexts was Æschines. Read

### THE LETTER OF PHILIP

" Philip, king of Macedon, to the magistrates and councillors of the confederate Peloponnesians and to all the other allies greeting: Whereas the Locrians surnamed Ozolian, dwelling in Amphissa, commit sacrilege against the temple of Apollo at Delphi, and coming with arms despoil the sacred plain, I propose with your assistance to avenge the god, and to chastise people who violate any part of our recognised religion. Wherefore meet me with arms in Phocis, bringing provisions for forty days, in the ensuing month of Lous, as we style it, Boedromion, as the Athenians, Panemus, as the Corinthians. Those who do not meet us with all their forces, we shall visit with punishment. Farewell."

[1] The archon is wrong. It was Theophrastus, as we learn from the speech of Æschines.

You see, he avoids all private pleas, and has recourse to an Amphictyonic. Who was it, I say, that helped him to this contrivance—that lent him these excuses? Who is most to blame for the misfortunes which have happened? Surely Æschines. Then go not about saying, O Athenians, that one man has inflicted these calamities on Greece. Heaven and earth! It was not a single man, but a number of miscreants in every state. Æschines was one of them; and, were I obliged to speak the truth without reserve, I should not hesitate to call him the common pest of all that have since been ruined, men, places, cities: for whoever supplies the seed, to him the crop is owing. I marvel, indeed, you turned not your faces away the moment you beheld him. But there is a thick darkness, it seems, between you and the truth.

The mention of this man's treasonable acts brings me to the part which I have myself taken in opposition to him. It is fair you should hear my account of it for many reasons, but chiefly, men of Athens, because it would be a shame, when I have undergone the toil of exertions on your behalf, that you should not endure the bare recital of them.

When I saw that the Thebans, and may I add the Athenians, were so led away by Philip's partisans and the corrupt men of either state, as to disregard and take no precaution against a danger which menaced both, and required the utmost precaution (I mean the suffering Philip's power to increase) and were readily disposed to enmity and strife with each other; I was constantly watchful to prevent it, not only because in my own judgment I deemed such vigilance expedient, but knowing that Aristophon, and again Eubulus, had all along desired to bring about that union, and, whilst they were frequently opposed upon other matters, were always agreed upon this. Men whom in their lifetime—you reptile! —you pestered with flattery, yet see not that you are accusing them in their graves: for the Theban policy that you reproach me with is a charge less affecting me than them, who

approved that alliance before I did. But I must return.—
I say, when Æschines had excited the war in Amphissa, and
his coadjutors had helped to establish enmity with Thebes,
Philip marched against us—that was the object for which
these persons embroiled the states—and had we not roused
up a little in time, we could never have recovered ourselves:
so far had these men carried matters. In what position you
then stood to each other, you will learn from the recital of
these decrees and answers. Here take and read them.

DECREE [1]

" In the archonship of Heropythus, on the twenty-fifth of
the month Elaphebolion, in the presidency of the Erechtheian
tribe, by the advice of the Council and the Generals: Whereas
Philip hath taken possession of certain neighbouring cities,
and is besieging others, and finally is preparing to advance
against Attica, setting our treaty at nought, and designs to
break his oaths and the peace, in violation of our common
engagements: The Council and People have resolved to send
unto him ambassadors, who shall confer with him, and exhort
him above all to maintain his relations of amity with us and
his convention, or if not, to give time to the Commonwealth
for deliberation, and conclude an armistice until the month
Thargelion. These have been chosen from the Council;
Simus of Anagyrus, Euthydemus of Phylus, Bulagoras of
Alopece."

ANOTHER DECREE

" In the archonship of Heropythus, on the last day of the
month Munychion, by the advice of the Polemarch: Whereas
Philip designs to put the Thebans at variance with us, and
hath prepared to advance with his whole army to the places

---

[1] The archon in this and the following decree is wrong, Lysimachides
having been archon in the year when these events happened.

nearest to Attica, violating the engagements that subsist between us, the Council and People have resolved to send unto him a herald and ambassadors, who shall request and call upon him to conclude an armistice, so that the people may take measures according to circumstances; for now they do not purpose to march out in the event of anything reasonable. Nearchus son of Sosinomus and Polycrates son of Epiphron have been chosen from the Council; and for herald, Eunomus of Anaphlystus from the People."

Now read the answers:—

### THE ANSWER TO THE ATHENIANS

" Philip king of Macedon to the Council and People of Athens greeting: Of the part which you have taken in reference to me from the beginning I am not ignorant, nor what exertions you are making to gain over the Thessalians and Thebans, and also the Bœotians.  Since they are more prudent, and will not submit their choice to your dictation, but stand by their own interest, you shift your ground, and sending ambassadors and a herald to me, you talk of engagements and ask for an armistice, although I have given you no offence.  However I have given audience to your ambassadors, and I agree to your request and am ready to conclude an armistice, if you will dismiss your evil counsellors and degrade them as they deserve.  Farewell."

### THE ANSWER TO THE THEBANS

" Philip king of Macedon to the Council and People of Thebes greeting: I have received your letter, wherein you renew peace and amity with me.  I am informed however that the Athenians are most earnestly soliciting you to accept their overtures.  I blamed you at first, for being inclined to put faith in their promises and to espouse their policy. But since I have discovered that you would rather maintain peace with me than follow the counsels of others, I praise you the more on divers accounts, but chiefly because you have consulted in this business for your safety, and preserve your attachment to me, which I trust will be of no small moment to you, if you persevere in that determination. Farewell."

Philip having thus disposed the states towards each other by his contrivances, and being elated by these decrees and answers, came with his army and seized Elatea, confident that, happen what might, you and the Thebans could never again unite. What commotion there was in the city you all know; but let me just mention the most striking circumstances.

It was evening. A person came with a message to the presidents that Elatea was taken. They rose from supper immediately, drove off the people from their market-stalls, and set fire to the wicker-frames; others sent for the generals and called the trumpeter; and the city was full of commotion. The next morning at daybreak the presidents summoned the council to their hall, and you went to the assembly, and before they could introduce or prepare the question, the whole people were up in their seats.[1] When the council had entered, and the presidents had reported their intelligence and presented the courier, and he had made his statement, the crier asked, " Who wishes to speak? " and no one came forward. The crier put the question repeatedly—still no man rose, though all the generals were present and all the orators, and our country with her common voice called for some one to speak and save her—for when the crier raises his voice according to law, it may justly be deemed the common voice of our country. If those who desired the salvation of Athens were the proper parties to come forward, all of you and the other Athenians would have risen and

[1] On the hill of the Pnyx.

mounted the platform; for I am sure you all desired her
salvation—if those of greatest wealth, the three-hundred—
if those who were both friendly to the state and wealthy,
the men who afterwards gave such ample donations, for
patriotism and wealth produced the gift. But that occasion, that day, as it seems, called not only for a patriot and
wealthy man, but for one who had closely followed the proceedings from their commencement, and rightly calculated
for what object and purpose Philip carried them on. A man
who was ignorant of these matters, or had not long and carefully studied them, let him be ever so patriotic or wealthy,
would neither see what measures were needful, nor be competent to advise you.

Well then—I was the man called for upon that day. I
came forward and addressed you. What I said, I beg you for
two reasons attentively to hear—first, to be convinced, that
of all your orators and statesmen I alone deserted not the
patriot's post in the hour of danger, but was found in the
very moment of panic speaking and moving what your necessities required—secondly, because at the expense of a little
time you will gain large experience for the future in all your
political concerns.

I said—those who were in such alarm under the idea that
Philip had got the Thebans with him did not, in my opinion,
understand the position of affairs; for I was sure had that
really been so, we should have heard not of his being at
Elatea, but upon our frontiers: he was come, however, I knew
for certain, to make all right for himself in Thebes. " Let
me inform you," said I, " how the matter stands.—All the
Thebans whom it was possible either to bribe or deceive he
has at his command; those who have resisted him from the
first and still oppose him he can in no way prevail upon:
what then is his meaning, and why has he seized upon
Elatea? He means, by displaying a force in the neighbourhood, and bringing up his troops, to encourage and embolden
his friends, to intimidate his adversaries, that they may either

concede from fear what they now refuse, or be compelled. Now "—said I—" if we determine on the present occasion to remember any unkindness which the Thebans have done us, and to regard them in the character of enemies with distrust, in the first place, we shall be doing just what Philip would desire; in the next place, I fear, his present adversaries embracing his friendship and all Philippising with one consent, they will both march against Attica. But if you will hearken to me, and be pleased to examine (not cavil at) what I say, I believe it will meet your approval, and I shall dispel the danger impending over Athens. What then do I advise?— First, away with your present fear; and rather fear all of ye for the Thebans—they are nearer harm than we are—to them the peril is more immediate:—next I say, march to Eleusis all the fighting-men and the cavalry, and show yourselves to the world in arms, that your partisans in Thebes may have equal liberty to speak up for the good cause, knowing that, as the faction who sell their country to Philip have an army to support them at Elatea, so the party that will contend for freedom have your assistance at hand if they are assailed. Further I recommend you to elect ten ambassadors, and empower them in conjunction with the generals to fix the time for going there and for the out-march. When the ambassadors have arrived at Thebes, how do I advise that you should treat the matter? Pray attend particularly to this— Ask nothing of the Thebans (it would be dishonourable at this time); but offer to assist them if they require it, on the plea that they are in extreme danger, and we see the future better than they do. If they accept this offer and hearken to our counsels, so shall we have accomplished what we desire, and our conduct will look worthy of the state: should we miscarry, they will have themselves to blame for any error committed now, and we shall have done nothing dishonourable or mean."

This and more to the like effect I spoke, and left the platform. It was approved by all; not a word was said against me.  Nor did I make the speech without moving, nor make the motion without undertaking the embassy, nor undertake the embassy without prevailing on the Thebans. From the beginning to the end I went through it all; I gave myself entirely to your service, to meet the dangers which encompassed Athens.

Produce me the decree which then passed.  Now, Æschines, how would you have me describe you, and how myself, upon that day?  Shall I call myself Batalus,[1] your nickname of reproach, and you not even a hero of the common sort, but one of those upon the stage, Cresphontes or Creon, or the Œnomaus whom you execrably murdered once at Colyttus?[2] Well; upon that occasion I the Batalus of Pæania was more serviceable to the state than you the Œnomaus of Cothocidæ. You were of no earthly use; I did everything which became a good citizen.  Read the decree.

THE DECREE OF DEMOSTHENES

" In the archonship of Nausicles,[3] in the presidency of the Æantian tribe, on the sixteenth of Scirophorion, Demosthenes son of Demosthenes of Pæania moved:  Whereas Philip king of Macedon hath in time past been violating the treaty of peace made between him and the Athenian people, in contempt of his oath and those laws of justice which are recognised among all the Greeks, and hath been annexing unto himself cities that no way belong to him, and hath besieged

---

[1] The origin of this nickname is doubtful.  The early critics were not agreed upon it, as we learn from Plutarch.  Libanius, in the *Life of Demosthenes*, says that Batalus was an effeminate fluteplayer in Asia Minor; which seems to agree with the words of Æschines, in his speech on the Embassy (p. 41), where he says that Demosthenes was called Batalus when a boy.

[2] Cresphontes, king of Messenia, and one of the Heraclidæ, was the hero of a lost play of Euripides; Creon is the well-known character in the *Œdipus* and *Antigone* of Sophocles: Œnomaus, the king of Elis, and father of Hippodamia, was the hero of a tragedy of Ischander, in the performance of which Æschines was hissed off the stage at Colyttus, one of the Attic townships.

[3] The archon was Lysimachides.

and taken some which belong to the Athenians without any
provocation by the people of Athens, and at the present
time he is making great advances in cruelty and violence,
forasmuch as in certain Greek cities he puts garrisons and
overturns their constitution, some he razes to the ground
and sells the inhabitants for slaves, in some he replaces a
Greek population with barbarians, giving them possession of
the temples and sepulchres, acting in no way foreign to his
own country or character, making an insolent use of his
present fortune, and forgetting that from a petty and insignificant person he has come to be unexpectedly great: and the
people of Athens, so long as they saw him annexing barbarian
or private cities of their own, less seriously regarded the
offence given to themselves, but now that they see Greek
cities outraged and some destroyed, they think it would be
monstrous and unworthy of their ancestral glory to look on
while the Greeks are enslaved: Therefore it is resolved by the
Council and People of Athens, that having prayed and sacrificed to the gods and heroes who protect the Athenian city
and territory, bearing in mind the virtue of their ancestors,
who deemed it of greater moment to preserve the liberty of
Greece than their own country, they will put two hundred
ships to sea, and their admiral shall sail up into the straits
of Thermopylæ, and their general and commander of horse
shall march with the infantry and cavalry to Eleusis, and
ambassadors shall be sent to the other Greeks, and first of all
to the Thebans, because Philip is nearest their territory,
and shall exhort them without dread of Philip to maintain
their own independence and that of Greece at large, and
assure them that the Athenian people, not remembering any
variance which has formerly arisen between the countries,
will assist them with troops and money and weapons and
arms, feeling that for them (being Greeks) to contend among
themselves for the leadership is honourable, but to be commanded and deprived of the leadership by a man of foreign
extraction is derogatory to the renown of the Greeks and the

virtue of their ancestors: further, the people of Athens do not regard the people of Thebes as aliens either in blood or race; they remember also the benefits conferred by their ancestors upon the ancestors of the Thebans; for they restored the children of Hercules who were kept by the Peloponnesians out of their hereditary dominion, defeating in battle those who attempted to resist the descendants of Hercules; and we gave shelter to Œdipus and his comrades in exile; and many other kind and generous acts have been done by us to the Thebans: wherefore now also the people of Athens will not desert the interests of the Thebans and the other Greeks: and let a treaty be entered into with them for alliance and intermarriage, and oaths be mutually exchanged. Ambassadors: Demosthenes son of Demosthenes of Pæania, Hyperides son of Cleander of Spettus, Mnesithides son of Antiphanes of Phrearrii, Democrates son of Sophilus of Phlyus, Callæschrus son of Diotimus of Cothocidæ."

That was the commencement and first step in the negotiation with Thebes: before then the countries had been led by these men into discord and hatred and jealousy. That decree caused the peril which then surrounded us to pass away like a cloud. It was the duty of a good citizen, if he had any better plan, to disclose it at the time, not to find fault now. A statesman and a pettifogger, while in no other respect are they alike, in this most widely differ. The one declares his opinion before the proceedings, and makes himself responsible to his followers, to fortune, to the times, to all men: the other is silent when he ought to speak; at any untoward event he grumbles. Now, as I said before, the time for a man who regarded the commonwealth, and for honest counsel, was then: however I will go to this extent—if any one now can point out a better course, or indeed if any other was practicable but the one which I adopted, I confess that I was wrong. For if there be any measure now discovered, which (executed them) would have been to our advantage, I say it ought not to have escaped me. But if there is none, if there was none, if none can be suggested even at this day, what was a statesman to do? Was he not to choose the best measures within his reach and view? That did I, Æschines, when the crier asked, " Who wishes to speak? "—not, " Who wishes to complain about the past, or to guarantee the future?" Whilst you on those occasions sat mute in the assembly, I came forward and spake. However, as you omitted then, tell us now. Say, what scheme that I ought to have devised, what favourable opportunity was lost to the state by my neglect?— what alliance was there, what better plan, to which I should have directed the people? But no! The past is with all the world given up; no one even proposes to deliberate about it: the future it is, or the present, which demands the action of a counsellor. At the time, as it appeared, there were dangers impending, and dangers at hand. Mark the line of my policy at that crisis; don't rail at the event. The end of all things is what the Deity pleases: his line of policy it is that shows the judgment of the statesman. Do not then impute it as a crime to me that Philip chanced to conquer in battle: that issue depended not on me, but on God. Prove that I adopted not all measures that according to human cal- culation were feasible—that I did not honestly and diligently and with exertions beyond my strength carry them out—or that my enterprises were not honourable and worthy of the state and necessary. Show me this, and accuse me as soon as you like. But if the hurricane that visited us hath been too powerful, not for us only, but for all Greece besides, what is the fair course? As if a merchant, after taking every pre- caution, and furnishing his vessel with everything that he thought would ensure her safety, because afterwards he met with a storm and his tackle was strained or broken to pieces, should be charged with the shipwreck! " Well, but I was not the pilot "—he might say—just as I was not the general.— " Fortune was not under my control: all was under hers."

Consider and reflect upon this—If, with the Thebans on

our side, we were destined so to fare in the contest, what was to be expected if we had never had them for allies, but they had joined Philip, as he used every effort of persuasion to make them do? And if, when the battle was fought three days march from Attica, such peril and alarm surrounded the city, what must we have expected if the same disaster had happened in some part of our territory? As it was (do you see?) we could stand, meet, breathe; mightily did one, two, three days, help to our preservation: in the other case —but it is wrong to mention things, of which we have been spared the trial by the favour of some deity, and by our protecting ourselves with the very alliance which you assail.

All this, at such length, have I addressed to you, men of the jury, and to the outer circle of hearers; for, as to the contemptible fellow, a short and plain argument would suffice. If the future was revealed to you, Æschines, alone, when the state was deliberating on these proceedings, you ought to have forewarned us at the time. If you did not foresee it, you are responsible for the same ignorance as the rest. Why then do you accuse me in this behalf, rather than I you? A better citizen have I been than you in respect of the matters of which I am speaking (others I discuss not at present) inasmuch as I gave myself up to what seemed for the general good, not shrinking from any personal danger, nor taking thought of any; whilst you neither suggested better measures (or mine would not have been adopted) nor lent any aid in the prosecuting of mine: exactly what the basest person and worst enemy of the state would do, are you found to have done after the event; and at the same time Aristratus in Naxos and Aristolaus in Thasos, the deadly foes of our state, are bringing to trial the friends of Athens, and Æschines at Athens is accusing Demosthenes. Surely the man, who waited to found his reputation upon the misfortunes of the Greeks, deserves rather to perish than to accuse another; nor is it possible that one, who has profited by the same conjunctures as the enemies of the commonwealth, can be a well-wisher of his country. You show yourself by your life and conduct, by your political action, and even your political inaction. Is anything going on that appears good for the people? Æschines is mute. Has anything untoward happened or amiss? Forth comes Æschines; just as fractures and sprains are put in motion, when the body is attacked with disease.

But since he insists so strongly on the event, I will even assert something of a paradox: and I beg and pray of you not to marvel at its boldness, but kindly to consider what I say. If then the results had been foreknown to all, if all had foreseen them, and you, Æschines, had foretold them and protested with clamour and outcry—you that never opened your mouth—not even then should the Commonwealth have abandoned her design, if she had any regard for glory, or ancestry, or futurity. As it is, she appears to have failed in her enterprise, a thing to which all mankind are liable, if the Deity so wills it: but then—claiming precedency over others, and afterwards abandoning her pretensions—she would have incurred the charge of betraying all to Philip. Why, had we resigned without a struggle that which our ancestors encountered every danger to win, who would not have spit upon you? Let me not say, the commonwealth or myself![1] With what eyes, I pray, could we have beheld strangers visiting the city, if the result had been what it is, and Philip had been chosen leader and lord of all, but other people without us had made the struggle to prevent it; especially when in former times our country had never preferred an ignominious security to the battle for honour? For what Grecian or what barbarian is ignorant, that by the Thebans, or by the Lacedæmonians who were in might before them, or by the Persian king, permission would thankfully and gladly have been given to our commonwealth, to take what she pleased and hold her own, provided she would accept foreign

---

[1] *I.e.* " Let me not say anything so shocking, so revolting to my feelings, as to suppose that the commonwealth or myself could deserve such an indignity! "

law and let another power command in Greece?  But, as it
seems, to the Athenians of that day such conduct would not
have been national, or natural, or endurable:  none could at
any period of time persuade the commonwealth to attach
herself in secure subjection to the powerful and unjust:
through every age has she persevered in a perilous struggle
for precedency and honour and glory.  And this you esteem
so noble and congenial to your principles, that among your
ancestors you honour most those who acted in such a spirit;
and with reason.  For who would not admire the virtue of
those men, who resolutely embarked in their galleys and
quitted country and home, rather than receive foreign law,
choosing Themistocles who gave such counsel for their general,
and stoning Cyrsilus to death who advised submission to the
terms imposed—not him only, but your wives also stoning
his wife? [1]  Yes; the Athenians of that day looked not for
an orator or a general, who might help them to a pleasant
servitude:  they scorned to live, if it could not be with
freedom.  For each of them considered that he was not
born to his father or mother only, but also to his country.
What is the difference?  He that thinks himself born for
his parents only, waits for his appointed or natural end:  he
that thinks himself born for his country also, will sooner
perish than behold her in slavery, and will regard the insults
and indignities, which must be borne in a commonwealth
enslaved, as more terrible than death.

Had I attempted to say, that I instructed you in sentiments worthy of your ancestors, there is not a man who would
not justly rebuke me.  What I declare is, that such principles
are your own;  I show that before my time such was the
spirit of the commonwealth;  though certainly in the execution of the particular measures I claim a share also for my-

---

[1] Cicero (*De Officiis*, III. 11) has borrowed this anecdote from Demosthenes.   The same story is related by Herodotus (IX. 4, 5), who calls
the person not Cyrsilus, but Lycidas.   The terms were offered by Mardonius to the Athenians, while they were in Salamis.   The advice of
Lycidas was given to the council, and the people outside hearing of it,
proceeded immediately to inflict summary punishment upon him.

self. The prosecutor, arraigning the whole proceedings, and embittering you against me as the cause of our alarms and dangers, in his eagerness to deprive me of honour for the moment, robs you of the eulogies that should endure for ever. For should you, under a disbelief in the wisdom of my policy, convict the defendant, you will appear to have done wrong not to have suffered what befell you by the cruelty of fortune. But never, never can you have done wrong, O Athenians, in undertaking the battle for the freedom and safety of all! I swear it by your forefathers—those that met the peril at Marathon, those that took the field at Platæa, those in the sea-fight at Salamis, and those at Artemisium, and many other brave men who repose in the public monuments, all of whom alike, as being worthy of the same honour, the country buried, Æschines, not only the successful or victorious! Justly! For the duty of brave men has been done by all: their fortune has been such as the Deity assigned to each.[1]

Accursed scribbler! you, to deprive me of the approbation and affection of my countrymen, speak of trophies and battles and ancient deeds, with none of which had this present trial the least concern; but I!—O you third-rate actor!—I, that rose to counsel the state how to maintain her pre-eminence! in what spirit was I to mount the hustings? In the spirit of one having unworthy counsel to offer?—I should have deserved to perish! You yourselves, men of Athens, may not try private and public causes on the same principles: the compacts of every-day life you are to judge of by particular laws and circumstances; the measures of statesmen, by reference to the dignity of your ancestors. And if you think it your duty to act worthily of them, you should every one of you consider, when you come into court to decide public questions, that together with your staff and ticket [2] the spirit of the commonwealth is delivered to you.

[1] So much criticism has been lavished, both in ancient and modern times, on the beauty of this celebrated passage, that to refer to all that has been said would be impossible.

[2] There were 6,000 jurors chosen by lot for the service of the year, 600 from each of the Attic tribes. The whole number was then divided

But in touching upon the deeds of your ancestors, there were some decrees and transactions which I omitted. I will return from my digression.

On our arrival at Thebes, we found ambassadors there from Philip, from the Thessalians and from his other allies; our friends in trepidation, his friends confident. To prove that I am not asserting this now to serve my own purposes, read me the letter which we ambassadors despatched on the instant. So outrageous is my opponent's malignity, that, if any advantage was procured, he attributes it to the occasion, not to me; while all miscarriages he attributes to me and my fortune. And according to him, as it seems, I, the orator and adviser, have no merit in results of argument and counsel, but am the sole author of misfortunes in arms and strategy. Could there be a more brutal calumniator or a more execrable? Read the letter.

*[The letter is read]* [1]

On the convening of the assembly, our opponents were introduced first, because they held the character of allies. And they came forward and spoke, in high praise of Philip and disparagement of you, bringing up all the hostilities that

into ten sections of 500 each, a thousand being left as supernumeraries, to supply deficiencies occasioned by death or any other cause. There were ten courts at Athens, among which the services of these jurors were to be distributed; and it was managed in the following way. Each court was designated by a colour, and also by a letter over the doorway. Each of the jury sections was likewise designated by a letter. When the juries had to be impanelled, the letters indicating the different sections were drawn out of one box, and the letters indicating the different courts were drawn out of another: each pair of lots so drawn out determined what section should be assigned to what court. When the whole section was not required, the individual jurors who were to form the panel were chosen by lot, each juror having a counter with his section and name marked upon it. The courts being thus allotted, every juryman received a staff and a ticket. The staff, on which was marked the letter and colour of his court, served to distinguish him from the crowd, and procure him instant admission. The ticket, which he returned to the magistrate when the business was concluded, entitled him to his fee.

[1] This, and all the documents subsequently referred to by the Orator, are lost.

you ever committed against the Thebans. In fine, they
urged them to show their gratitude for the services done by
Philip, and to avenge themselves for the injuries which you
had done them, either—it mattered not which—by giving
them a passage against you, or by joining in the invasion of
Attica; and they proved, as they fancied, that by adopting
their advice the cattle and slaves and other effects of Attica
would come into Bœotia, whereas, by acting as they said we
should advise, Bœotia would suffer pillage through the war.
And much they said besides, tending all to the same point.
The reply that we made I would give my life to recapitulate,
but I fear, as the occasion is past, you will look upon it as if
a sort of deluge had overwhelmed the whole proceedings, and
regard any talk about them as a useless troubling of you.
Hear then what we persuaded them and what answer they
returned. Take and read this:

*[The answer of the Thebans]*

After this they invited and sent for you. You marched to
their succour, and—to omit what happened between—their
reception of you was so friendly, that, while their infantry
and cavalry were outside the walls, they admitted your army
into their houses and citadel, among their wives and children
and all that was most precious. Why, upon that day three
of the noblest testimonies were before all mankind borne in
your favour by the Thebans, one to your courage, one to
your justice, one to your good behaviour. For when they
preferred fighting on your side to fighting against you, they
held you to be braver and juster in your demands than
Philip; and when they put under your charge what they and
all men are most watchful to protect, their wives and children, they showed that they had confidence in your good
behaviour. In all which, men of Athens, it appeared they
had rightly estimated your character. For after your forces
entered the city, not so much as a groundless complaint was

preferred against you by any one; so discreetly did you behave yourselves: and twice arrayed on their side in the earlier battles, that by the river and the winter-battle, you proved yourselves not irreproachable only, but admirable in your discipline, your equipments, and your zeal: which called forth eulogies from other men to you, sacrifice and thanks-giving from you to the Gods. And I would gladly ask Æschines—while these things were going on, and the city was full of enthusiasm and joy and praise, whether he joined with the multitude in sacrifice and festivity, or sat at home sorrowing and moaning and repining at the public success. For if he was present and appeared with the rest, is not his conduct monstrous, or rather impious, when measures, which he himself called the Gods to witness were excellent, he now requires you to condemn—you that have sworn by the Gods? If he was not present, does he not deserve a thousand deaths for grieving to behold what others rejoiced at? Read me now the decrees.

*[The decrees for sacrifice]*

We thus were engaged in sacrifice; the Thebans were in the assurance that they had been saved through us; and it had come about, that a people, who seemed likely to want assistance through the practices of these men, were them-selves assisting others in consequence of my advice which you followed. What language Philip then uttered, and in what trouble he was on this account, you shall learn from his letters which he sent to Peloponnesus. Take and read them, that the jury may know what my perseverance and journeys and toils, and the many decrees which this man just now pulled to pieces, accomplished.

Athenians, you have had many great and renowned orators before me; the famous Callistratus, Aristophon, Cephalus, Thrasybulus, hundreds of others; yet none of them ever thoroughly devoted himself to any measure of state: for instance, the mover of a resolution would not be ambassador; the ambassador would not move a resolution; each one left for himself some relief, and also, should anything happen, an excuse. How then—it may be said—did you so far surpass others in might and boldness as to do everything yourself? I don't say that: but such was my conviction of the danger impending over us, that I considered it left no room or thought for individual security; a man should have been only too happy to perform his duty without neglect. As to myself I was persuaded, perhaps foolishly, yet I was persuaded, that none would move better resolutions than myself, none would execute them better, none as ambassador would show more zeal and honesty. Therefore I undertook every duty myself. Read the letters of Philip.

[*The letters*]

To this did my policy, Æschines, reduce Philip. This language he uttered through me, he that before had lifted his voice so boldly against Athens! For which I was justly crowned by the people; and you were present and opposed it not, and Diondas who preferred an indictment obtained not his share of the votes. Here, read me the decrees which were then absolved, and which this man never indicted.

[*The decrees*]

These decrees, men of Athens, contain the very words and syllables which Aristonicus drew up formerly, and Ctesiphon the defendant has now. And Æschines neither arraigned these himself, nor aided the party who preferred an indictment. Yet, if his present charge against me be true, he might then have arraigned Demomeles the mover and Hyperides with more show of reason than he can the defendant. Why? Because Ctesiphon may refer to them, and to the decisions of the courts, and to the fact of Æschines not having accused them, although they moved the same decrees which he has now, and to the laws which bar any further proceedings in such a case, and to many points besides:— whereas then the question would have been tried on its own merits, before any such advantages had been obtained. But then, I imagine, it would have been impossible to do what Æschines now does—to pick out of a multitude of old dates and decrees what no man knew before, and what no man would have expected to hear to-day, for the purpose of slander—to transpose dates, and assign measures to the wrong causes instead of the right, in order to make a plausible case. That was impossible then. Every statement must have been according to the truth, soon after the facts, while you still remembered the particulars and had them almost at your fingers' ends. Therefore it was that he shunned all investigation at the time, and has come at this late period; thinking, as it appears to me, that you would make it a contest of orators, instead of an inquiry into political conduct; that words would be criticised, and not interests of state.

Then he plays the sophist, and says, you ought to disregard the opinion of us which you came from home with— that, as when you audit a man's account under the impression that he has a surplus, if it casts up right and nothing remains, you allow it, so should you now accept the fair conclusion of the argument. Only see, how rotten in its nature (and justly so) is every wicked contrivance! For by this very cunning simile he has now acknowledged it to be your conviction, that I am my country's advocate and he is Philip's. Had not this been your opinion of each, he would not have tried to persuade you differently. That he has however no reasonable ground for requiring you to change your belief, I can easily show, not by casting accounts—for that mode of reckoning applies not to measures—but by calling the circumstances briefly to mind, taking you that hear me both for auditors and witnesses.

Through my policy, which he arraigns, instead of the

Thebans invading this country with Philip, as all expected, they joined our ranks and prevented him;—instead of the war being in Attica, it took place seven hundred furlongs from the city, on the confines of Bœotia—instead of corsairs issuing from Eubœa to plunder us, Attica was in peace on the coast-side during the whole war;—instead of Philip being master of the Hellespont by taking Byzantium, the Byzantines were our auxiliaries against him. Does this computation of services, think you, resemble the casting of accounts? Or should we strike these out on a balance, and not look that they be kept in everlasting remembrance? I will not set down that of the cruelty remarkable in cases were Philip got people all at once into his power, others have had the trial; whilst of the generosity, which, casting about for his future purposes, he assumed towards Athens, you have happily enjoyed the fruits. I pass that by.

Yet this I do not hesitate to say; that any one desirous of truly testing an orator, not of calumniating him, would never have made the charges that you advanced just now, inventing similes, mimicking words and gestures: (doubtless it hath determined the fortune of Greece, whether I spoke this word or that, whether I moved my hand one way or the other!) no! he would have examined the facts of the case, what means and resources our country possessed, when I entered on the administration, what, when I applied myself to it, I collected for her, and what was the condition of our adversaries. Then, if I had lessened her resources, he would have shown me to be guilty; if I had greatly increased them, he would not have calumniated me. However, as you have declined this course, I will adopt it. See if I state the case fairly.

For resources—our country possessed the islanders; not all, but the weakest; for neither Chios, nor Rhodes, nor Corcyra was with us: subsidies [1] she had amounting to five-and-forty talents; and they were anticipated: infantry or cavalry, none besides the native. But what was most alarming

[1] The tribute from the islanders.

and wrought most in favour of the enemy—these men had got
all our neighbours to be hostile rather than friendly to us;
Megarians, Thebans, Eubœans.  Such were the circumstances
of our state; no man can say anything to the contrary: look
now at those of Philip, whom we had to contend with.   In
the first place, he ruled his followers with unlimited sway, the
most important thing for military operations:  in the next
place, they had arms always in their hands: besides, he had
plenty of money, and did what he pleased, not giving notice
by decrees, not deliberating openly, not brought to trial by
calumniators, not defending indictments for illegal measures,
not responsible to any one, but himself absolute master,
leader, and lord of all.   I, who was matched against him—for
it is right to examine this—what had I under my control?
Nothing.   Public speech, for instance, the only thing open to
me—even to this you invited his hirelings as well as myself; and whenever they prevailed over me (as often happened
for some cause or other) your resolutions were passed for
the enemy's good.   Still under these disadvantages I got you
for allies Eubœans, Achæans, Corinthians, Thebans, Megarians,
Leucadians, Corcyræans; from whom were collected fifteen
thousand mercenaries and two thousand horse, besides the
national troops.   Of money too I procured as large a contribution as possible.

If you talk about just conditions with the Thebans,[1] Æschines, or with the Byzantines or Eubœans, or discuss now
the question of equal terms, first I say—you are ignorant
that of those galleys formerly which defended Greece, being
three hundred in number, our commonwealth furnished two
hundred, and never (as it seemed) thought herself injured by
having done so, never prosecuted those who advised it or expressed any dissatisfaction;—shame on her if she had!—but
was grateful to the gods, that, when a common danger beset
the Greeks, she alone furnished double what the rest did for

---

[1] Æschines, in his speech (73), complains that the terms of the
treaty, concluded by Demosthenes with the Thebans, were most
disadvantageous to Athens.

the preservation of all. Besides, it is but a poor favour you do your countrymen by calumniating me. For what is the use of telling us now what we should have done?—Why, being in the city and present, did you not make your proposals then; if indeed they were practicable at a crisis, when we had to accept not what we liked but what the circumstances allowed? Remember, there was one ready to bid against us, to welcome eagerly those that we rejected, and give money into the bargain.

But if I am accused for what I have actually done, how would it have been, if, through my hard bargaining, the states had gone off and attached themselves to Philip, and he had become master at the same time of Euboea, Thebes, and Byzantium? What think ye these impious men would have said or done? Said, doubtless, that the states were abandoned—that they wished to join us and were driven away—that he had got command of the Hellespont by the Byzantines, and become master of the corn-trade of Greece—that a heavy neighbour-war had by means of the Thebans been brought into Attica—that the sea had become unnavigable by the excursion of pirates from Euboea! All this would they have said sure enough, and a great deal besides. A wicked, wicked thing, O Athenians, is a calumniator always, every way spiteful and fault-finding. But this creature is a reptile by nature, that from the beginning never did anything honest or liberal; a very ape of a tragedian, village Oenomaus, counterfeit orator! What advantage has your eloquence been to your country? Now do you speak to us about the past? As if a physician should visit his patients, and not order or prescribe anything to cure the disease, but on the death of any one, when the last ceremonies were performing, should follow him to the grave and expound, how, if the poor fellow had done this and that, he never would have died! Idiot! do you speak now?

Even the defeat—if you exult in that which should make you groan, you accursed one!—by nothing that I have done will it appear to have befallen us. Consider it thus,

O Athenians. From no embassy, on which I was commissioned by you, did I ever come away defeated by the ambassadors of Philip—neither from Thessaly, nor from Ambracia, nor from the kings of Thrace, nor from Byzantium, nor from any other place, nor on the last recent occasion from Thebes; but where his ambassadors were vanquished in argument, he came with arms and carried the day. And for this you call me to account; and are not ashamed to jeer the same person for cowardice whom you require singlehanded to overcome the might of Philip—and that too by words! For what else had I at my command? Certainly not the spirit of each individual, nor the fortune of the army, nor the conduct of the war, for which you would make me accountable; such a blunderer are you!

Yet understand me. Of what a statesman may be responsible for I allow the utmost scrutiny; I deprecate it not. What are his functions? To observe things in the beginning, to foresee and foretell them to others,—this I have done: again; wherever he finds delays, backwardness, ignorance, jealousies, vices inherent and unavoidable in all communities, to contract them into the narrowest compass, and on the other hand, to promote unanimity and friendship and zeal in the discharge of duty. All this too I have performed; and no one can discover the least neglect on my part. Ask any man by what means Philip achieved most of his successes, and you will be told, by his army, and by his bribing and corrupting men in power. Well; your forces were not under my command or control; so that I cannot be questioned for anything done in that department. But by refusing the price of corruption I have overcome Philip: for as the offerer of a bribe, if it be accepted, has vanquished the taker, so the person who refuses it and is not corrupted has vanquished the person offering. Therefore is the commonwealth undefeated as far as I am concerned.

These and such as these (besides many others) are the grounds furnished by myself to justify the defendant's motion in my behalf. Those which you, my fellow-citizens, furnished I will proceed to mention. Immediately after the battle the people, knowing and having witnessed everything which I did, in the very midst of their alarm and terror, when it would not have been surprising if the great body of them had even treated me harshly, passed my resolutions for the safety of the country; all their measures of defence, the disposition of the garrisons, the trenches, the levies for our fortifications, were carried on under my decrees: and further, upon the election of a commissioner of grain, they chose me in preference to all. Afterwards, when those who were bent to do me a mischief conspired, and brought indictments, audits, impeachments and the rest of it against me, not at first in their own persons, but in such names as they imagined would most effectually screen themselves (for you surely know and remember that every day of that first period I was arraigned, and neither the desperation of Sosicles, nor the malignity of Philocrates, nor the madness of Diondas and Melantus, nor anything else was left untried by them against me;) on all those occasions, chiefly through the Gods, secondly through you and the other Athenians, I was preserved. And with justice. Yes, that is the truth, and to the honour of the juries who so conscientiously decided. Well then: on the impeachments, when you acquitted me and gave not the prosecutors their share of the votes, you pronounced that my policy was the best: by my acquittal on the indictments my counsels and motions were shown to be legal; by your passing of my accounts you acknowledged my whole conduct to have been honest and incorruptible. Under these circumstances, what name could Ctesiphon with decency or justice give to my acts? Not that which he saw the people give— which he saw the jurors give—which he saw truth establish to the world?

Aye, says he; but that was a fine thing of Cephalus, never to have been indicted. Yes, and a lucky one too. But why should a man, who has often been charged, but never convicted of crime, be a whit the more liable to reproach? However, men of Athens, against my opponent I have a right to use the boast of Cephalus; for he never preferred or prosecuted any indictment against me; therefore I am a citizen as good as Cephalus by his admission.

From many things one may see his unfeelingness and malignity, but especially from his discourse about fortune. For my part, I regard any one who reproaches his fellow-man with fortune, as devoid of sense. He that is best satisfied with his condition, he that deems his fortune excellent, cannot be sure that it will remain so until the evening: how then can it be right to bring it forward, or upbraid another man with it? As Æschines, however, has on this subject (besides many others) expressed himself with insolence, look, men of Athens, and observe how much more truth and humanity there shall be in my discourse upon fortune than in his.

I hold the fortune of our commonwealth to be good, and so I find the oracles of Dodonæan Jupiter and Pythian Apollo declaring to us. The fortune of all mankind, which now prevails, I consider cruel and dreadful: for what Greek, what barbarian, has not in these times experienced a multitude of evils? That Athens chose the noblest policy, that she fares better than those very Greeks who thought, if they abandoned us, they should abide in prosperity, I reckon as part of her good fortune: if she suffered reverses, if all happened not to us as we desired, I conceive she has had that share of the general fortune which fell to our lot. As to my fortune (personally speaking) or that of any individual among us, it should, as I conceive, be judged of in connection with personal matters. Such is my opinion upon the subject of fortune, a right and just one, as it appears to me, and I think you will agree with it. Æschines says that my individual fortune is paramount to that of the commonwealth, the small and mean to the good and great. How can this possibly be?

However, if you are determined, Æschines, to scrutinise my fortune, compare it with your own, and, if you find my fortune better than yours, cease to revile it. Look then from the very beginning. And I pray and entreat that I may not be condemned for bad taste. I don't think any person wise who insults poverty, or who prides himself on having been bred in affluence: but by the slander and malice of this cruel man I am forced into such a discussion; which I will conduct with all the moderation which circumstances allow.

I had the advantage, Æschines, in my boyhood of going to proper schools, and having such allowance as a boy should have who is to do nothing mean from indigence. Arrived at man's estate, I lived suitably to my breeding; was choir-master, ship-commander, ratepayer; backward in no acts of liberality public or private, but making myself useful to the commonwealth and to my friends. When I entered upon state affairs, I chose such a line of politics that both by my country and many people of Greece I have been crowned many times, and not even you, my enemies, venture to say that the line I chose was not honourable. Such, then, has been the fortune of my life: I could enlarge upon it, but I forbear, lest what I pride myself in should give offence.

But you, the man of dignity, who spit upon others, look what sort of fortune is yours compared with mine. As a boy you were reared in abject poverty, waiting with your father on the school, grinding the ink, sponging the benches, sweeping the room, doing the duty of a menial rather than a free-man's son. After you were grown up, you attended your mother's initiations,[1] reading her books and helping in all the ceremonies: at night wrapping the noviciates in fawn-skin, swilling, purifying, and scouring them with clay and bran, raising them after the lustration, and bidding them say, " Bad I have scaped, and better I have found; " priding yourself that no one ever howled so lustily—and I believe him! for

[1] The rites, which Demosthenes represents to have been performed by the mother of Æschines, were brought into Greece from Phrygia and the east, and from Thrace. They appear not to have been of the most reputable kind, at all events the officiating parties were a low class of people.

don't suppose that he who speaks so loud is not a splendid howler! In the daytime you led your noble orgiasts, crowned with fennel and poplar, through the highways, squeezing the big-cheeked serpents, and lifting them over your head, and shouting Evœ Sabœ, and capering to the words Hyes Attes, Attes Hyes, saluted by the beldames as Leader, Conductor, Chest-bearer, Fan-bearer, and the like, getting as your reward tarts and biscuits and rolls; for which any man might well bless himself and his fortune!

When you were enrolled among your fellow-townsmen—by what means I stop not to inquire—when you were enrolled, however, you immediately selected the most honourable of employments, that of clerk and assistant to our petty magistrates. From this you were removed after a while, having done yourself all that you charge others with; and then, sure enough, you disgraced not your antecedents by your subsequent life, but hiring yourself to those ranting players, as they were called, Simylus and Socrates, you acted third parts, collecting figs and grapes and olives like a fruiterer from other men's farms, and getting more from them than from the playing, in which the lives of your whole company were at stake; for there was an implacable and incessant war between them and the audience, from whom you received so many wounds, that no wonder you taunt as cowards people inexperienced in such encounters.[1]

But passing over what may be imputed to poverty, I will

---

[1] The commentators and translators have all misunderstood this passage, imagining that Æschines and his troop are charged with strolling about the country and robbing orchards. Nothing could be more foreign to the meaning. The explanation is simply as follows: Æschines and his fellow-players acted so badly that they were pelted by the audience with figs, grapes, and olives—as we should say, with oranges. The players picked up these missiles, and were glad to pocket the affront. Such quantities were showered upon the stage, that they got enough to stock a fruiterer's shop; so they were supplied like a dealer in fruit, who purchases his stock from various farmers and gardeners. From this source Æschines derived more profit than from the dramatic contests, for which the company were ill paid, and in which they ran the risk of their lives every day from the indignation of the audience.

come to the direct charges against your character. You
espoused such a line of politics (when at last you thought of
taking to them) that, if your country prospered, you lived
the life of a hare, fearing and trembling and ever expecting to
be scourged for the crimes of which your conscience accused
you; though all have seen how bold you were during the
misfortunes of the rest. A man who took courage at the
death of a thousand citizens—what does he deserve at the
hands of the living? A great deal more that I could say
about him I shall omit: for it is not all I can tell of his
turpitude and infamy which I ought to let slip from my
tongue, but only what is not disgraceful to myself to
mention.

Contrast now the circumstances of your life and mine,
gently and with temper, Æschines; and then ask these people
whose fortune they would each of them prefer. You taught
reading, I went to school: you performed initiations, I
received them: you danced in the chorus, I furnished it: you
were assembly-clerk, I was a speaker: you acted third parts,
I heard you: you broke down, and I hissed: you have
worked as a statesman for the enemy, I for my country.[1]  I
pass by the rest; but this very day I am on my probation
for a crown, and am acknowledged to be innocent of all
offence; whilst you are already judged to be a pettifogger,
and the question is, whether you shall continue that trade, or
at once be silenced by not getting a fifth part of the votes.
A happy fortune, do you see, you have enjoyed, that you
should denounce mine as miserable!

Come now, let me read the evidence to the jury of public

---

[1] Milton has imitated this passage in the Apology for Smectymnuus
(vol. i. p. 221, Symmons' Edition.) Speaking of the young divines and
students at college, whom he had seen so often upon the stage prosti-
tuting the shame of that ministry which they either had or were nigh
having, to the eyes of courtiers and court ladies, he proceeds thus:—
"There while they acted and overacted, among other young scholars
I was a spectator: they thought themselves gallant men, and I thought
them fools; they made sport, and I laughed; they mispronounced,
and I misliked; and, to make up the Atticism, they were out, and I
hissed."

services which I have performed.    And by way of comparison do you recite me the verses which you murdered:

> From Hades and the dusky realms I come.

And

> Ill news, believe me, I am loath to bear.

Ill betide thee, say I, and may the Gods, or at least the Athenians, confound thee for a vile citizen and a vile third-rate actor!

Read the evidence.

### [*Evidence*]

Such has been my character in political matters.    In private, if you do not all know that I have been liberal and humane and charitable to the distressed, I am silent, I will say not a word, I will offer no evidence on the subject, either of persons whom I ransomed from the enemy, or of persons whose daughters I helped to portion, or anything of the kind. For this is my maxim.    I hold that the party receiving an obligation should ever remember it, the party conferring should forget it immediately, if the one is to act with honesty, the other without meanness.    To remind and speak of your own bounties is next door to reproaching.    I will not act so:    nothing shall induce me.    Whatever my reputation is in these respects, I am content with it.

I will have done then with private topics, but say another word or two upon public.    If you can mention, Æschines, a single man under the sun, whether Greek or barbarian, who has not suffered by Philip's power formerly and Alexander's now, well and good;    I concede to you, that my fortune, or misfortune (if you please), has been the cause of everything. But if many that never saw me or heard my voice have been grievously afflicted, not individuals only but whole cities and nations, how much juster and fairer is it to consider that to the common fortune apparently of all men, to a tide of events overwhelming and lamentable, these disasters are to be attributed. You, disregarding all this, accuse me whose ministry has been among my countrymen, knowing all the while that a part (if not the whole) of your calumny falls upon the people, and yourself in particular. For if I assumed the sole and absolute direction of our counsels, it was open to you the other speakers to accuse me: but if you were constantly present in all the assemblies, if the state invited public discussion of what was expedient, and if these measures were then believed by all to be the best, and especially by you (for certainly from no goodwill did you leave me in possession of hopes and admiration and honours, all of which attended on my policy, but doubtless because you were compelled by the truth and had nothing better to advise) is it not iniquitous and monstrous to complain now of measures, than which you could suggest none better at the time?

Among all other people I find these principles in a manner defined and settled—Does a man wilfully offend? He is the object of wrath and punishment. Hath a man erred unintentionally? There is pardon instead of punishment for him. Has a man devoted himself to what seemed for the general good, and without any fault or misconduct been in common with all disappointed of success? Such a one deserves not obloquy or reproach, but sympathy. These principles will not be found in our statutes only: Nature herself has defined them by her unwritten laws and the feelings of humanity. Æschines, however, has so far surpassed all men in brutality and malignity that even things which he cited himself as misfortunes he imputes to me as crimes.

And besides—as if he himself had spoken everything with candour and goodwill—he told you to watch me, and mind that I did not cajole and deceive you, calling me a great orator, a juggler, a sophist, and the like: as though, if a man says of another what applies to himself, it must be true, and the hearers are not to inquire who the person is that makes the charge. Certain am I that you are all acquainted with my opponent's character, and believe these charges to be more applicable to him than to me. And of this I am sure, that my oratory—let it be so: though indeed I find that the speaker's power depends for the most part on the hearers; for according to your reception and favour it is, that the wisdom of a speaker is esteemed—if I, however, possess any ability of this sort, you will find it has been exhibited always in public business on your behalf, never against you or on personal matters; whereas that of Æschines has been displayed not only in speaking for the enemy, but against all persons who ever offended or quarrelled with him. It is not for justice or the good of the commonwealth that he employs it. A citizen of worth and honour should not call upon judges impanelled in the public service to gratify his anger or hatred or anything of that kind; nor should he come before you upon such grounds. The best thing is not to have these feelings; but, if it cannot be helped, they should be mitigated and restrained.

On what occasions ought an orator and statesman to be vehement? Where any of the commonwealth's main interests are in jeopardy, and he is opposed to the adversaries of the people. Those are the occasions for a generous and brave citizen. But for a person who never sought to punish me for any offence either public or private, on the state's behalf or on his own, to have got up an accusation because I am crowned and honoured, and to have expended such a multitude of words—this is a proof of personal enmity and spite and meanness, not of anything good. And then his leaving the controversy with me, and attacking the defendant, comprises everything that is base.

I should conclude, Æschines, that you undertook this cause to exhibit your eloquence and strength of lungs, not to obtain satisfaction for any wrong. But it is not the language of an orator, Æschines, that has any value, not yet the tone of his voice, but his adopting the same views with the people, and his hating and loving the same persons that his country does.

He that is thus minded will say everything with loyal intention: he that courts persons from whom the commonwealth apprehends danger to herself, rides not on the same anchorage with the people, and therefore has not the same expectation of safety. But—do you see?—I have: for my objects are the same with those of my countrymen; I have no interest separate or distinct. Is that so with you? How can it be— when immediately after the battle you went as ambassador to Philip, who was at that period the author of your country's calamities, notwithstanding that you had before persisted in refusing that office,[1] as all men know?

And who is it that deceives the state? Surely the man who speaks not what he thinks. On whom does the crier pronounce a curse?[2] Surely on such a man. What greater crime can an orator be charged with than that his opinions and his language are not the same? Such is found to be your character. And yet you open your mouth, and dare to look these men in the faces! Do you think they don't know you?—or are sunk all in such slumber and oblivion as not to remember the speeches which you delivered in the assembly, cursing and swearing that you had nothing to do with Philip, and that I brought that charge against you out of personal enmity without foundation? No sooner came the news of the battle, than you forgot all that; you acknowledged and avowed that between Philip and yourself there subsisted a relation of hospitality and friendship—new names these for your contract of hire. For upon what plea of equality or justice could Æschines, son of Glaucothea the timbrel-player,[3]

---

[1] This is to be understood only of the last six years before Chæronea.

[2] This curse was pronounced at every assembly of the people and every meeting of the council, before the business began. It was included in a form of prayer prescribed by law, in which the gods were implored to bless and prosper the consultations of the citizens, and to destroy and extirpate all persons who were ill-affected to the commonwealth, or plotted or conspired against the people, or were bribed to mislead or deceive them. There are many allusions to this curse in the Attic orators.

[3] The drum or timbrel was an instrument peculiarly used in the orgies of Bacchus and Cybele, derived from Phrygia.

be the friend or acquaintance of Philip? I cannot see. No!
You were hired to ruin the interests of your countrymen:
and yet, though you have been caught yourself in open
treason, and informed against yourself after the fact, you
revile and reproach me for things which you will find any
man is chargeable with sooner than I.

Many great and glorious enterprises has the commonwealth,
Æschines, undertaken and succeeded in through me; and
she did not forget them. Here is the proof—On the election
of a person to speak the funeral oration immediately after
the event, you were proposed, but the people would not have
you, notwithstanding your fine voice, nor Demades, though
he had just made the peace, nor Hegemon, nor any other of
your party—but me. And when you and Pythocles came for-
word in a brutal and shameful manner (O merciful heaven!)
and urged the same accusations against me which you now do,
and abused me, they elected me all the more. The reason—
you are not ignorant of it—yet I will tell you. The Athenians
knew as well the loyalty and zeal with which I conducted
their affairs as the dishonesty of you and your party; for
what you denied upon oath in our prosperity you confessed
in the misfortunes of the republic. They considered, therefore, that men who got security for their politics by the
public disasters had been their enemies long before, and were
then avowedly such. They thought it right also that the
person who was to speak in honour of the fallen and celebrate their valour should not have sat under the same roof
or at the same table with their antagonists; that he should
not revel there and sing a pæan over the calamities of Greece
in company with their murderers, and then come here and
receive distinction; that he should not with his voice act the
mourner of their fate, but that he should lament over them
with his heart. This they perceived in themselves and in
me, but not in any of you: therefore they elected me, and
not you. Nor, while the people felt thus, did the fathers and
brothers of the deceased, who were chosen by the people to

perform their obsequies, feel differently. For having to order
the funeral banquet (according to custom) at the house of
the nearest relative to the deceased, they ordered it at mine.
And with reason: because, though each to his own was
nearer of kin than I was, none was so near to them all collectively. He that had the deepest interest in their safety
and success had upon their mournful disaster the largest
share of sorrow for them all.

Read him this epitaph, which the state chose to inscribe on
their monument, that you may see even by this, Æschines,
what a heartless and malignant wretch you are. Read.

### THE EPITAPH.

These are the patriot brave, who side by side
Stood to their arms, and dash'd the foeman's pride:
Firm in their valour, prodigal of life,
Hades they chose the arbiter of strife;
That Greeks might ne'er to haughty victors bow,
Nor thraldom's yoke, nor dire oppression know;
They fought, they bled, and on their country's breast
(Such was the doom of heaven) these warriors rest.
Gods never lack success, nor strive in vain,
But man must suffer what the fates ordain.

Do you hear, Æschines, in this very inscription, that "Gods
never lack success, nor strive in vain?" Not to the statesman
does it ascribe the power of giving victory in battle, but to
the Gods. Wherefore, then, execrable man, do you reproach
me with these things? Wherefore utter such language? I
pray that it may fall upon the heads of you and yours.

Many other accusations and falsehoods he urged against
me, O Athenians, but one thing surprised me more than all,
that, when he mentioned the late misfortunes of the country,
he felt not as became a well-disposed and upright citizen, he
shed no tear, experienced no such emotion: with a loud voice,
exulting, and straining his throat, he imagined apparently
that he was accusing me, whilst he was giving proof against
himself that our distresses touched him not in the same
manner as the rest. A person who pretends, as he did, to
care for the laws and constitution, ought at least to have this

about him, that he grieves and rejoices for the same cause as the people, and not by his politics to be enlisted in the ranks of the enemy, as Æschines has plainly done, saying that I am the cause of all, and that the commonwealth has fallen into troubles through me, when it was not owing to my views or principles that you began to assist the Greeks; for, if you conceded this to me, that my influence caused you to resist the subjugation of Greece, it would be a higher honour than any that you have bestowed upon others. I myself would not make such an assertion—it would be doing you injustice —nor would you allow it, I am sure; and Æschines, if he acted honestly, would never, out of enmity to me, have disparaged and defamed the greatest of your glories.

But why do I censure him for this, when with calumny far more shocking has he assailed me? He that charges me with Philippising—O heaven and earth!—what would he not say? By Hercules and the Gods! if one had honestly to inquire, discarding all expression of spite and falsehood, who the persons really are, on whom the blame of what has happened may by common consent fairly and justly be thrown, it would be found, they are persons in the various states like Æschines, not like me—persons who, while Philip's power was feeble and exceedingly small, and we were constantly warning and exhorting and giving salutary counsel, sacrificed the general interests for the sake of selfish lucre, deceiving and corrupting their respective countrymen, until they made them slaves—Daochus, Cineas, Thrasylaus, the Thessalians; Cercidas, Hieronymus, Eucampidas, the Arcadians; Myrtis, Teledamus, Mnaseas, the Argives; Euxitheus, Cleotimus, Aristæchmus, the Eleans; Neon and Thrasylochus, sons of the accursed Philiades, the Messenians; Aristratus, Epichares, the Sicyonians; Dinarchus, Demaratus, the Corinthians; Ptœodorus, Helixus, Perilaus, the Megarians; Timolaus, Theogiton, Anemœtas, the Thebans; Hipparchus, Clitarchus Sosistratus, the Eubœans. The day will not last me to recount the names of the traitors. All these, O Athenians, are men of the same politics in their own countries as this party among you,—profligates, and parasites, and miscreants, who have each of them crippled their fatherlands; toasted away their liberty, first to Philip and last to Alexander; who measure happiness by their belly and all that is base, while freedom and independence, which the Greeks of olden time regarded as the test and standard of well-being, they have annihilated.

Of this base and infamous conspiracy and profligacy—or rather, O Athenians, if I am to speak in earnest, of this betrayal of Grecian liberty—Athens is by all mankind acquitted, owing to my counsels; and I am acquitted by you. Then do you ask me, Æschines, for what merit I claim to be honoured? I will tell you. Because, while all the statesmen in Greece, beginning with yourself, have been corrupted formerly by Philip and now by Alexander, me neither opportunity, nor fair speeches, nor large promises, nor hope, nor fear, nor anything else could tempt or induce to betray ought that I considered just and beneficial to my country. Whatever I have advised my fellow-citizens, I have never advised like you men, leaning as in a balance to the side of profit: all my proceedings have been those of a soul upright, honest, and incorrupt: entrusted with affairs of greater magnitude than any of my contemporaries, I have administered them all honestly and faithfully. Therefore do I claim to be honoured.

As to this fortification, for which you ridiculed me,[1] of the wall and fosse, I regard them as deserving of thanks and praise, and so they are; but I place them nowhere near my acts of administration. Not with stones nor with bricks did I fortify Athens: nor is this the ministry on which I most pride myself. Would you view my fortifications aright, you

---

[1] Æschines had urged in his speech—" that the merit of repairing the fortifications was far outweighed by the guilt of having rendered such repairs necessary; that a good statesman should not seek to be honoured for strengthening the ramparts, but for doing some real service to the commonwealth."

will find arms, and states, and posts, and harbours, and galleys, and horses, and men for their defence. These are the bulwarks with which I protected Attica, as far as was possible by human wisdom; with these I fortified our territory, not the circle of Piræus or the city. Nay more; I was not beaten by Philip in estimates or preparations; far from it; but the generals and forces of the allies were overcome by his fortune. Where are the proofs of this? They are plain and evident. Consider.

What was the course becoming a loyal citizen—a statesman serving his country with all possible forethought and zeal and fidelity? Should he not have covered Attica on the seaboard with Eubœa, on the midland frontier with Bœotia, on the Peloponnesian with the people of that confine? Should he not have provided for the conveyance of corn along a friendly coast all the way to Piræus? preserved certain places that belonged to us by sending off succours, and by advising and moving accordingly,—Proconnesus, Chersonesus, Tenedos? brought others into alliance and confederacy with us,—Byzantium, Abydus, Eubœa?—cut off the principal resources of the enemy, and supplied what the commonwealth was deficient in? All this has been accomplished by my decrees and measures; and whoever will examine them without prejudice, men of Athens, will find they were rightly planned and faithfully executed; that none of the proper seasons were lost or missed or thrown away by me, nothing which depended on one man's ability and prudence was neglected. But if the power of some deity or of fortune, or the worthlessness of commanders, or the wickedness of you that betrayed your countries, or all these things together, injured and eventually ruined our cause, of what is Demosthenes guilty? Had there in each of the Greek cities been one such man as I was in my station among you; or rather, had Thessaly possessed one single man, and Arcadia one, of the same sentiments as myself, none of the Greeks either beyond or within Thermopylæ would have suffered their present calamities: all would have been free and independent, living prosperously in their own countries with perfect safety and security, thankful to you and the rest of the Athenians for such manifold blessings through me.

To show you that I greatly understate my services for fear of giving offence, here—read me this—the list of auxiliaries procured by my decrees.

*[The list of auxiliaries]*

These and the like measures, Æschines, are what become an honourable citizen (by their success—O earth and heaven —we should have been the greatest people incontestably, and deserved to be so: even under their failure the result is glory, and no one blames Athens or her policy; all condemn fortune that so ordered things); but never will he desert the interests of the commonwealth, nor hire himself to her adversaries, and study the enemy's advantage instead of his country's; nor on a man who has courage to advise and propose measures worthy of the state, and resolution to persevere in them, will he cast an evil eye, and, if any one privately offends him, remember and treasure it up; no, nor keep himself in a criminal and treacherous retirement, as you so often do. There is indeed a retirement just and beneficial to the state, such as you, the bulk of my countrymen, innocently enjoy; that however is not the retirement of Æschines; far from it. Withdrawing himself from public life when he pleases (and that is often) he watches for the moment when you are tired of a constant speaker, or when some reverse of fortune has befallen you, or anything untoward has happened (and many are the casualties of human life), at such a crisis he springs up an orator, rising from his retreat like a wind; in full voice,[1]

---

[1] It appears from the testimony of ancient writers, as well as from the sneers of Demosthenes, that Æschines had a remarkably fine voice, and was not a little proud of it. A good voice must indeed have been a great advantage to an Athenian speaker, who had to address thousands of people in the open air. But Æschines not only possessed a voice that was loud and clear, but had a wonderful ease and fluency of speech, in these natural gifts surpassing Demosthenes himself.

with words and phrases collected, he rolls them out audibly
and breathlessly, to no advantage or good purpose whatsoever, but to the detriment of some or other of his fellow-
citizens and to the general disgrace.

Yet from this labour and diligence, Æschines, if it proceeded from an honest heart, solicitous for your country's
welfare, the fruits should have been rich and noble and
profitable to all—alliances of states, supplies of money, conveniences of commerce, enactment of useful laws, opposition
to our declared enemies. All such things were looked for in
former times; and many opportunities did the past afford
for a good man and true to show himself; during which time
you are nowhere to be found, neither first, second, third,
fourth, fifth, nor sixth—not in any rank at all—certainly
in no service by which your country was exalted. For what
alliance has come to the state by your procurement? What
succours, what acquisition of goodwill or credit? What
embassy or agency is there of yours, by which the reputation
of the country has been increased? What concern domestic,
Hellenic, or foreign, of which you have had the management,
has improved under it? What galleys? what ammunition?
what arsenals? what repair of walls? what cavalry? What
in the world are you good for? What assistance in money
have you ever given, either to the rich or the poor, out of
public spirit or liberality? None. But, good sir, if there is
nothing of this, there is at all events zeal and loyalty. Where?
when? You infamous fellow! Even at a time when all
who ever spoke upon the platform gave something for the
public safety, and last Aristonicus gave the sum which he had
amassed to retrieve his franchise,[1] you neither came forward
nor contributed a mite—not from inability—no! for you
have inherited above five talents from Philo, your wife's
father, and you had a subscription of two talents from the
chairmen of the Boards for what you did to cut up the navy-

---

[1] His civic privileges were suspended until he had discharged the
debt due from him to the state.

law. But, that I may not go from one thing to another and lose sight of the question, I pass this by. That it was not poverty prevented your contributing, already appears: it was, in fact, your anxiety to do nothing against those to whom your political life is subservient. On what occasions then do you show your spirit? When do you shine out? When aught is to be spoken against your countrymen!— then it is you are splendid in voice, perfect in memory, an admirable actor, a tragic Theocrines.[1]

You mention the good men of olden times; and you are right so to do. Yet it is hardly fair, O Athenians, that he should get the advantage of that respect which you have for the dead, to compare and contrast me with them—me who am living among you; for what mortal is ignorant, that towards the living there exists always more or less of illwill, whereas the dead are no longer hated even by an enemy? Such being human nature, am I to be tried and judged by the standard of my predecessors? Heaven forbid! It is not just or equitable, Æschines. Let me be compared with you, or any persons you like of your party who are still alive. And consider this—whether it is more honourable and better for the state, that because of the services of a former age, prodigious though they are beyond all power of expression, those of the present generation should be unrequited and spurned, or that all who give proof of their good intentions should have their share of honour and regard from the people? Yet indeed—if I must say so much—my politics and principles, if considered fairly, will be found to resemble those of the illustrious ancients, and to have had the same objects in view, while yours resemble those of their calumniators: for it is certain there were persons in those times who ran down the living and praised people dead and gone with a malignant purpose like yourself.

You say that I am nothing like the ancients. Are you like

---

[1] Theocrines was a notorious informer and slanderer. There is an oration attributed to Demosthenes against such a person.

them, Æschines? Is your brother, or any of our speakers? I assert that none is. But pray, my good fellow (that I may give you no other name), try the living with the living and with his competitors, as you would in all cases—poets, dancers, athletes. Philammon did not, because he was inferior to Glaucus of Carystus and some other champions of a bygone age, depart uncrowned from Olympia, but, because he beat all who entered the ring against him, was crowned and proclaimed conqueror.[1] So I ask you to compare me with the orators of the day, with yourself, with any one you like: I yield to none. When the commonwealth was at liberty to choose for her advantage, and patriotism was a matter of emulation, I showed myself a better counsellor than any, and every act of state was pursuant to my decrees and laws and negotiations: none of your party was to be seen, unless you had to do the Athenians a mischief. After that lamentable occurrence, when there was a call no longer for advisers, but for persons obedient to command, persons ready to be hired against their country and willing to flatter strangers, then all of you were in occupation, grand people with splendid equipages; I was powerless, I confess, though more attached to my countrymen than you.[2]

Two things, men of Athens, are characteristic of a well-disposed citizen—so may I speak of myself and give the least offence—In authority, his constant aim should be the dignity and pre-eminence of the commonwealth; in all times and circumstances his spirit should be loyal. This depends upon nature; power and might upon other things. Such a

[1] An anecdote of this Glaucus is told by Pausanias (vi. 10). He used to drive his father's plough, and one day, when the coulter was loose, he knocked it in with his fist. His father, having seen this feat, took him to Olympia, and entered him in the ring as a pugilist. He was nearly beaten for want of skill, when his father called out, " Strike as you did the coulter," on which he redoubled his efforts, and won the battle.

[2] Æschines declares (cont. Ctes. 76) that soon after the battle of Chæronea Demosthenes rose in the assembly, trembling and half-dead, and asked that he might be appointed to draw up the terms of peace; but the Athenians would not allow his name to be subscribed to their decrees.

spirit, you will find, I have ever sincerely cherished. Only see. When my person was demanded—when they brought Amphictyonic suits against me—when they menaced—when they promised—when they set these miscreants like wild beasts upon me—never in any way have I abandoned my affection for you. From the very beginning I chose an honest and straightforward course in politics, to support the honour, the power, the glory of my fatherland, these to exalt, in these to have my being. I do not walk about the market-place gay and cheerful because the stranger has prospered, holding out my right hand and congratulating those who I think will report it yonder, and on any news of our own success shudder and groan and stoop to the earth, like these impious men who rail at Athens, as if in so doing they did not rail at themselves; who look abroad, and if the foreigner thrives by the distresses of Greece, are thankful for it, and say we should keep him so thriving to all time.

Never, O ye Gods, may those wishes be confirmed by you! If possible, inspire even in these men a better sense and feeling! But if they are indeed incurable, destroy them by themselves; exterminate them on land and sea; and for the rest of us, grant that we may speedily be released from our present fears, and enjoy a lasting deliverance!

PART II

# PART II

## THE FIRST OLYNTHIAC

### ARGUMENT

OLYNTHUS was a city in Macedonia, at the head of the Toronaic gulf, and north of the peninsula of Pallene. It was colonised by a people from Chalcis in Eubœa, and commanded a large district called Chalcidice, in which there were thirty-two cities. Over all this tract the sway of Olynthus was considerable, and she had waged wars anciently with Athens and Sparta, and been formidable to Philip's predecessors on the throne of Macedon. Soon after Philip's accession, the Olynthians had disputes with him, which were at first accommodated, and he gratified them by the cession of Anthemus. They then joined him in a war against Athens, and he gave up to them Potidæa, which had yielded to their united arms. After the lapse of some years, during which Philip had greatly increased his power, and acquired considerable influence in Thessaly and Thrace, the Olynthians became alarmed, and began to think him too dangerous a neighbour. The immediate cause of rupture was an attack which he made on one of the Chalcidian towns. An embassy was instantly sent to Athens to negotiate an alliance. Philip, considering this as an infraction of their treaty with him, declared war against them, and invaded their territory. A second embassy was sent to Athens, pressing for assistance. The question was debated in the popular assembly. Demades, an orator of considerable ability, but profligate character, opposed the alliance. Many speakers were heard; and at length Demosthenes rose to support the prayer of the embassy, delivering one of those clear and forcible speeches which seldom failed to make a strong impression on his audience. The alliance was accepted, and succours voted.

The orator here delicately touches on the law of Eubulus, which had made it capital to propose that the Theoric fund should be applied to military service. This fund was in fact the surplus revenue of the civil administration, which by the ancient law was appropriated to the defence of the commonwealth; but it had by various means been diverted from that purpose, and expended in largesses to the people, to enable them to attend the theatre, and other public shows and amusements. The law of Eubulus perpetuated this abuse. Demosthenes, seeing the necessity of a war supply, hints that this absurd law ought to be abolished, but does not openly propose it.

There has been much difference of opinion among the learned as to the order of the three Olynthiac orations; nor is it certain whether they were spoken on the occasion of one embassy, or several embassies. The curious may consult Bishop Thirlwall's Appendix to the fifth volume of his Grecian History, and Jacobs' Introduction to his translation. I have followed the common order, as adopted by Bekker, whose edition of Demosthenes is the text of this translation; and indeed my opinion is, on the whole, in favour of preserving the common order, though the plan of this work prevents my entering into controversy on the question.    The historical abstract prefixed to this volume is intended chiefly to assist the reader in reference to dates. Such occurrences only are noticed as may be useful to illustrate Demosthenes.

I BELIEVE, men of Athens, you would give much to know, what is the true policy to be adopted in the present matter of inquiry.    This being the case, you should be willing to hear with attention those who offer you their counsel.    Besides that you will have the benefit of all preconsidered advice, I esteem it part of your good fortune that many fit suggestions will occur to some speakers at the moment, so that from them all you may easily choose what is profitable.

The present juncture, Athenians, all but proclaims aloud that you must yourselves take these affairs in hand, if you care for their success.    I know not how we seem disposed in the matter.    My own opinion is, vote succour immediately and make the speediest preparations for sending it off from Athens, that you may not incur the same mishap as before; send also ambassadors to announce this, and watch the proceedings.    For the danger is that this man, being unscrupulous and clever at turning events to account, making concessions when it suits him, threatening at other times (his threats may well be believed), slandering us and urging our absence against us, may convert and wrest to his use some of our main resources.    Though, strange to say, Athenians, the very cause of Philip's strength is a circumstance favourable to you.    His having it in his sole power to publish or conceal his designs, his being at the same time general, sovereign, paymaster, and everywhere accompanying his army, is a great advantage for quick and timely operations in war; but, for a peace with the Olynthians, which he would gladly make, it has a contrary effect.    For it is plain to the Olynthians that now they are fighting, not for glory or a slice of territory, but to save their country from destruction and servitude.    They know how he treated those Amphipolitans who surrendered to him their city, and those Pydneans who gave him admittance.[1] And generally, I believe, a despotic power is mistrusted by free states, especially if their dominions are adjoining. All this being known to you, Athenians, all else of importance considered, I say, you must take heart and spirit, and apply yourselves more than ever to the war, contributing promptly, serving personally, leaving nothing undone. No plea or pretence is left you for declining your duty. What you were all so clamorous about, that the Olynthians should be pressed into a war with Philip, has of itself come to pass, and in a way most advantageous to you. For, had they undertaken the war at your instance, they might have been slippery allies, with minds but half resolved perhaps: but since they hate him on a quarrel of their own, their enmity is like to endure on account of their fears and their wrongs. You must not then, Athenians, forego this lucky opportunity, nor commit the error which you have often done heretofore. For example, when we returned from succouring the Eubœans, and Hierax and Stratocles of Amphipolis came to this platform,[2] urging us to sail and receive possession of their city, if we had shown the same zeal for ourselves as for the safety of Eubœa, you would have held Amphipolis then and been rid of all the

---

[1] Amphipolis was a city at the head of the Strymonic gulf, in that part of Macedonia which approaches western Thrace. It had been built formerly by an Athenian colony, and was taken by the Spartan general Brasidas in the Peloponnesian war. Ever since Athens regained her character of an imperial state, she had desired to recover Amphipolis, which was important for its maritime position, its exportation of iron, and especially from the vicinity of the forests near the Strymon, which afforded an inexhaustible supply of ship-timber. But she had never been able to accomplish that object. Philip, who at that time possessed no maritime town of importance, was for obvious reasons anxious to win Amphipolis for himself; and he got possession of it partly by force of arms, partly by the treachery of certain Amphipolitans who were attached to his interest. It seems the Athenians had been amused by a promise of Philip to give up the town to them. The non-performance of this compact led to their first long war with him. Immediately after the capture of Amphipolis, Philip marched against Pydna, and was admitted into the town.

[2] The hustings from which the speakers addressed the people. It was cut to the height of ten feet out of the rock which formed the boundary wall of the assembly; and was ascended by a flight of steps.

troubles that ensued.   Again, when news came that Pydna,[1]
Potidæa, Methone, Pagasæ, and the other places (not to
waste time in enumerating them) were besieged, had we to
any one of these in the first instance carried prompt and
reasonable succour, we should have found Philip far more
tractable and humble now.   But, by always neglecting the
present, and imagining the future would shift for itself, we,
O men of Athens, have exalted Philip, and made him greater
than any king of Macedon ever was.   Here then is come a
crisis, this of Olynthus, self-offered to the state, inferior to
none of the former.   And methinks, men of Athens, any man
fairly estimating what the gods have done for us, notwithstanding many untoward circumstances, might with reason
be grateful to them.   Our numerous losses in war may justly
be charged to our own negligence; but that they happened
not long ago, and that an alliance, to counterbalance them,
is open to our acceptance, I must regard as manifestations
of divine favour.   It is much the same as in money matters.
If a man keep what he gets, he is thankful to fortune; if he
lose it by imprudence, he loses withal his memory of the
obligation.   So in political affairs, they who misuse their
opportunities forget even the good which the gods send them;
for every prior event is judged commonly by the last result.
Wherefore, Athenians, we must be exceedingly careful of our
future measures, that by amendment therein we may efface
the shame of the past.   Should we abandon these men [2] too,
and Philip reduce Olynthus, let any one tell me what is to
prevent him marching where he pleases?   Does any one of
you Athenians compute or consider the means by which

---

[1] Potidæa was in the peninsula of Pallene, near Olynthus, and was
therefore given by Philip to the Olynthians, as mentioned in the argument.   Methone and Pydna are on the Macedonian coast approaching
Thessaly.   Pagasæ is a Thessalian town in the Magnesian district.   It
was the seaport of Pheræ, capital of the tyrant Lycophron, against
whom Philip was invited to assist the Thessalians.   Philip overcame
Lycophron, and restored republican government at Pheræ; but Pagasæ
he garrisoned himself, and also Magnesia, a coast-town in the same
district.

[2] Here he points to the Olynthian ambassadors.

Philip, originally weak, has become great? Having first taken Amphipolis, then Pydna, Potidæa next, Methone afterwards, he invaded Thessaly. Having ordered matters at Pheræ, Pegasæ, Magnesia, everywhere exactly as he pleased, he departed for Thrace; where, after displacing some kings and establishing others, he fell sick; again recovering, he lapsed not into indolence, but instantly attacked the Olynthians. I omit his expeditions to Illyria and Pæonia, that against Arymbas,[1] and some others.

Why, it may be said, do you mention all this now? That you, Athenians, may feel and understand both the folly of continually abandoning one thing after another, and the activity which forms part of Philip's habit and existence, which makes it impossible for him to rest content with his achievements. If it be his principle, ever to do more than he has done, and yours, to apply yourselves vigorously to nothing, see what the end promises to be. Heavens! which of you is so simple as not to know that the war yonder will soon be here, if we are careless? And should this happen, I fear, O Athenians, that as men who thoughtlessly borrow on large interest, after a brief accommodation, lose their estate, so will it be with us: found to have paid dear for our idleness and self-indulgence, we shall be reduced to many hard and unpleasant shifts, and struggle for the salvation of our country.

To censure, I may be told, is easy for any man; to show what measures the case requires, is the part of a counsellor. I am not ignorant, Athenians, that frequently, when any disappointment happens, you are angry, not with the parties in fault, but with the last speakers on the subject; yet never, with a view to self-protection, would I suppress what I deem for your interest. I say then, you must give a two-fold assistance here; first, save the Olynthians their towns,[2] and

---

[1] Arymbas was a king of the Molossians in Epirus, and uncle of Olympias, Philip's wife.
[2] The Chalcidian towns. See the Argument. Philip commenced his aggressions upon the Olynthians by reducing several of these.

send out troops for that purpose; secondly, annoy the enemy's country with ships and other troops; omit either of these courses, and I doubt the expedition will be fruitless. For should he, suffering your incursion, reduce Olynthus, he will easily march to the defence of his kingdom; or, should you only throw succour into Olynthus, and he, seeing things out of danger at home, keep up a close and vigilant blockade, he must in time prevail over the besieged. Your assistance therefore must be effective, and two-fold.

Such are the operations I advise. As to a supply of money: you have money, Athenians; you have a larger military fund than any people; and you receive it just as you please. If ye will assign this to your troops, ye need no further supply; otherwise ye need a further, or rather ye have none at all. How then? some man may exclaim: do you move that this be a military fund? Verily, not I.[1] My opinion indeed is, that there should be soldiers raised, and a military fund, and one and the same regulation for receiving and performing what is due; only you just without trouble take your allowance for the festivals. It remains then, I imagine, that all must contribute, if much be wanted, much, if little, little. Money must be had; without it nothing proper can be done. Other persons propose other ways and means. Choose which ye think expedient; and put hands to the work, while it is yet time.

It may be well to consider and calculate how Philip's affairs now stand. They are not as they appear, or as an inattentive observer might pronounce, in very good trim,

[1] There is some studied obscurity in this passage, owing to the necessity under which the speaker lay of avoiding the penalty of the law; and a little quiet satire on his countrymen, who seemed desirous of eating their pudding and having it too. The logic of the argument runs thus—My opinion is, that we ought to have a military fund, and that no man should receive public money without performing public service. However, as you prefer taking the public money to pay for your places at the festivals, I will not break the law by moving to apply that money to another purpose. Only you gain nothing by it; for, as the troops must be paid, there must be an extraordinary contribution, or property tax, to meet the exigency of the case.

or in the most favourable position. He would never have commenced this war had he imagined he must fight. He expected to carry everything on the first advance, and has been mistaken. This disappointment is one thing that troubles and dispirits him; another is, the state of Thessaly.[1] That people were always, you know, treacherous to all men; and just as they ever have been, they are to Philip. They have resolved to demand the restitution of Pagasæ, and have prevented his fortifying Magnesia; and I was told, they would no longer allow him to take the revenue of their harbours and markets, which they say should be applied to the public business of Thessaly, not received by Philip. Now, if he be deprived of this fund, his means will be much straitened for paying his mercenaries. And surely we must suppose, that Pæonians and Illyrians, and all such people, would rather be free and independent than under subjection; for they are unused to obedience, and the man is a tyrant. So report says, and I can well believe it; for undeserved success leads weak-minded men into folly; and thus it appears often, that to maintain prosperity is harder than to acquire it. Therefore must you, Athenians, looking on his difficulty as your opportunity, assist cheerfully in the war, sending embassies where required, taking arms yourselves, exciting all other people; for if Philip got such an opportunity against us, and there was a war on our frontier, how eagerly think ye he would attack you! Then are you not ashamed that the

[1] Philip's influence in Thessaly was of material assistance to him in his ambitious projects. It was acquired in this way. The power established by Jason of Pheræ, who raised himself to a sort of royal authority under the title of Tagus, had devolved upon Lycophron. His sway extended more or less over the whole of Thessaly; but was, if not generally unpopular, at least unacceptable to the great families in the northern towns, among whom the Aleuadæ of Larissa held a prominent place. They invoked Philip's aid, while Lycophron was assisted by the Phocian Onomarchus. After various success, Onomarchus was defeated and slain, and Lycophron expelled from Pheræ. This established Philip's influence, and led to his being afterwards called in to terminate the Sacred War. How far the assertions of Demosthenes, respecting the discontent of the Thessalians, are true, cannot exactly be told. They are confirmed, however, in some degree by the fact, that at the close of the Sacred War Philip restored to them Magnesia.

very damage which you would suffer, if he had the power, you dare not seize the moment to inflict on him?

And let not this escape you, Athenians, that you have now the choice, whether you shall fight there, or he in your country. If Olynthus hold out, you will fight there and distress his dominions, enjoying your own home in peace. If Philip take that city, who shall then prevent his marching here? Thebans? I wish it be not too harsh to say, they will be ready to join in the invasion. Phocians? who cannot defend their own country without your assistance. Or some other ally? But, good sir, he will not desire! Strange indeed, if, what he is thought fool-hardy for prating now, this he would not accomplish if he might. As to the vast difference between a war here or there, I fancy there needs no argument. If you were obliged to be out yourselves for thirty days only, and take the necessaries for camp-service from the land (I mean, without an enemy therein) your agricultural population would sustain, I believe, greater damage than what the whole expense of the late war [1] amounted to. But if a war should come, what damage must be expected? There is the insult, too, and the disgrace of the thing, worse than any damage to right-thinking men.

On all these accounts, then, we must unite to lend our succour, and drive off the war yonder; the rich, that, spending a little for the abundance which they happily possess, they may enjoy the residue in security; the young,[2] that gaining military experience in Philip's territory, they may become redoubtable champions to preserve their own; the orators, that they may pass a good account of their statesmanship; for on the result of measures will depend your judgment of their conduct. May it for every cause be prosperous.

[1] The Amphipolitan war, said to have cost fifteen hundred talents.
[2] Strictly, *those of the military age,* which was from eighteen years to sixty. Youths between eighteen and twenty were liable only to serve in Attica, and were chiefly employed to garrison the walls. Afterwards they were compellable to perform any military service, under the penalty of losing their privileges as citizens.

# THE SECOND OLYNTHIAC

### ARGUMENT

THE Athenians had voted an alliance with the Olynthians, and resolved to send succours. But the sending of them was delayed, partly by the contrivance of the opposite faction, partly from the reluctance of the people themselves to engage in a war with Philip. Demosthenes stimulates them to exertion, and encourages them, by showing that Philip's power is not so great as it appears.

ON many occasions, men of Athens, one may see the kindness of the gods to this country manifested, but most signally, I think, on the present. That here are men prepared for a war with Philip, possessed of a neighbouring territory and some power, and (what is most important) so fixed in their hostility as to regard any accommodation with him as insecure, and even ruinous to their country; this really appears like an extraordinary act of divine beneficence. It must then be our care, Athenians, that we are not more unkind to ourselves than circumstances have been; as it would be a foul, a most foul reproach, to have abandoned not only cities and places that once belonged to us, but also the allies and advantages provided by fortune.

To dilate, Athenians, on Philip's power, and by such discourse to incite you to your duty, I think improper: and why? Because all that may be said on that score involves matter of glory for him, and misconduct on our part. The more he has transcended his repute, the more is he universally admired; you, as you have used your advantages unworthily, have incurred the greater disgrace. This topic, then, I shall pass over. Indeed, Athenians, a correct observer will find the source of his greatness here, [1] and not in himself. But

[1] In this assembly, by the contrivance of venal orators, or through the supineness of the people. In the first Philippic there is a more pointed allusion to the practices of Philip's adherents, who are charged with sending him secret intelligence of what passed at home. Such men as Aristodemus, Neoptolemus, perhaps Demades and others are referred to. Æschines had not yet begun to be a friend of Philip.

of measures, for which Philip's partisans deserve his gratitude and your vengeance, I see no occasion to speak now. Other things are open to me, which it concerns you all to know, and which must, on a due examination, Athenians, reflect great disgrace on Philip. To these will I address myself.

To call him perjured and treacherous, without showing what he has done, might justly be termed idle abuse. But to go through all his actions and convict him in detail, will take, as it happens, but a short time, and is expedient, I think, for two reasons: first, that his baseness may appear in its true light; secondly, that they, whose terror imagines Philip to be invincible, may see he has run through all the artifices by which he rose to greatness, and his career is just come to an end. I myself, men of Athens, should most assuredly have regarded Philip as an object of fear and admiration, had I seen him exalted by honourable conduct; but, observing and considering, I find that in the beginning, when certain persons drove away the Olynthians who desired a conference with us, he gained over our simplicity by engaging to surrender Amphipolis and to execute the secret article [1] once so famous; afterwards he got the friendship of the Olynthians by taking Potidæa from you, wronging you, his former allies, and delivering it to them; and lastly now the Thessalians, by promising to surrender Magnesia, and undertake the Phocian war on their behalf. In short, none who have dealt with him has he not deceived. He has risen by conciliating and cajoling the weakness of every people in turn who knew him not. As, therefore, by such means he rose, when every people imagined he would advance their interest, so ought he by the same means to be pulled down again, when the selfish aim of his whole policy is exposed. To this crisis, O Athenians, are Philip's affairs come; or let

---

[1] A secret intrigue was carried on between Philip and the Athenians, by which he engaged to put Amphipolis in their hands, but on the understanding that they would deliver up Pydna to him. Demosthenes only mentions the former part of the arrangement, the latter not being honourable to his countrymen.

any man stand forward and prove to me, or rather to you, that my assertions are false, or that men whom Philip has once overreached will trust him hereafter, or that the Thessalians who have been degraded into servitude would not gladly become free.

But if any among you, though agreeing in these statements, thinks that Philip will maintain his power by having occupied forts and havens and the like, this is a mistake. True, when a confederacy subsists by good-will, and all parties to the war have a common interest, men are willing to co-operate and bear hardships and persevere. But when one has grown strong, like Philip, by rapacity and artifice, on the first pretext, the slightest reverse, all is overturned and broken up. Impossible is it—impossible, Athenians—to acquire a solid power by injustice and perjury and falsehood. Such things last for once, or for a short period; maybe, they blossom fairly with hope; but in time they are discovered and drop away. As a house, a ship, or the like, ought to have the lower parts firmest, so in human conduct, I ween, the principle and foundation should be just and true. But this is not so in Philip's conduct.

I say, then, we should at once aid the Olynthians (the best and quickest way that can be suggested will please me most) and send an embassy to the Thessalians, to inform some of our measures, and to stir up the rest; for they have now resolved to demand Pagasæ, and remonstrate about Magnesia. But look to this, Athenians, that our envoys shall not only make speeches, but have some real proof that we have gone forth as becomes our country, and are engaged in action. All speech without action appears vain and idle, but especially that of our commonwealth; as the more we are thought to excel therein, the more is our speaking distrusted by all. You must show yourselves greatly reformed, greatly changed, contributing, serving personally, acting promptly, before any one will pay attention to you. And if ye will perform these duties properly and becomingly,

Athenians, not only will it appear that Philip's alliances are weak and precarious, but the poor state of his native empire and power will be revealed.

To speak roundly, the Macedonian power and empire is very well as a help, as it was for you in Timotheus' time against the Olynthians; likewise for them against Potidæa the conjunction was important; and lately it aided the Thessalians in their broils and troubles against the regnant house: and the accession of any power, however small, is undoubtedly useful. But the Macedonian is feeble of itself, and full of defects. The very operations which seem to constitute Philip's greatness, his wars and his expeditions, have made it more insecure than it was originally. Think not, Athenians, that Philip and his subjects have the same likings. He desires glory, makes that his passion, is ready for any consequence of adventure and peril, preferring to a life of safety the honour of achieving what no Macedonian king ever did before. They have no share in the glorious result; ever harassed by these excursions up and down, they suffer and toil incessantly, allowed no leisure for their employments or private concerns, unable even to dispose of their hard earnings, the markets of the country being closed on account of the war. By this then may easily be seen, how the Macedonians in general are disposed to Philip. His mercenaries and guards, indeed, have the reputation of admirable and well-trained soldiers, but, as I heard from one who had been in the country, a man incapable of falsehood, they are no better than others. For if there be any among them experienced in battles and campaigns, Philip is jealous of such men and drives them away, he says, wishing to keep the glory of all actions to himself; his jealousy (among other failings) being excessive. Or if any man be generally good and virtuous, unable to bear Philip's daily intemperances, drunkenness, and indecencies,[1] he is pushed aside and

_____
[1] The original signifies a certain dance, which formed a part of riotous festivities. We gather from history that the orator's description here is not wholly untrue, though exaggerated.

accounted as nobody. The rest about him are brigands and parasites, and men of that character, who will get drunk and perform dances which I scruple to name before you. My information is undoubtedly true; for persons whom all scouted here as worse rascals than mountebanks, Callias the town-slave and the like of him, antic-jesters, and composers of ribald songs to lampoon their companions, such person Philip caresses and keeps about him. Small matters these may be thought, Athenians, but to the wise they are strong indications of his character and wrongheadedness. Success perhaps throws a shade over them now; prosperity is a famous hider of such blemishes; but, on any miscarriage, they will be fully exposed. And this (trust me, Athenians) will appear in no long time, if the gods so will and you determine. For as in the human body, a man in health feels not partial ailments, but, when illness occurs, all are in motion, whether it be a rupture or a sprain or anything else unsound; so with states and monarchs, whilst they wage external war, their weaknesses are undiscerned by most men, but the tug of a frontier war betrays all.

If any of you think Philip a formidable opponent, because they see he is fortunate, such reasoning is prudent, Athenians. Fortune has indeed a great preponderance—nay, is everything, in human affairs. Not but that, if I had the choice, I should prefer our fortune to Philip's, would you but moderately perform your duty. For I see you have many more claims to the divine favour than he has. But we sit doing nothing; and a man idle himself cannot require even his friends to act for him, much less the gods. No wonder then that he, marching and toiling in person, present on all occasions, neglecting no time or season, prevails over us delaying and voting and inquiring. I marvel not at that; the contrary would have been marvellous, if we doing none of the duties of war had beaten one doing all. But this surprises me, that formerly, Athenians, you resisted the Lacedæmonians for the rights of Greece, and rejecting many opportunities of selfish gain, to secure the rights of others, expended your property in contributions, and bore the brunt of the battle; yet now you are loth to serve, slow to contribute, in defence of your own possessions, and, though you have often saved the other nations of Greece collectively and individually, under your own losses you sit still. This surprises me, and one thing more, Athenians; that not one of you can reckon, how long your war with Philip has lasted, and what you have been doing while the time has passed. You surely know, that while you have been delaying, expecting others to act, accusing, trying one another, expecting again, doing much the same as ye do now, all the time has passed away. Then are ye so senseless, Athenians, as to imagine that the same measures which have brought the country from a prosperous to a poor condition will bring it from a poor to a prosperous? Unreasonable were this and unnatural; for all things are easier kept than gotten. The war now has left us nothing to keep; we have all to get, and the work must be done by ourselves. I say then, you must contribute money, serve in person with alacrity, accuse no one, till you have gained your objects; then, judging from facts, honour the deserving, punish offenders; let there be no pretences or defaults on your own part; for you cannot harshly scrutinise the conduct of others, unless you have done what is right yourselves. Why, think you, do all the generals [1] whom you commission avoid this war, and seek wars of their own? (for of the generals, too, must a little truth be told.) Because here the prizes of the war are yours; for

---

[1] A system of employing mercenary troops sprang up at the close of the Peloponnesian war, when there were numerous Grecian bands accustomed to warfare and seeking employment. Such troops were eagerly sought for by the Persian satraps and their king, by such men as Jason of Pheræ, Dionysius of Syracuse, or Philomelus of Phocis. Athens, which had partially employed mercenaries before, began to make use of them on a large scale, while her citizens preferred staying at home to attend to commerce, politics, and idle amusements. The ill effects, however, were soon apparent. Athenian generals, ill supplied with money, and having little control over their followers, were tempted or obliged to engage in enterprises unconnected with, and often adverse to, the interests of their country.

example, if Amphipolis be taken, you will immediately
recover it; the commanders have all the risk and no reward.
But in the other case the risks are less, and the gains belong
to the commanders and soldiers; Lampsacus,[1] Sigeum, the
vessels which they plunder. So they proceed to secure their
several interests: you, when you look at the bad state of your
affairs, bring the generals to trial; but when they get a hearing and plead these necessities, you dismiss them. The
result is that, while you are quarrelling and divided, some
holding one opinion, some another, the commonwealth goes
wrong. Formerly, Athenians, you had boards[2] for taxes;
now you have boards for politics. There is an orator presiding on either side, a general under him, and three hundred
men to shout; the rest of you are attached to the one party
or the other. This you must leave off; be yourselves again;
establish a general liberty of speech, deliberation, and action.
If some are appointed to command as with royal authority,
some to be ship-captains, tax-payers, soldiers by compulsion,
others only to vote against them, and help in nothing besides,
no duty will be seasonably performed; the aggrieved parties
will still fail you, and you will have to punish them instead
of your enemies. I say, in short; you must all fairly contribute, according to each man's ability; take your turns of
service till you have all been afield; give every speaker a
hearing, and adopt the best counsel, not what this or that
person advises. If ye act thus, not only will ye praise the
speaker at the moment, but yourselves afterwards, when the
condition of the country is improved.

[1] Chares, the Athenian general, was said to have received these
Asiatic cities from Artabazus, the Persian satrap, in return for the
service he had performed. Probably it was some authority or privileges in those cities, not the actual dominion, that was conferred upon
him. Sigeum, which is near the mouth of the Hellespont, and was a
convenient situation for his adventures, was the ordinary residence of
Chares.

[2] This refers to the institution of the boards for management of the
property-tax at Athens.

# THE THIRD OLYNTHIAC

### ARGUMENT

THE Athenians had despatched succours to Olynthus, and received, as
Libanius says, some favourable intelligence; more probably, however,
some vague rumours, which led them to imagine the danger was for
the time averted. They began, very prematurely, as the result showed,
to be confident of success, and talked of punishing Philip for his pre-
sumption. In this they were encouraged by certain foolish orators,
who sought to flatter the national prejudices. Demosthenes in this
oration strives to check the arrogance of the people; reminds them of
the necessity of defensive rather than offensive measures, and especially
of the importance of preserving their allies. He again adverts (and
this time more boldly) to the law of Eubulus, which he intimates ought
to be repealed; and he exhorts the Athenians generally to make
strenuous exertions against Philip.

NOT the same ideas, men of Athens, are presented to me,
when I look at our condition, and when at the speeches which
are delivered. The speeches, I find, are about punishing
Philip; but our condition is come to this, that we must mind
we are not first damaged ourselves. Therefore, it seems to
me, these orators commit the simple error of not laying
before you the true subject of debate. That once we might
safely have held our own and punished Philip too, I know
well enough; both have been possible in my own time, not
very long ago. But now, I am persuaded, it is sufficient in
the first instance to effect the preservation of our allies.
When this has been secured, one may look out for revenge
on Philip; but before we lay the foundation right, I deem it
idle to talk about the end.

The present crisis, O Athenians, requires, if any ever did,
much thought and counsel. Not that I am puzzled what
advice to give in the matter; I am only doubtful in what
way, Athenians, to address you thereupon. For I have been
taught, both by hearsay and experience, that most of your

advantages have escaped you from unwillingness to do your duty not from ignorance. I request you, if I speak my mind, to be patient, and consider only, whether I speak the truth, and with a view to future amendment. You see to what wretched plight we are reduced by some men haranguing for popularity.

I think it necessary, however, first to recall to your memory a few past events. You remember, Athenians, when news came three or four years ago that Philip was in Thrace besieging Heræum.[1] It was then the fifth month,[2] and after much discussion and tumult in the assembly you resolved to launch forty galleys, that every citizen under forty-five should embark, and a tax be raised of sixty talents. That year passed; the first, second, third month arrived; in that month, reluctantly, after the mysteries,[3] you despatched Charidemus with ten empty ships and five talents in money; for as Philip was reported to be sick or dead (both rumours came) you thought there was no longer any occasion for succours, and discontinued the armament. But that was the very occasion; if we had then sent our succours quickly, as we resolved, Philip would not have been saved to trouble us now.

Those events cannot be altered. But here is the crisis of another war, the cause why I mentioned the past, that you may not repeat your error. How shall we deal with it, men of Athens? If you lend not the utmost possible aid, see how you will have manœuvred everything for Philip's benefit. There were the Olynthians, possessed of some power; and matters stood thus: Philip distrusted them, and they Philip. We negotiated for peace with them; this hampered (as it were) and annoyed Philip, that a great city, reconciled to us,

[1] A fortress on the Propontis (now Sea of Marmora), near Perinthus. This was a post of importance to the Athenians, who received large supplies of corn from that district.
[2] Corresponding nearly to our November. The Attic year began in July, and continued twelve lunar months, of alternately 29 and 30 days.
[3] The Eleusinian Mysteries, in honour of Ceres and Proserpine, called *The* Mysteries from their peculiar sanctity.

should be watching opportunities against him. We thought it necessary by all means to make that people his enemies; and lo, what erewhile you clamoured for, has somehow or other been accomplished. Then what remains, Athenians, but to assist them vigorously and promptly? I know not. For besides the disgrace that would fall upon us, if we sacrificed any of our interests, I am alarmed for the consequences, seeing how the Thebans are affected towards us, the Phocian treasury exhausted, nothing to prevent Philip when he has subdued what lies before him, from turning to matters here. Whoever postpones until then the performance of his duty, wishes to see the peril at hand, when he may hear of it elsewhere, and to seek auxiliaries for himself, when he may be auxiliary to others; for that this will be the issue, if we throw away our present advantage, we all know pretty well.

But, it may be said, we have resolved that succours are necessary, and we will send them; tell us only how. Marvel not then, Athenians, if I say something to astonish the multitude. Appoint law-revisors: at their session enact no statutes, for you have enough, but repeal those which are at present injurious; I mean, just plainly, the laws concerning our theatrical fund, and some concerning the troops, whereof the former divide the military fund among stayers-at-home for theatrical amusement, the latter indemnify deserters, and so dishearten men well inclined to the service. When you have repealed these, and made the road to good counsel safe, then find a man to propose what you all know to be desirable. But before doing so, look not for one who will advise good measures and be destroyed by you for his pains. Such a person you will not find, especially as the only result would be, for the adviser and mover to suffer wrongfully, and, without forwarding matters, to render good counsel still more dangerous in future. Besides, Athenians, you should require the same men to repeal these laws who have introduced them. It is unjust that their authors should enjoy a popularity which has injured the commonwealth, while the adviser of salutary measures suffers by a displeasure that may lead to general improvement. Till this is set right, Athenians, look not that any one should be so powerful with you as to transgress these laws with impunity, or so senseless as to plunge into ruin right before him.

Another thing, too, you should observe, Athenians, that a decree is worth nothing, without a readiness on your part to do what you determine. Could decrees of themselves compel you to perform your duty, or execute what they prescribe, neither would you with many decrees have accomplished little or nothing, nor would Philip have insulted you so long. Had it depended on decrees, he would have been chastised long ago. But the course of things is otherwise. Action, posterior in order of time to speaking and voting, is in efficacy prior and superior. This requisite you want; the others you possess. There are among you, Athenians, men competent to advise what is needful, and you are exceedingly quick at understanding it; aye, and you will be able now to perform it, if you act rightly. For what time or season would you have better than the present? When will you do your duty, if not now? Has not the man got possession of all our strongholds? And if he become master of this country, shall we not incur foul disgrace? Are not they to whom we promised sure protection in case of war at this moment in hostilities? Is he not an enemy, holding our possessions—a barbarian [1]—anything you like to call him? But, O heavens! after permitting, almost helping him to accomplish these things, shall we inquire who were to blame for them? I know we shall not take the blame to ourselves. For so in battles, no runaway accuses himself, but his general,

---

[1] *Barbarians* (among the Greeks) designates persons who were not of Hellenic origin. Alexander, an ancestor of Philip, had obtained admission to the Olympic games by proving himself to be of Argive descent. But the Macedonian people were scarcely considered as Greeks till a much later period; and Demosthenes speaks rather with reference to the nation than to Philip personally.

his neighbour, any one rather; though, sure enough, the defeat is owing to all the runaways; for each who accuses the rest might have stood his ground, and had each done so, they would have conquered. Now then, does any man not give the best advice? Let another rise and give it, but not censure the last speaker. Does a second give better advice? Follow it, and success attend you! Perhaps it is not pleasant: but that is not the speaker's fault, unless he omits some needful prayer.[1] To pray is simple enough, Athenians, collecting all that one desires in a short petition: but to decide, when measures are the subject of consideration, is not quite so easy; for we must choose the profitable rather than the pleasant, where both are not compatible.

But if any one can let alone our theatrical fund, and suggest other supplies for the military, is he not cleverer? it may be asked. I grant it, if this were possible: but I wonder if any man ever was or will be able, after wasting his means in useless expenses, to find means for useful. The wishes of men are indeed a great help to such arguments, and therefore the easiest thing in the world is self-deceit, for every man believes what he wishes, though the reality is often different. See then, Athenians, what the realities allow, and you will be able to serve and have pay. It becomes not a wise or magnanimous people to neglect military operations for want of money, and bear disgraces like these; or, while you snatch up arms to march against Corinthians and Megarians, to let Philip enslave Greek cities for lack of provisions for your troops.

I have not spoken for the idle purpose of giving offence: I am not so foolish or perverse as to provoke your displeasure without intending your good: but I think an upright citizen should prefer the advancement of the commonwealth to the gratification of his audience. And I hear, as perhaps you do,

---

[1] Demosthenes sneers at the custom of introducing into the debate sententious professions of good-will, and prayers for prosperity; a poor substitute (he would say) for good counsel.

that the speakers in our ancestors' time, whom all that
address you praise, but not exactly imitate, were politicians
after this form and fashion;—Aristides, Nicias, my namesake,[1]
Pericles. But since these orators have appeared who ask,
What is your pleasure? what shall I move? how can I oblige
you? the public welfare is complimented away for a moment's
popularity, and these are the results; the orators thrive, you
are disgraced. Mark, O Athenians, what a summary contrast may be drawn between the doings in our olden time and
in yours. It is a tale brief and familiar to all; for the
examples by which you may still be happy are found not
abroad, men of Athens, but at home. Our forefathers,
whom the speakers humoured not nor caressed, as these men
caress you, for five-and-forty years took the leadership of
the Greeks by general consent, and brought above ten thousand talents into the citadel; and the king of this country
was submissive to them, as a barbarian should be to Greeks;
and many glorious trophies they erected for victories won
by their own fighting on land and sea, and they are the sole
people in the world who have bequeathed a renown superior
to envy. Such were their merits in the affairs of Greece:
see what they were at home, both as citizens and as men.
Their public works are edifices and ornaments of such beauty
and grandeur in temples and consecrated furniture, that
posterity have no power to surpass them. In private they
were so modest and attached to the principle of our constitution, that whoever knows the style of house which
Aristides had, or Miltiades, and the illustrious of that day,
perceives it to be no grander than those of the neighbours.
Their politics were not for money-making; each felt it his
duty to exalt the commonwealth. By a conduct honourable
towards the Greeks, pious to the gods, brotherlike among
themselves, they justly attained a high prosperity.

---

[1] Demosthenes, the general so distinguished in the Peloponnesian
war, who defeated the Spartans at Pylus, and afterwards lost his life in
Sicily.

So fared matters with them under the statesmen I have mentioned. How fare they with you under the worthies of our time? Is there any likeness or resemblance? I pass over other topics on which I could expatiate; but observe: in this utter absence of competitors (Lacedæmonians depressed, Thebans employed, none of the rest capable of disputing the supremacy with us) when we might hold our own securely and arbitrate the claims of others, we have been deprived of our rightful territory, and spent above fifteen hundred talents to no purpose; the allies, whom we gained in war, these persons have lost in peace, and we have trained up against ourselves an enemy thus formidable. Or let any one come forward and tell me, by whose contrivance but ours Philip has grown strong. Well, sir, this looks bad, but things at home are better. What proof can be adduced? The parapets that are whitewashed? The roads that are repaired? fountains, and fooleries? Look at the men of whose statesmanship these are the fruits. They have risen from beggary to opulence, or from obscurity to honour; some have made their private houses more splendid than the public buildings; and in proportion as the state has declined, their fortunes have been exalted.

What has produced these results? How is it that all went prosperously then, and now goes wrong? Because anciently the people, having the courage to be soldiers, controlled the statesmen, and disposed of all emoluments; any of the rest was happy to receive from the people his share of honour, office, or advantage. Now, contrariwise, the statesmen dispose of emoluments; through them everything is done; you the people, enervated, stripped of treasure and allies, are become as underlings and hangers-on, happy if these persons dole you out show-money or send you paltry beeves; and, the unmanliest part of all, you are grateful for receiving your own. They, cooping you in the city, lead you to your pleasures, and make you tame and submissive to their hands. It is impossible, I say, to have a high and noble spirit, while you are engaged in petty and mean employments: whatever be the pursuits of men, their characters must be similar. By Ceres, I should not wonder, if I, for mentioning these things, suffered more from your resentment than the men who have brought them to pass. For even liberty of speech you allow not on all subjects; I marvel indeed you have allowed it here.

Would you but even now, renouncing these practices, perform military service and act worthily of yourselves; would you employ these domestic superfluities as a means to gain advantage abroad; perhaps, Athenians, perhaps you might gain some solid and important advantage, and be rid of these perquisites, which are like the diet ordered by physicians for the sick. As that neither imparts strength, nor suffers the patient to die, so your allowances are not enough to be of substantial benefit, nor yet permit you to reject them and turn to something else. Thus do they increase the general apathy? What? I shall be asked: mean you stipendiary service? Yes, and forthwith the same arrangement for all, Athenians, that each, taking his dividend from the public, may be what the state requires. Is peace to be had? You are better at home, under no compulsion to act dishonourably from indigence. Is there such an emergency as the present? Better to be a soldier, as you ought, in your country's cause, maintained by those very allowances. Is any one of you beyond the military age? What he now irregularly takes without doing service, let him take by just regulation, superintending and transacting needful business. Thus, without derogating from or adding to our political system, only removing some irregularity, I bring it into order, establishing a uniform rule for receiving money, for serving in war, for sitting on juries, for doing what each according to his age can do, and what occasion requires. I never advise we should give to idlers the wages of the diligent, or sit at leisure, passive and helpless, to hear that such a one's mercenaries are victorious; as we now do.

Not that I blame any one who does you a service: I only call upon you, Athenians, to perform on your own account those duties for which you honour strangers, and not to surrender that post of dignity which, won through many glorious dangers, your ancestors have bequeathed.

I have said nearly all that I think necessary. I trust you will adopt that course which is best for the country and yourselves.

# THE FIRST PHILIPPIC

## ARGUMENT

PHILIP, after the defeat of Onomarchus, had marched towards the
pass of Thermopylæ, which, however, he found occupied by the
Athenians, who had sent a force for the purpose of preventing his
advance.   Being baffled there, he directed his march into Thrace, and
alarmed the Athenians for the safety of their dominions in the Chersonese.   At the same time he sent a fleet to attack the islands of
Lemnos and Imbrus, infested the commerce of Athens with his cruisers,
and even insulted her coast.   In Thrace he became involved in the
disputes between the rival kings Amadocus and Cersobleptes, espousing
the cause of the former;  and for some time he was engaged in the
interior of the country, either at war with Cersobleptes, or extending
his own influence over other parts of Thrace, where he established or
expelled the rulers, as it suited him.   It was just at that time that
Demosthenes spoke the following oration, the first on which he called
the attention of his countrymen to the dangerous increase of Philip's
power.   He had become convinced by the course of events, and by
observing the restless activity of Philip, that Athens had more to fear
from him than from Thebes, or from any new combination of the
Grecian republics.   The orator himself, perhaps, hardly appreciated
the extent of Philip's resources, strengthened as he was now by the
friendship of Thessaly, possessed of a navy and maritime towns, and
relieved from the presence of any powerful neighbours.   What were
the precise views of Demosthenes as to the extent of the impending
danger, we cannot say.   It was not for him to frighten the Athenians
too much, but to awaken them from their lethargy.   This he does in
a speech, which, without idle declamation or useless ornament, is
essentially practical.   He alarms, but encourages, his countrymen;
points out both their weakness and their strength;  rouses them to a
sense of danger, and shows the way to meet it;  recommends not any
extraordinary efforts, for which at the moment there was no urgent
necessity, and to make which would have exceeded their power, but
unfolds a scheme, simple and feasible, suiting the occasion, and calculated (if Athenians had not been too degenerate) to lay the foundation
of better things.

HAD the question for debate been anything new, Athenians,
I should have waited till most of the usual speakers [1] had

---

[1] By an ancient ordinance of Solon, those who were above fifty years
of age were first called on to deliver their opinion.   The law had ceased
to be in force;  but, as a decent custom, the older men usually commenced the debate.   There would be frequent occasions for departing
from such a custom, and Demosthenes, who was now thirty-three,
assigns his reason for speaking first.

been heard; if any of their counsels had been to my liking, I had remained silent, else proceeded to impart my own. But as the subject of discussion is one upon which they have spoken oft before, I imagine, though I rise the first, I am entitled to indulgence. For if these men had advised properly in time past, there would be no necessity for deliberating now.

First I say, you must not despond, Athenians, under your present circumstances, wretched as they are; for that which is worst in them as regards the past, is best for the future. What do I mean? That your affairs are amiss, men of Athens, because you do nothing which is needful; if, notwithstanding you performed your duties, it were the same, there would be no hope of amendment.

Consider next, what you know by report, and men of experience remember; how vast a power the Lacedæmonians had not long ago, yet how nobly and becomingly you con sulted the dignity of Athens, and undertook the war [1] against them for the rights of Greece. Why do I mention this? To show and convince you, Athenians, that nothing, if you take precaution, is to be feared, nothing, if you are negligent, goes as you desire. Take for examples the strength of the Lacedæmonians then, which you overcame by attention to your duties, and the insolence of this man now, by which through neglect of our interests we are confounded. But if any among you, Athenians, deem Philip hard to be conquered, looking at the magnitude of his existing power, and the loss by us of all our strongholds, they reason rightly, but should reflect, that once we held Pydna and Potidæa and Methone and all the region round about as our own, and many of the nations now leagued with him were independent and free, and preferred our friendship to his. Had Philip then taken it into his head, that it was difficult to contend

[1] He refers to the war in which Athens assisted the Thebans against Lacedæmon, and in which Chabrias won the naval battle of Naxos. That war commenced twenty-six years before the speaking of the first Philippic, and would be well remembered by many of the hearers.

with Athens, when she had so many fortresses to infest his country, and he was destitute of allies, nothing that he has accomplished would he have undertaken, and never would he have acquired so large a dominion. But he saw well, Athenians, that all these places are the open prizes of war, that the possessions of the absent naturally belong to the present, those of the remiss to them that will venture and toil. Acting on such principle, he has won everything and keeps it, either by way of conquest, or by friendly attachment and alliance; for all men will side with and respect those whom they see prepared and willing to make proper exertion. If you, Athenians, will adopt this principle now, though you did not before, and every man, where he can and ought to give his service to the state, be ready to give it without excuse, the wealthy to contribute, the able-bodied to enlist; in a word, plainly, if you will become your own masters, and cease each expecting to do nothing himself, while his neighbour does everything for him, you shall then with heaven's permission recover your own, and get back what has been frittered away, and chastise Philip. Do not imagine that his empire is everlastingly secured to him as a god. There are who hate and fear and envy him, Athenians, even among those that seem most friendly; and all feelings that are in other men belong, we may assume, to his confederates. But now they are all cowed, having no refuge through your tardiness and indolence, which I say you must abandon forthwith. For you see, Athenians, the case, to what pitch of arrogance the man has advanced who leaves you not even the choice of action or inaction, but threatens and uses (they say) outrageous language, and, unable to rest in possession of his conquests, continually widens their circle, and, whilst we dally and delay, throws his net all around us. When then, Athenians, when will ye act as becomes you? In what event? In that of necessity, I suppose. And how should we regard the events happening now? Methinks, to freemen the strongest necessity is the disgrace of their condition. Or

tell me, do ye like walking about and asking one another:—
Is there any news? Why, could there be greater news than
a man of Macedonia subduing Athenians, and directing the
affairs of Greece? Is Philip dead? No, but he is sick. And
what matters it to you? Should anything befall this man,
you will soon create another Philip, if you attend to business
thus. For even he has been exalted not so much by his own
strength as by our negligence. And again; should anything
happen to him; should fortune, which still takes better care
of us than we of ourselves, be good enough to accomplish
this; observe that, being on the spot, you would step in
while things were in confusion, and manage them as you
pleased; but as you now are, though occasion offered Amphipolis, you would not be in a position to accept it, with
neither forces nor counsels at hand.

However, as to the importance of a general zeal in the
discharge of duty, believing you are convinced and satisfied,
I say no more.

As to the kind of force which I think may extricate you
from your difficulties, the amount, the supplies of money,
the best and speediest method (in my judgment) of providing all the necessaries, I shall endeavour to inform you
forthwith, making only one request, men of Athens. When
you have heard all, determine; prejudge not before. And
let none think I delay our operations, because I recommend
an entirely new force. Not those that cry, quickly! to-day!
speak most to the purpose (for what has already happened
we shall not be able to prevent by our present armament);
but he that shows what and how great and whence procured
must be the force capable of enduring, till either we have
advisedly terminated the war, or overcome our enemies: for
so shall we escape annoyance in future. This I think I am
able to show, without offence to any other man who has a
plan to offer. My promise indeed is large; it shall be tested
by the performance; and you shall be my judges.

First, then, Athenians, I say we must provide fifty warships,[1] and hold ourselves prepared, in case of emergency, to embark and sail. I require also an equipment of transports for half the cavalry [2] and sufficient boats. This we must have ready against his sudden marches from his own country to Thermopylæ, the Chersonese, Olynthus, and anywhere he likes. For he should entertain the belief, that possibly you may rouse from this over-carelessness, and start off, as you did to Eubœa,[3] and formerly (they say) to Haliartus,[4] and very lately to Thermopylæ. And although you should not pursue just the course I would advise, it is no slight matter that Philip, knowing you to be in readiness—know it he will for certain; there are too many among our own people who report everything to him—may either keep quiet from apprehension, or, not heeding your arrangements, be taken off his guard, there being nothing to prevent your sailing, if he give you a chance, to attack his territories. Such an armament, I say, ought instantly to be agreed upon and provided. But besides, men of Athens, you should keep in hand some force that will incessantly make war and annoy him: none of your ten or twenty thousand mercenaries, not your forces on paper, but one that shall belong to the state, and, whether you appoint one or more generals, or this or that man or any other, shall obey and follow him. Subsistence too I require for it. What the force shall be, how large, from what source maintained, how rendered efficient, I will show you, stating every particular. Mercenaries I recommend—and beware of

[1] The Athenian ship of war at this time was the Trireme, or galley with three ranks of oars. It had at the prow a beak with a sharp iron head, which, in a charge (generally made at the broadside), was able to shatter the planks of the enemy's vessel. An ordinary trireme carried two hundred men, including the crew and marines. These last were usually ten for each ship, but the number was often increased.

[2] The total number was one thousand, each tribe furnishing one hundred.

[3] The expedition about five years before, when the Thebans had sent an army to Eubœa, and Timotheus roused his countrymen to expel them from the island. Of this, Demosthenes gives an animated account at the close of the oration on the Chersonese.

[4] B.C. 395, when the war between Thebes and Sparta had begun, and Lysander besieged Haliartus. He was slain in a sally by the Thebans and Athenians.

doing what has often been injurious—thinking all measures below the occasion, adopting the strongest in your decrees, you fail to accomplish the least—rather, I say, perform and procure a little, add to it afterwards, if it prove insufficient. I advise then two thousand soldiers in all, five hundred to be Athenians, of whatever age you think right, serving a limited time, not long, but such time as you think right, so as to relieve one another: the rest should be mercenaries. And with them two hundred horse, fifty at least Athenians, like the foot, on the same terms of service; and transports for them. Well; what besides? Ten swift galleys: for, as Philip has a navy, we must have swift galleys also, to convoy our power. How shall subsistence for these troops be provided? I will state and explain; but first let me tell you why I consider a force of this amount sufficient, and why I wish the men to be citizens.

Of that amount, Athenians, because it is impossible for us now to raise an army capable of meeting him in the field: we must plunder and adopt such kind of warfare at first: our force, therefore, must not be over-large (for there is not pay or subsistence) nor altogether mean. Citizens I wish to attend and go on board, because I hear that formerly the state maintained mercenary troops at Corinth,[1] commanded by Polystratus and Iphicrates and Chabrias and some others, and that you served with them yourselves; and I am told that these mercenaries fighting by your side and you by theirs defeated the Lacedæmonians. But ever since your hirelings have served by themselves, they have been vanquishing your friends and allies, while your enemies have become unduly great. Just glancing at the war of our state, they go off to Artabazus[2] or anywhere rather, and the

---

[1] He alludes to the time when Corinth, Athens, Thebes, and Argos were allied against Sparta, and held a congress at Corinth, B.C. 394. The allies were at first defeated, but Iphicrates gained some successes, and acquired considerable reputation by cutting off a small division of Spartan infantry.

[2] Diodorus relates that Chares, in the Social War, having no money to pay his troops, was forced to lend them to Artabazus, then in

general follows, naturally; for it is impossible to command
without giving pay. What therefore ask I? To remove
the excuses both of general and soldiers, by supplying pay,
and attaching native soldiers, as inspectors of the general's
conduct. The way we manage things now is a mockery.
For if you were asked: Are you at peace, Athenians? No,
indeed, you would say; we are at war with Philip. Did you
not choose from yourselves ten captains and generals, and
also captains and two generals[1] of horse? How are they
employed? Except one man, whom you commission on
service abroad, the rest conduct your processions with the
sacrificers. Like puppet-makers, you elect your infantry
and cavalry officers for the market-place, not for war. Consider, Athenians, should there not be native captains, a
native general of horse, your own commanders, that the
force might really be the state's? Or should your general
of horse sail to Lemnos,[2] while Menelaus commands the
cavalry fighting for your possessions? I speak not as object-
ing to the man, but he ought to be elected by you, whoever
the person be.

Perhaps you admit the justice of these statements, but
wish principally to hear about the supplies, what they must
be and whence procured. I will satisfy you. Supplies, then,
for maintenance, mere rations for these troops, come to

rebellion against the king of Persia. Chares gained a victory for the
satrap, and received a supply of money. But this led to a complaint
and menace of war by the king, which brought serious consequences.

[1] There were chosen at Athens every year

> Ten generals (one for each tribe),
> Ten captains (one for each tribe),
> Two generals of cavalry,
> Ten cavalry officers (one for each tribe).

In a regular army of citizens, when each tribe formed its own division, both of horse and foot, all these generals and officers would be
present. Thus, there were ten generals at Marathon. A change took
place in later times when the armies were more miscellaneous. Three
Athenian generals were frequently employed, and at a still later period
only one. Demosthenes here touches on a very important matter,
which we can well understand, viz., the necessity of officering the foreign
mercenaries from home.

[2] To assist at a religious ceremony held annually at Lemnos, where
many Athenians resided.

ninety talents and a little more: for ten swift galleys forty talents, twenty minas a month to every ship; for two thousand soldiers forty more, that each soldier may receive for rations ten drachms a month; and for two hundred horsemen, each receiving thirty drachms a month, twelve talents.[1] Should any one think rations for the men a small provision, he judges erroneously. Furnish that, and I am sure the army itself will, without injuring any Greek or ally, procure everything else from the war, so as to make out their full pay. I am ready to joint the fleet as a volunteer, and submit to anything, if this be not so. Now for the ways and means of the supply which I demand from you.

[*Statement*[2] *of ways and means*]

This, Athenians, is what we have been able to devise. When you vote upon the resolutions, pass what you approve that you may oppose Philip, not only by decrees and letters but by action also.

I think it will assist your deliberations about the war and the whole arrangements, to regard the position, Athenians, of the hostile country, and consider that Philip by the winds and seasons of the year gets the start in most of his operations, watching for the trade-winds[3] or the winter to commence them, when we are unable (he thinks) to reach the spot. On this account, we must carry on the war not with hasty levies (or we shall be too late for everything) but with a permanent force and power. You may use as winter quarters for your troops Lemnos, and Thasus, and Sciathus, and the islands[4] in that neighbourhood, which have harbours

[1] As to Athenian money, see Appendix I.
[2] Here the clerk or secretary reads the scheme drawn up by Demosthenes, in the preparing of which he was probably assisted by the financial officers of the state. What follows was, according to Dionysius, spoken at a different time.
[3] The Etesian winds blowing from the north-west in July, which would impede a voyage from Athens to Macedonia and Thrace.
[4] As Scopelus, Halonnesus, Peparethus, which were then subject to Athens.

and corn and all necessaries for an army. In the season of the year, when it is easy to put ashore and there is no danger from the winds, they will easily take their station off the coast itself and at the entrances of the seaports.

How and when to employ the troops, the commander appointed by you will determine as occasion requires. What you must find is stated in my bill. If, men of Athens, you will furnish the supplies which I mention, and then, after completing your preparations of soldiers, ships, cavalry, will oblige the entire force by law to remain in the service, and, while you become your own paymasters and commissaries, demand from your general an account of his conduct, you will cease to be always discussing the same questions without forwarding them in the least, and besides, Athenians, not only will you cut off his greatest revenue—What is this? He maintains war against you through the resources of your allies, by his piracies on their navigation—But what next? You will be out of the reach of injury yourselves: he will not do as in time past, when falling upon Lemnos and Imbrus he carried off your citizens captive, seizing the vessels at Geræstus he levied an incalculable sum, and lastly, made a descent at Marathon and carried off the sacred galley [1] from our coast, and you could neither prevent these things nor send succours by the appointed time. But how is it, think you, Athenians, that the Panathenaic and Dionysian festivals [2] take place always at the appointed time, whether expert or unqualified persons be chosen to conduct either of them, whereon you expend larger sums than upon any armament, and which are more numerously attended and

[1] A ship called Paralus, generally used on religious missions or to carry public despatches.
[2] The Panathenaic festivals were in honour of Pallas or Athene, the protectress of Athens, and commemorated also the union of the old Attic towns under one government. There were two, the greater held every fourth year, the lesser annually. They were celebrated with sacrifices, races, gymnastic and musical contests, and various other amusements and solemnities, among which was the carrying the pictured robe of Pallas to her temple. The Dionysian festival was in honour of Bacchus.

magnificent than almost anything in the world; whilst all your armaments are after the time, as that to Methone, to Pagasæ, to Potidæa? Because in the former case everything is ordered by law, and each of you knows long beforehand, who is the choir-master[1] of his tribe, who the gymnastic[2] master, when, from whom, and what he is to receive, and what to do. Nothing there is left unascertained or undefined: whereas in the business of war and its preparations all is irregular, unsettled, indefinite. Therefore, no sooner have we heard anything than we appoint ship-captains, dispute with them on the exchanges,[3] and consider about ways and means; then it is resolved that resident aliens and house-holders[4] shall embark, then to put yourselves on board instead: but during these delays the objects of our expedition are lost; for the time of action we waste in preparation, and favourable moments wait not our evasions and delays. The forces that we imagine we possess in the meantime are found, when the crisis comes, utterly insufficient. And

[1] The choregus, or choir-master, of each tribe, had to defray the expense of the choruses, whether dramatic, lyric, or musical, which formed part of the entertainment on solemn occasions. This was one of the burdensome offices to which men of property were liable at Athens.

[2] The gymnasiarch, like the choregus, had a burden imposed on him by his tribe, to make certain provisions for the gymnasium, public place or school of exercise. Some of the contests at the festivals being of a gymnastic nature, such as the Torch-race, it was his duty to make arrangements for them, and more particularly to select the ablest youths of the school for performers.

[3] For every ship of war a captain, or trierarch, was appointed, whose duty it was, not merely to command, but take charge of the vessel, keep it in repair, and bear the expense (partly or wholly) of equipping it. In the Peloponnesian war we find the charge laid upon two joint captains, and afterwards it was borne by an association formed like the Symmoriæ of the Property Tax. Demosthenes, when he came to the head of affairs, introduced some useful reforms in the system of the Trierarchy. The exchange was a clumsy contrivance to enforce the performance of these public duties by persons capable of bearing them. A party charged might call upon any other person to take the office, or exchange estates with him. If he refused, complaint was made to the magistrate who had cognisance of the business, and the dispute was judicially heard and decided.

[4] Freedman, who had quitted their masters' house, and lived independently.

Philip has arrived at such a pitch of arrogance, as to send the following letter to the Eubœans:

[*The letter is read*]

Of that which has been read, Athenians, most is true, unhappily true; perhaps not agreeable to hear. And if what one passes over in speaking, to avoid offence, one could pass over in reality, it is right to humour the audience: but if graciousness of speech, where it is out of place, does harm in action, shameful is it, Athenians, to delude ourselves, and by putting off everything unpleasant to miss the time for all operations, and be unable even to understand, that skilful makers of war should not follow circumstances, but be in advance of them; that just as a general may be expected to lead his armies, so are men of prudent counsel to guide circumstances, in order that their resolutions may be accomplished, not their motions determined by the event. Yet you, Athenians, with larger means than any people,—ships, infantry, cavalry, and revenue—have never up to this day made proper use of any of them; and your war with Philip differs in no respect from the boxing of barbarians. For among them the party struck feels always for the blow; strike him somewhere else, there go his hands again; ward or look in the face he cannot nor will. So you, if you hear of Philip in the Chersonese, vote to send relief there, if at Thermopylæ, the same; if anywhere else, you run after his heels up and down, and are commanded by him; no plan have you devised for the war, no circumstance do you see beforehand, only when you learn that something is done, or about to be done. Formerly perhaps this was allowable: now it is come to a crisis, to be tolerable no longer. And it seems, men of Athens, as if some god, ashamed for us at our proceedings, has put this activity into Philip. For had he been willing to remain quiet in possession of his conquests and prizes, and attempted nothing further, some of you, I think, would be satisfied with a state of things, which brands our nation with the shame of cowardice and the foulest disgrace. But by continually encroaching and grasping after more, he may possibly rouse you, if you have not altogether despaired. I marvel, indeed, that none of you, Athenians, notices with concern and anger, that the beginning of this war was to chastise Philip, the end is to protect ourselves against his attacks. One thing is clear: he will not stop, unless some one oppose him. And shall we wait for this? And if you despatch empty galleys and hopes from this or that person, think ye all is well? Shall we not embark? Shall we not sail with at least a part of our national forces, now though not before? Shall we not make a descent upon his coast? Where, then, shall we land? some one asks. The war itself, men of Athens, will discover the rotten parts of his empire, if we make a trial; but if we sit at home, hearing the orators accuse and malign one another, no good can ever be achieved. Methinks, where a portion of our citizens, though not all, are commissioned with the rest, Heaven blesses, and Fortune aids the struggle: but where you send out a general and an empty decree and hopes from the hustings, nothing that you desire is done; your enemies scoff, and your allies die for fear of such an armament. For it is impossible—aye, impossible, for one man to execute all your wishes: to promise,[1] and assert, and accuse this or that person, is possible; but so your affairs are ruined. The general commands wretched unpaid hirelings; here are persons easily found, who tell you lies of his conduct; you vote at random from what you hear: what then can be expected?

How is this to cease, Athenians? When you make the same persons soldiers, and witnesses of the general's conduct, and judges when they return home at his audit;[2] so that you

[1] Chares is particularly alluded to. The " promises of Chares " passed into a proverb.

[2] The audit or scrutiny of his conduct which every officer of the republic had to undergo, before a jury, if necessary, at the end of his administration. In the case of a general, the scrutiny would be like a court-martial. The Athenian people (says Demosthenes), as repre-

may not only hear of your own affairs, but be present to see them. So disgraceful is our condition now, that every general is twice or thrice tried [1] before you for his life, though none dares even once to hazard his life against the enemy: they prefer the death of kidnappers and thieves to that which becomes them; for it is a malefactor's part to die by sentence of the law, a general's to die in battle. Among ourselves, some go about and say that Philip is concerting with the Lacedæmonians the destruction of Thebes and the dissolution of republics; some, that he has sent envoys to the king; [2] others, that he is fortifying cities in Illyria: so we wander about, each inventing stories. For my part, Athenians, by the gods I believe, that Philip is intoxicated with the magnitude of his exploits, and has many such dreams in his imagination, seeing the absence of opponents, and elated by success; but most certainly he has no such plan of action as to let the silliest people among us know what his intentions are; for the silliest are these newsmongers. Let us dismiss such talk, and remember only that Philip is an enemy who robs us of our own and has long insulted us; that wherever we have expected aid from any quarter, it has been found hostile, and that the future depends on ourselves, and unless we are willing to fight him there, we shall perhaps be compelled to fight here. This let us remember, and then we shall have determined wisely, and have done with idle conjectures. You need not pry into the future, but assure yourselves it will be disastrous, unless you attend to your duty, and are willing to act as becomes you.

As for me, never before have I courted favour, by speaking what I am not convinced is for your good, and now I have spoken my whole mind frankly and unreservedly. I could

sented by the citizen soldiers, would themselves be witnesses of the general's conduct. These same soldiers, when they came home, or at least a portion of them, might serve on the jury; and so the people would be both witnesses and judges.

[1] Chares was tried several times. Capital charges were preferred also against Autocles, Cephisodotus, Leosthenes, Callisthenes.

[2] The king of Persia, generally called *the king* by the Greeks.

have wished, knowing the advantage of good counsel to you, I were equally certain of its advantage to the counsellor: so should I have spoken with more satisfaction. Now, with an uncertainty of the consequence to myself, but with a conviction that you will benefit by adopting it, I proffer my advice. I trust only that what is most for the common benefit will prevail.

# THE ORATION ON THE PEACE

### ARGUMENT

To understand as well the subject of this oration, as the motives of
Demosthenes, who here recommends a course of action different from
the vigorous measures counselled by him on other occasions, it is
necessary to take a short review of the preceding events, and observe
the position in which Athens stood at the time when the speech was
delivered.

Philip, after taking Olynthus, turned his thoughts to new objects, of
which the more immediate were, first, to get possession of the Greek
towns on the Hellespont and the Chersonese; secondly, to get a footing in southern Greece. The first of these seemed comparatively easy
since the reduction of Olynthus; the second was more difficult, and
could only be accomplished by the aid or sufferance of certain Greek
states. But the continuance of the Sacred war afforded Philip an
opportunity of which he skilfully availed himself. Phalæcus, son of
Onomarchus, had maintained his ground against the enemy, and both
Thebans and Thessalians began to be desirous of Macedonian aid.
But Athens was in alliance with Phocis, and Philip had seen some
few years before, when the Athenians occupied the pass of Thermopylæ,
that they were still capable of vigorous efforts, if under able direction
or any strong excitement. It became therefore his policy to conciliate
Athens for the present. He caused it to be announced by means of
his agents and partisans, that he was desirous of peace, and reports
of various acts of kindness done by him to Athenian citizens in Macedonia were studiously disseminated. This seems to have been the
period at which Philip gained over to his interest, or even retained
in his service, divers active members of the Athenian assembly. Among
them was Philocrates, who first made a formal motion that Philip
should have leave to open a negotiation. Soon after he carried a
decree to send ambassadors to Philip, and ten were despatched, among
them Philocrates himself, Æschines, and Demosthenes. They returned
with a letter from Philip, and were soon followed by three Macedonian
envoys of high distinction, Antipater, Parmenio, and Eurylochus.
The Athenians met in assembly; peace was determined on, and the
ambassadors were again ordered to sail to Macedonia to receive the
oath of Philip. In the meantime Philip had marched into Thrace,
where he defeated Cersobleptes, the king of that country, and took
possession of a part of his dominions. From this expedition he had
not returned when the Athenian ambassadors arrived at Pella, the
Macedonian capital. Here they waited a month, and, on Philip's
return, were induced by that monarch, who had secretly prepared for
his invasion of Phocis, to accompany him as far as Pheræ in Thessaly.
From Pheræ they departed for Athens, and Philip marched straight
to Thermopylæ. The Athenians, deceived by his promises, were lulled
into security; Phalæcus, seeing no hope of assistance, withdrew from
Phocis, while Philip, strengthened by the forces of Thessaly and Thebes,
overran the country, and took possession of Delphi. An Amphic-

tyonic council was conveyed to sit in judgment on the sacrilegious Phocians. Sentence was passed on them, which (besides other penalties) deprived them of their seat in the council of Amphictyons, and transferred their privileges to the king of Macedonia.

The first intelligence of these transactions was received at Athens with consternation. Measures were taken to put the city in a state of defence, as if an invasion were threatened. Philip sent a calm letter of remonstrance, which allayed the fears of the people, but did not abate their anger and ill-humour. A feeling of disappointment was mingled with shame for their own credulity, and alarm at the increase of Macedonian influence. They saw too, with deep vexation, that Philip, instead of conferring any benefit upon Athens, as they had fondly hoped he would, had excited himself to promote the advantage of Thebes, which, by his assistance, recovered her subject Bœotian towns, and even obtained some of the Phocian territory for herself. Nothing more strongly marked the state of public feeling at Athens than her refusal at this time to attend the Pythian games, at which Philip had been chosen to preside by the Amphictyonic decree. The Athenians by absenting themselves made a sort of protest against his election.

It was in this state of things that Macedonian ambassadors, accompanied by Thessalian and Bœotian, arrived at Athens, to demand from her a formal sanction of the decree by which Philip had become a member of the Amphictyonic council. An assembly was held to consider the question. The people were exceedingly clamorous, and applauded those orators who opposed the claim of Philip. Æschines, who supported it, could scarcely obtain a hearing. Demosthenes at length addressed the assembly, and, without advising any dishonourable submission, or even direct concession to what the envoys required, strongly dissuaded his countrymen from taking any course which might draw Athens into a war. It was not that Philip was less to be dreaded now than he was before; on the contrary, his power had greatly increased; but this was not the time to provoke his hostility, backed as he was by Thessaly and Thebes; and even if Athens could stand alone against such a combination, a mere Amphictyonic title was not a proper subject of quarrel.

It appears that the Athenians came to no formal vote on this matter, but their anger was so far calmed by the arguments of Demosthenes, that the envoys departed with full confidence that the peace would not be broken.

I SEE, men of Athens, our affairs are in great perplexity and confusion, not only because many interests have been sacrificed, and it is useless to make fine speeches about them, but because, for preserving what remains, you cannot agree upon any single expedient, some holding one opinion, and some another. And besides, perplexing and difficult as deliberation of itself is, you, Athenians, have rendered it far more so. For other men usually hold counsel before action, you hold it after: the result of which during all the time of my remembrance has been, that the censurer of your errors gets repute and credit as a good speaker, while your interests and objects of deliberation are lost. Yet, even under these circumstances, I believe, and I have risen with the persuasion, that if you will desist from wrangling and tumult, and listen as becomes men on a political consultation of such importance, I shall be able to suggest and advise measures by which our affairs may be improved and our losses retrieved.

Well as I know, Athenians, that to talk before you of oneself and one's own counsels is a successful artifice with unscrupulous men, I think it so vulgar and offensive that I shrink from it even in a case of necessity. However, I think you will better appreciate what I shall say now, by calling to mind a little that I said on former occasions. For example, Athenians, when they were advising you in the troubles of Euboea to assist Plutarch,[1] and undertake a discreditable and expensive war, I, and I alone, stood forward to oppose it, and was nearly torn to pieces by the men who for petty lucre have seduced you into many grievous errors. A short time later, when you incurred disgrace, and suffered what no mortals ever did from parties whom they assisted, you all acknowledged the worthlessness of their counsels who misled you, and the soundness of mine. Again, Athenians, when I saw that Neoptolemus[2] the actor, privileged under colour of his profession, was doing serious mischief to the state, managing and directing things at Athens on Philip's behalf, I came and informed you, not from any private enmity or malice, as subsequent occurrences have shown. And herein I shall not blame the advocates of Neoptolemus (for there were none) but you yourselves; for had you been

---

[1] Callias, sovereign of Chalcis, had invited Philip into Euboea, to assist him against Plutarch, sovereign of Eretria: Plutarch applied to Athens for assistance, and Phocion was sent with an army into Euboea, where, by the carelessness or treachery of Plutarch, he was exposed in a defile at Tamynæ, and attacked by Callias with a superior force of Chalcidians and Macedonians. He gained the victory, but to punish Plutarch expelled him from Eretria.

[2] Neoptolemus on some professional engagement at Pella had probably been bribed by Philip. He was active in promoting the peace and afterwards abandoned his country for Macedonia.

seeing a tragedy in the temple of Bacchus, instead of it being a debate on the public weal and safety, you could not have heard him with more partiality, or me with more intolerance. But I suppose you all now understand that he made his journey to the enemy, in order (as he said) to get the debts there owing to him, and defray thereout his public charges at home; and, after urging this argument, that it was hard to reproach men who brought over their effects from abroad, as soon as he obtained security through the peace, he converted into money all the real estate which he possessed here, and has gone off with it to Philip. Thus two of my warnings, justly and rightfully pronounced in accordance with the truth, testify in my favour as a counsellor. A third, men of Athens, I will mention, this one only, and straight proceed to the subject of my address. When we ambassadors, after receiving the oath on the peace, had returned, and certain men were promising that Thespiæ and Platæa [1] would be repeopled; that Philip, if he got the mastery, would save the Phocians, and disperse the population of Thebes; that Oropus [2] would be yours, and Eubœa given as compensation for Amphipolis, with more of the like hopes and delusions, which led you on, against policy, equity, and honour, to abandon the Phocians; you will find, I neither aided in any of these deceits, nor held my tongue. I warned you, as you surely remember, that I knew not of these things nor expected them, and deemed it all idle gossip.

These instances, wherein I have shown greater foresight than others, I mention not by way of boast, nor ascribe, Athenians, to any sagacity of my own, nor will I pretend to discover or discern the future from any but two causes, which I will state: first, men of Athens, through good fortune, which I observe beats all the craft and cleverness of man;

[1] Thespiæ and Platæa were taken and rased to the ground by the Thebans under Epaminondas, B.C. 373.
[2] Oropus was a border town, for the possession of which Thebes and Athens had long contended. Themison of Eretria had taken it from Athens, and put it in the hands of the Thebans.

secondly, because I judge and estimate things disinterestedly, and no one can show that any lucre is attached to my politics or my speeches. Therefore, whatever be your true policy, as indicated by the circumstances, I have a correct view of it; but when you put money on one side as in a balance, it carries away and pulls down the judgment with it, and he that does so can no longer reason upon anything justly or soundly.

The first thing which I maintain to be necessary is this. Whether you seek to obtain allies, or contribution,[1] or aught else for the state, do it without disturbing the present peace; not that it is very glorious or worthy of you, but, whatever be its character, it had better suited our interests never to have made peace, than to break it ourselves: for we have thrown away many advantages, which would have rendered the war then safer and easier for us than it can be now Secondly, Athenians, we must take care that these people assembled and calling themselves Amphictyons[2] are not by us necessitated, or furnished with a plea, to make a common war against us. I grant, if we renewed the war with Philip on account of Amphipolis, or any such private quarrel, in which Thessalians, Argives and Thebans are not concerned,

---

[1] *I.e.*, money contributed by allies. When the Athenians re-established their confederacy, which had been dissolved by the Peloponnesian war, the payments received from the allies received the name of *contributions* as less obnoxious than *tribute*.

[2] The Amphictyonic league, at the head of which Philip was now placed, was a federal union of Hellenic (or Greek) tribes, having for its object the maintenance of a common religion and nationality. The various deputies met twice a year, in the spring at Delphi, in the autumn at Anthela near Thermopylæ. They met, not only to celebrate games and festivals, but to transact the business of the league, to determine questions of international law and religion. The oracular sanctity of Delphi gave a dignity to these meetings, but the rivalry and jealousies of the more powerful Greek states did not permit them (in general) to be controlled by Amphictyonic decrees. The three Sacred wars are instances in which their decrees were enforced by combination; but in the two last, for which Philip's aid was invited, there was but little enthusiasm in the cause from any motive of religion or patriotism. The meeting at which Philip had been chosen president was so tumultuous and irregular, that the Athenians would not allow it to be a legal convocation of the Amphictyonic body. Philip greatly resented this, because his election was considered to establish the title of his countrymen to rank among the Greek nations.

none of them would join in it, and least of all—hear me before you cry out—the Thebans: not that they are kindly disposed to us, or would not gratify Philip, but they see clearly, stupid as one may think them,[1] that, if they had a war with you, the hardships would all be theirs, while another sat waiting for the advantages. Therefore they would not throw themselves into it, unless the ground and origin of the war were common. So if we again went to war with the Thebans for Oropus or any private cause, I should fear no disaster, because our respective auxiliaries would assist us or them, if either country were invaded, but would join with neither in aggression. Such is the spirit of alliances that are worth regard, and so the thing naturally is. People are not friendly either to us or the Thebans, to the extent of equally desiring our safety and our predominance. Safe they would all have us for their own sakes; dominant, so as to become their masters, they would not have either of us. What then, say I, is the danger? what to be guarded against? Lest in the coming war there be found a common plea, a common grievance for all. If Argives, and Messenians, and Megalopolitans, and some of the other Peloponnesians, who are in league with them, are hostile to us on account of our negotiating with the Lacedæmonians and seeming to take up some of their enterprises; if the Thebans are (as they say) our enemies, and will be more so, because we harbour their exiles and in every way manifest our aversion to them; Thessalians again, because we harbour the Phocian exiles, and Philip, because we oppose his admission to the Amphictyonic body; I fear that, each incensed on a private quarrel, they will combine to bring war upon you, setting up the decrees of the Amphictyons, and be drawn on (beyond what their single interests require) to battle it with us, as they did with the Phocians. For you are surely aware that now the Thebans and Philip and the Thessalians have co-operated, without having each exactly the same views. For example,

[1] Bœotian stupidity was proverbial.

the Thebans could not hinder Philip from advancing and occupying the passes, nor yet from coming last and having the credit of their labours. True, in respect of territorial acquisition, something has been done for them; but in regard to honour and reputation, they have fared wretchedly; since, had Philip not stept in, they would (it seems) have got nothing. This was not agreeable to them, but having the wish without the power to obtain Orchomenos and Coronea, they submitted to it all. Of Philip, you know, some persons venture to say, that he would not have given Orchomenos and Coronea to the Thebans, but was compelled to do so. I wish them joy of their opinion, but thus far I believe that he cared not so much about that business, as he desired to occupy the passes, and have the glory of the war, as being determined by his agency, and the direction of the Pythian games. Such were the objects of his ambition. The Thessalians wished not either Philip or Thebes to be aggrandised, since in both they saw danger to themselves; but sought to obtain these two advantages, the synod at Thermopylæ, and the privileges at Delphi;[1] for which objects they aided the confederacy. Thus you will find that each party has been led into many acts unwillingly: and against this danger, being such as I describe, you must take precautions.

Must we then do as we are bidden, for fear of the consequences? and do you recommend this? Far from it. I advise you so to act, as not to compromise your dignity, to avoid war, to prove yourselves right-thinking, just-speaking

[1] The Thessalians were peculiarly aggrieved by their exclusion (during the Sacred war) from the national synod, and from the oracle and festivities of Delphi. Their country had been the cradle of the Hellenic race, their deputies were the most numerous in the council, and their vicinity to the places of meeting gave them a greater interest in the proceedings. Hence they most eagerly pressed for punishment of the Phocians. The tribes of Mount Œta proposed that the male population of Phocis should be precipitated from the Delphian rock; which cruelty was not permitted by Philip. To gratify the Thessalians, Philip put them in possession of Nicæa, one of the towns near the pass of Thermopylæ, but even there he kept a Macedonian garrison. The Thebans had expected to have that town themselves, and were disappointed.

men. With those who think we should boldly suffer any-thing, and do not foresee the war, I would reason thus. We permit the Thebans to have Oropus; and if one asked us why, and required a true answer, we should say, To avoid war. And to Philip now we have ceded Amphipolis by treaty, and allow the Cardians [1] to be excepted from the other people of the Chersonese; and the Carian [2] to seize the islands Chios, Cos, and Rhodes, and the Byzantines to detain [3] our vessels; evidently because we think the tranquillity of peace more beneficial than strife and contest about such questions. It were folly then and utter absurdity, after dealing thus with each party singly on matters of vital moment to ourselves, to battle now with them all for a shadow at Delphi.

[1] Cardia was a city at the north-western extremity of the Chersonese, and from its position on the isthmus was considered the key of the peninsula. Among the towns ceded to Athens by Cersobleptes, Cardia had not been included; but the Athenians afterwards laid claim to it, and Philip supported the Caridans in resisting that claim.

[2] Idrieus, king of Caria, who was now in possession of these islands, which had revolted from Athens in the Social war.

[3] Compel them to go into their port to pay harbour duties.

# THE SECOND PHILIPPIC

## ARGUMENT

SOON after the close of the Phocian war, the attention of Philip was called to Peloponnesus, where the dissensions between Sparta and her old enemies afforded him an occasion of interference. The Spartans had never abandoned their right to the province of Messenia, which had been wrested from them by Epaminondas; and since Thebes was no longer to be feared, they seem to have conceived hopes of regaining their lost power. The Argives and the Arcadians of Megalopolis were in league with Messenia, but Sparta had her allies in the Peloponnesus, and even Athens was suspected of favouring her cause. It does not appear that any open hostilities had taken place; but about this time the fears of the Messenians induced them to solicit the alliance of Philip. He willingly promised them his protection, and sent a body of troops into the Peninsula. The progress which Macedonian influence was making there having alarmed the Athenians, they sent Demosthenes with an embassy to counteract it. He went to Messene and to Argos, addressed the people, and pointed out the dangers to which all Greece was exposed by Philip's ambition. It seems that he failed in rousing their suspicions, or they were too much occupied by an immediate peril to heed one that appeared remote. Philip however resented this proceeding on the part of the Athenians, and sent an embassy to expostulate with them, especially on the charge of bad faith and treachery which had been preferred against him by Demosthenes. Ambassadors from Argos and Messene accompanied those of Macedon, and complained of the connection that appeared to subsist between Athens and Lacedæmon, hostile (they thought) to the liberties of Peloponnesus. In answer to these complaints, Demosthenes addressed his second Philippic to the Popular Assembly; repeating the substance of what he had said to the Peloponnesians, vindicating his own conduct, and denouncing the Macedonian party at Athens. The embassy led to no immediate result; but the influence of Demosthenes at home was increased.

IN all the speeches, men of Athens, about Philip's measures and infringements of the peace, I observe that statements made on our behalf are thought just and generous,[1] and all who accuse Philip are heard with approbation; yet nothing (I may say) that is proper, or for the sake of which the speeches are worth hearing, is done. To this point are the

---

[1] *Generous*, as regards the Greek states, whose independence the Athenians stand up for. This praise Demosthenes frequently claims for his countrymen, and, compared with the rest of the Greeks, they deserved it.

affairs of Athens brought, that the more fully and clearly one convicts Philip of violating the peace with you, and plotting against the whole of Greece, the more difficult it becomes to advise you how to act. The cause lies in all of us, Athenians, that, when we ought to oppose an ambitious power by deeds and actions, not by words, we men of the hustings shrink from our duty, of moving and advising, for fear of your displeasure, and only declaim on the heinousness and atrocity of Philip's conduct; you of the assembly, though better instructed than Philip to argue justly, or comprehend the argument of another, to check him in the execution of his designs are totally unprepared. The result is inevitable, I imagine, and perhaps just. You each succeed better in what you are busy and earnest about; Philip in actions, you in words. If you are still satisfied with using the better arguments, it is an easy matter, and there is no trouble: but if we are to take measures for the correction of these evils, to prevent their insensible progress, and the rising up of a mighty power, against which we could have no defence, then our course of deliberation is not the same as formerly; the orators, and you that hear them, must prefer good and salutary counsels to those which are easy and agreeable.

First, men of Athens, if any one regards without uneasiness the might and dominion of Philip, and imagines that it threatens no danger to the state, or that all his preparations are not against you, I marvel, and would entreat you every one to hear briefly from me the reasons why I am led to form a contrary expectation, and wherefore I deem Philip an enemy; that, if I appear to have the clearer foresight, you may hearken to me; if they, who have such confidence and trust in Philip, you may give your adherence to them.

Thus then I reason, Athenians. What did Philip first make himself master of after the peace? Thermopylæ and the Phocian state. Well, and how used he his power? He chose to act for the benefit of Thebes, not of Athens. Why so? Because, I conceive, measuring his calculations by ambition, by his desire of universal empire, without regard to peace, quiet, or justice, he saw plainly that to a people of our character and principles nothing could he offer or give, that would induce you for self-interest to sacrifice any of the Greeks to him. He sees that you, having respect for justice, dreading the infamy of the thing, and exercising proper forethought, would oppose him in any such attempt as much as if you were at war: but the Thebans he expected (and events prove him right) would, in return for the services done them, allow him in everything else to have his way, and, so far from thwarting or impeding him, would fight on his side if he required it. From the same persuasion he befriended lately the Messenians and Argives, which is the highest panegyric upon you, Athenians; for you are adjudged by these proceedings to be the only people incapable of betraying for lucre the national rights of Greece, or bartering your attachment to her for any obligation or benefit. And this opinion of you, that (so different) of the Argives and Thebans, he has naturally formed, not only from a view of present times, but by reflection on the past. For assuredly he finds and hears that your ancestors, who might have governed the rest of Greece on terms of submitting to Persia, not only spurned the proposal, when Alexander,[1] this man's ancestor, came as herald to negotiate, but preferred to abandon their country and endure any suffering, and thereafter achieved such exploits as all the world loves to mention, though none could ever speak them worthily, and therefore I must be silent; for their deeds are too mighty to be uttered in words. But the forefathers of the Argives and Thebans, they either joined the barbarian's army, or did not oppose it; and therefore he knows that both will selfishly embrace

[1] Alexander of Macedon, son of Amyntas, was sent by Mardonius, the Persian commander, to offer the most favourable terms to the Athenians, if they would desert the cause of the Greeks. The Spartans at the same time sent an embassy, to remind them of their duty. The spirited reply which the Athenians made to both embassies is related by Herodotus.

their advantage, without considering the common interest of the Greeks. He thought then, if he chose your friendship, it must be on just principles; if he attached himself to them, he should find auxiliaries of his ambition. This is the reason of his preferring them to you both then and now. For certainly he does not see them with a larger navy than you, nor has he acquired an inland empire and renounced that of the sea and the ports, nor does he forget the professions and promises on which he obtained the peace.

Well, it may be said, he knew all this, yet he so acted, not from ambition or the motives which I charge, but because the demands of the Thebans were more equitable than yours. Of all pleas, this now is the least open to him. He that bids the Lacedæmonians resign Messene, how can he pretend, when he delivered Orchomenos and Coronea to the Thebans, to have acted on a conviction of justice?

But, forsooth, he was compelled—this plea remains—he made concessions against his will, being surrounded by Thessalian horse and Theban infantry. Excellent! So of his intentions they talk; he will mistrust the Thebans; and some carry news about, that he will fortify Elatea. All this he intends and will intend, I dare say; but to attack the Lacedæmonians on behalf of Messene and Argos he does not intend; he actually sends mercenaries and money into the country, and is expected himself with a great force. The Lacedæmonians, who are enemies of Thebes, he overthrows; the Phocians, whom he himself before destroyed, will he now preserve?

And who can believe this? I cannot think that Philip either if he was forced into his former measures, or if he were now giving up the Thebans, would pertinaciously oppose their enemies; his present conduct rather shows that he adopted those measures by choice. All things prove to a correct observer that his whole plan of action is against our state. And this has now become to him a sort of necessity. Consider. He desires empire: he conceives you to be his only opponents. He has been for some time wronging you, as his own conscience best informs him, since, by retaining what belongs to you, he secures the rest of his dominion: had he given up Amphipolis and Potidæ, he deemed himself unsafe at home. He knows therefore, both that he is plotting against you, and that you are aware of it; and, supposing you to have intelligence, he thinks you must hate him; he is alarmed, expecting some disaster, if you get the chance, unless he hastes to prevent you. Therefore he is awake, and on the watch against us; he courts certain people, Thebans, and people in Peloponnesus of the like views, who from cupidity, he thinks, will be satisfied with the present, and from dullness of understanding will foresee none of the consequences. And yet men of even moderate sense might notice striking facts, which had occasion to quote to the Messenians and Argives, and perhaps it is better they should be repeated to you.

Ye men of Messene, said I, how do ye think the Olynthians would have brooked to hear anything against Philip at those times, when he surrendered to them Anthemus, which all former kings of Macedonia claimed, when he cast out the Athenian colonists and gave them Potidæa, taking on himself your enmity, and giving them the land to enjoy? Think ye they expected such treatment as they got, or would have believed it if they had been told? Nevertheless, said I, they, after enjoying for a short time the land of others, are for a long time deprived by him of their own, shamefully expelled, not only vanquished, but betrayed by one another and sold. In truth, these too close connections with despots are not safe for republics. The Thessalians, again, think ye, said I, when he ejected their tyrants, and gave back Nicæa and Magnesia, they expected to have the decemvirate [1] which is now estab-

---

[1] Thessaly was anciently divided into four districts, each called a *tetras*, and this, as we learn from the third Philippic, was restored soon after the termination of the Sacred war. The object of Philip in effecting this arrangement was, no doubt, to weaken the influence of the great Thessalian families by a division of power; otherwise the Pheræan tyranny might have been exchanged for an oligarchy

lished? or that he who restored the meeting at Pylæ [1] would take away their revenues? Surely not. And yet these things have occurred, as all mankind may know. You behold Philip, I said, a dispenser of gifts and promises: pray, if you are wise, that you may never know him for a cheat and a deceiver. By Jupiter, I said, there are manifold contrivances for the guarding and defending of cities, as ramparts, walls, trenches, and the like: these are all made with hands, and require expense; but there is one common safeguard in the nature of prudent men, which is a good security for all, but especially for democracies against despots. What do I mean? Mistrust. Keep this, hold to this; preserve this only, and you can never be injured. What do ye desire? Freedom. Then see ye not that Philip's very titles are at variance therewith? Every king and despot is a foe to freedom, an antagonist to laws. Will ye not beware, I said, lest, seeking deliverance from war, you find a master?

They heard me with a tumult of approbation; and many other speeches they heard from the ambassadors, both in my presence and afterwards; yet none the more, as it appears, will they keep aloof from Philip's friendship and promises. And no wonder, that Messenians and certain Peloponnesians should act contrary to what their reason approves; but you, who understand yourselves, and by us orators are told, how you are plotted against, how you are inclosed! you, I fear, to escape present exertion, will come to ruin ere you are aware. So doth the moment's ease and indulgence prevail over distant advantage.

As to your measures, you will in prudence, I presume, consult hereafter by yourselves. I will furnish you with such an answer as it becomes the assembly to decide upon.

powerful enough to be independent of Macedonia. The decemvirate here spoken of was a further contrivance to forward Philip's views.

[1] *Pylæ*, which signifies *gates*, was a name applied by the Greeks to divers passes, or defiles, but especially to the pass of *Thermopylæ*, which opened through the ridges of Mont Œta into the country of the Epicnemidian Locrians, and was so called from the hot sulphureous springs that gushed from the foot of the mountain.

*[Here the proposed answer was read]*

It were just, men of Athens, to call the persons who brought those promises, on the faith whereof you concluded peace. For I should never have submitted to go as ambassador, and you would certainly not have discontinued the war, had you supposed that Philip, on obtaining peace, would act thus; but the statements then made were very different. Aye, and others you should call. Whom? The men who declared—after the peace, when I had returned from my second mission, that for the oaths, when, perceiving your delusion, I gave warning, and protested, and opposed the abandonment of Thermopylæ and the Phocians—that I, being a water-drinker,[1] was naturally a churlish and morose fellow, that Philip, if he passed the straits, would do just as you desired, fortify Thespiæ and Platæ, humble the Thebans, cut through the Chersonese [2] at his own expense, and give you Oropus and Eubœa in exchange for Amphipolis. All these declarations on the hustings I am sure you remember, though you are not famous for remembering injuries. And, the most disgraceful thing of all, you voted in your confidence, that this same peace should descend to your posperity, so completely were you misled. Why mention I this now, and desire these men to be called? By the gods, I will tell you the truth frankly and without reserve. Not that I may fall a-wrangling, to provoke recrimination before you, and afford my old adversaries a fresh pretext for getting more from Philip, nor for the purpose of idle garrulity. But I imagine that what Philip is doing will grieve you hereafter more than it does now. I see the thing progressing, and would that my surmises were false; but I doubt it is too near already. So when you are able no longer to disregard events, when,

---

[1] It was Philocrates who said this. There were many jokes against Demosthenes as a water-drinker.

[2] This peninsula being exposed to incursions from Thrace, a plan was conceived of cutting through the isthmus from Pteleon to Leuce Acte, to protect the Athenian settlements.

instead of hearing from me or others that these measures are against Athens, you all see it yourselves, and know it for certain, I expect you will be wrathful and exasperated. I fear then, as your ambassadors have concealed the purpose for which they know they were corrupted, those who endeavour to repair what the others have lost may chance to encounter your resentment; for I see it is a practice with many to vent their anger, not upon the guilty, but on persons most in their power. Whilst therefore the mischief is only coming and preparing, whilst we hear one another speak, I wish every man, though he knows it well, to be reminded, who it was [1] persuaded you to abandon Phocis and Thermo-pylæ, but the command of which Philip commands the road to Attica and Peloponnesus, and has brought it to this, that your deliberation must be, not about claims and interests abroad, but concerning the defence of your home and a war in Attica, which will grieve every citizen when it comes, and indeed it has commenced from that day. Had you not been then deceived, there would be nothing to distress the state. Philip would certainly never have prevailed at sea and come to Attica with a fleet, nor would he have marched with a land-force by Phocis and Thermopylæ: he must either have acted honourably, observing the peace and keeping quiet, or been immediately in a war similar to that which made him desire the peace. Enough has been said to awaken recol-lection. Grant, O ye gods, it be not all fully confirmed! I would have no man punished, though death he may deserve, to the damage and danger of the country.

[1] He means Æschines.

# THE ORATION ON THE CHERSONESE

## ARGUMENT

THE Athenians had sent a body of citizens, commanded by Diopithes, to receive allotments of land in the Chersonese, and at the same time to protect the interests of Athens by acting as an army of observation. They soon fell into disputes with the Cardians about the limits of their territory. Philip, who at this time was engaged in a Thracian war, sent assistance to the Cardians; but Diopithes, having collected a troop of mercenaries, kept the field successfully, and, not content with acting on the defensive, carried the war into Thrace, assisted the enemies of Philip, and wrested from him some of his conquests. Philip, who, as we have seen in the last oration, had written before to the Athenians on the subject of Cardia, now wrote them a letter complaining of the conduct of Diopithes, charging them with an infringement of the peace. This letter arrived early in the summer of the year B.C. 342, and an assembly was immediately called to consider what measures should be taken. The Macedonian party were vehement in denouncing Diopithes, and urging his recall. Demosthenes, seeing that Athens, though nominally at peace with Philip, was really defending herself against his aggressions, rose to justify Diopithes, insisted on the necessity, which he had so strongly urged in the first Philippic, of keeping a permanent force on the northern coast, and contended that the army of Diopithes should rather be reinforced than recalled at a time when its presence was peculiarly necessary. He again warns his countrymen of impending danger, and points out the measures which, as men of spirit and prudence, they ought to pursue.

This oration is full of good sense and manly eloquence. It had the success which it deserved. Diopithes was continued in his command; and the exertions of Athens in the next few years had the effect of preserving the Chersonese and the Bosphorus.

Diopithes was father to Menander, the celebrated comic poet, whose plays have been copied by Terence.

IT were just, men of Athens, that the orators in your assembly should make no speeches to gratify either friendship or malice, but every one declare what he considers for the best, especially when you are deliberating on public measures of importance. However, since there are persons who are impelled to address you from factious motives, or others which I cannot name, it becomes you, Athenians, the majority laying all else aside, to determine and to do what you find beneficial to the state. The serious question here is, the position of the Chersonese, and the campaign in Thrace, which Philip has now for upwards of ten months been carrying on; yet most of the speeches have been about Diopithes, his conduct and designs. It seems to me, that on a charge against any of these men, whom according to the laws you may punish when you please, it is in your option either to proceed immediately or at a later time, and needless for me, or for any one, to argue the point strongly: but for the defence of our dominions, which Philip, our standing enemy, and now in great force about the Hellespont, is making haste to conquer, and, if we are once too late, we shall never recover, our duty is to consult and prepare with the utmost speed, and not for clamours and charges about other matters to run off from this.

I wonder at many things which are commonly said here, but I have been particularly surprised, Athenians, at what I lately heard a man declare in the Council,[1] that a statesman's advice should be, either to make war decidedly, or to observe the peace. True; if Philip keeps quiet, neither holding any of our territories contrary to the treaty, nor packing a world of enemies against us, there is nothing to say: peace we must absolutely observe, and I see every readiness on your part. But if the conditions of the peace, which we swore to, are recorded and open to inspection; if it appears that from the beginning (before Diopithes and the settlers,[2] who are accused as authors of the war, ever sailed from Athens) Philip has robbed us of divers territories, of which you still complain in these unrepealed resolutions, and has been all along incessantly gathering the spoil of other nations, Greek and barbarian, for the materials of an attack upon you, what mean they by saying we must have war or

[1] The Council or Senate of Five Hundred, of which Demosthenes became a member when he was thirty-six years of age.

[2] The settlers were citizens sent out to receive parcels of land in some country dependent on Athens, but who still retained rights of Athenian citizenship, whether or not they permanently resided abroad. The word signifies " allotment-holders," or " allottees of lands."

peace? We have no choice in the matter: there remains but one most just and necessary course, which these men purposely overlook. What is it? To defend ourselves against an aggressor. Unless indeed they mean, that, so long as Philip keeps aloof from Attica and Piræus, he neither wrongs you nor commits hostility.[1] But if they put our rights on this principle, and so define the peace, besides that the argument is iniquitous, monstrous, and perilous for Athens, as I imagine is evident to all, it happens also to be inconsistent with their complaint against Diopithes. For why, I wonder, should we give Philip licence to do what he pleases, provided he abstain from Attica, while Diopithes is not suffered even to assist the Thracians, without our saying that he makes war? Here, it will be granted, they are shown in the wrong: but the mercenaries make sad work ravaging the Hellespontine coast, and Diopithes has no right to detain vessels, and we must not allow him! Well; be it so! I am content. Yet I think, if they really give this counsel in good faith, as their object is to disband a force in your service, while they denounce the general who maintains it, they ought likewise to show that Philip's army will be disbanded if you follow their advice. Otherwise, observe, they just bring the country into the same way, through which all our past measures have miscarried. For you surely know that by nothing in the world has Philip beaten us so much as by being earlier in his operations. He with an army always attending him, knowing his own designs, pounces on whom he pleases in a moment: we, when we hear that something is going on, begin to bustle and prepare. Methinks the result is that he very quietly secures what he goes for; we arrive too late, and have incurred all the expense for nothing. Our enmity and our hostile intention we manifest, and get the disgrace of missing the time for action.

[1] Philip sought to conquer Athens in Thrace, as Napoleon to conquer England in Egypt or Portugal. And we shall find that precisely the same arguments were used in our Parliament, to show the necessity of continuing the French war, which Demosthenes here urges to alarm the Athenians against Philip.

Then be sure, Athenians, now, that all the rest is talk and pretence, the real aim and contrivance is, that while you remain at home, and the country has no force abroad, Philip may accomplish what he pleases without interruption. First, consider what is actually going on. Philip is staying with a large army in Thrace, and sending for reinforcements, as eye-witnesses report, from Macedonia and Thessaly. Now, should he wait for the trade-winds, and then march to the siege of Byzantium,[1] think ye the Byzantines would persist in their present folly, and would not invite you and implore your assistance? I don't believe it. No; they will receive any people, even those they distrust more than us, sooner than surrender their city to Philip; unless indeed he is beforehand with them and captures it. If then we are unable to sail northwards, and there be no help at hand, nothing can prevent their destruction. Well! the men are infatuated and besotted. Very likely; yet they must be rescued for all that, because it is good for Athens. And this also is not clear to us, that he will not attack the Chersonese: nay, if we may judge from the letter which he sent us, he says he will chastise the people in the Chersonese. Then if the present army be kept on foot, it will be able to defend that country, and attack some of Philip's dominions; but if it be once disbanded, what shall we do if he march against the Chersonese? Try Diopithes, I suppose. And how will our affairs be bettered? But we shall send succour from Athens. And suppose the winds prevent us? Oh, but he won't come! And who will insure that? Do you mark and consider, men of Athens, the approaching season of the year, against which certain persons desire to get the Hellespont clear of you, and deliver it up to Philip? Suppose he should leave Thrace, and without going near Chersonesus or Byzantium (I beg

---

[1] Athens and Byzantium had not been on good terms since the Social war. Even at this period the Byzantines looked with more suspicion upon the Athenians than upon Philip. Yet less than a year elapsed before the predictions of Demosthenes were fulfilled. Athens was in alliance with Byzantium, and defending her successfully against Philip.

you also to consider this) he should invade Chalcis or Megara, as he lately did Oreus,[1] think you it is better to resist him here and suffer the war to approach Attica, or to find employment for him yonder?   I think the last.

With such facts and arguments before you, so far from disparaging and seeking to disband this army, which Diopithes is endeavouring to organise for Athens, you ought yourselves to provide an additional one, to support him with money and other friendly co-operation.   For if Philip were asked, " Which would you prefer, that these soldiers of Diopithes, whatever be their character (I dispute not about that) should thrive and have credit at Athens, and be reinforced with the assistance of the state, or that they should be dispersed and destroyed at the instance of calumniators and accusers? " —I think he would say, the latter.   And what Philip would pray to the gods for, certain persons among us are bringing about; and after this you ask how the state is ruined!

I wish, therefore, to examine with freedom our present affairs, to consider how we are dealing with them, and what we are ourselves about.   We like not to contribute money, we dare not take the field, we cannot abstain from the public funds, we neither give supplies to Diopithes nor approve what he finds for himself, but grumble and inquire how he got them, and what he intends to do, and the like; and yet, though thus disposed, we are not willing to mind our own business, but with our mouths applaud those who speak worthily of the state, whilst in action we co-operate with their adversaries.   You like always to ask the speaker—What must we do?   I will ask you this—What must I say?   For if you will neither contribute, nor take the field, nor abstain from the public funds, nor give supplies to Diopithes, nor let alone what he finds for himself, nor be content to mind your own business, I have nothing to say.   If to these men, so prompt to accuse and calumniate, you already give such a

---

[1] Oreus of Eubœa was betrayed to Philip not long before this time, as explained in the third Philippic.   The designs of Philip on Megara were baffled.

licence, as to hear them complain by anticipation of projects which they impute to Diopithes, what can one say?

But the probable effect of such conduct some of you should hear. I will speak frankly; indeed, I could not speak otherwise. All the generals who have ever sailed from Athens (or let me suffer any penalty) take money from Chians, from Erythræans,[1] from whom they severally can, I mean from the people who dwell in Asia. Those who have one or two galleys take less, those who have a greater fleet, more. And the givers give not, either the small or the larger sums, for nothing (they are not so mad), but by way of bargain, that the merchants who leave their harbours may not be wronged or plundered, that their vessels may be convoyed, or the like. They say they give benevolences:[2] that is the name of the presents. And so Diopithes, having an army, is well aware that all these people will give money: for how else do you suppose that a man who has received nothing from you, and has nothing of his own to pay withal, can maintain his troops? From the skies? Impossible. He goes on with what he collects, begs, or borrows. Therefore they, who accuse him before you, in effect warn all people to give him nothing, as being sure to be punished for his intentions, much more for his acts, either as principal or auxiliary. Hence their clamours—he is preparing a siege! he is giving up the Greeks! So concerned are many of these persons for the Asiatic Greeks: perhaps quicker to feel for strangers than for their country. And this is the meaning of our sending another general to the Hellespont. Why, if Diopithes commits outrage and detains vessels, a small, very small summons, men of Athens, can stop it all; and the laws prescribe this, to impeach the guilty parties, but not to watch them ourselves at a great expense and with a large

---

[1] Erythræ is a city of Asia Minor.

[2] It is singular that the same name should be given so many centuries after to the illegal contributions which were extorted by some of our English kings from their subjects, under the pretence of their being voluntary gifts. Edward IV. and Henry VII. were most oppressive in this way.

navy, for that were the extreme of madness. Against our enemies, whom we cannot bring under the laws, it is right and needful to maintain troops, and despatch a fleet, and contribute money; but against ourselves a decree, an impeachment, the state-galley,[1] are sufficient. Thus would men of discretion act; malignant and mischievous politicians would proceed as these do. And that certain of these men are thus disposed, bad though it be, is not the worst. For you of the assembly are so minded now that if any one comes forward and says that Diopithes is the author of all your misfortunes, or Chares, or Aristophon, or what citizen he likes to name, you instantly assent and shout approbation; but if one rises to speak the truth—Athenians, you are trifling; of all these misfortunes and troubles Philip is the cause; had he only kept quiet, the state would have had no trouble—you are unable to contradict these statements, yet, methinks, you are annoyed, and feel as if something were lost. The reason is—and pray allow me, when I speak for the best, to speak freely—certain statesmen have long since got you to be severe and terrible in the assemblies, in warlike preparations feeble and contemptible. If the party blamed be one whom you are certain to find within your reach, you say aye, and are content: but if one be accused, whom you cannot punish without vanquishing him by arms, you appear confounded and pained at the exposure. It ought, Athenians, to have been the reverse; your statesmen should have accustomed you to be mild and merciful in the assembly, since there your dealings are with citizens and allies; in warlike preparations they should have shown you to be terrible and severe, since in them the contest is with adversaries and foes. But by excessive coaxing and humouring they have brought you to such a condition, that in the assembly you give yourselves airs and are flattered at hearing nothing but compliments,

---

[1] The Paralus, or the Salaminia, which were employed for state purposes, and sometimes to fetch home criminals to be tried or punished. Thus the Salaminia was despatched to bring Alcibiades back from Sicily.

whilst in your measures and proceedings you are putting everything to hazard.

By Jupiter! suppose the Greeks called you to account for the opportunities which you have indolently lost, and asked you, saying, " Men of Athens, you send us ambassadors on every occasion, and assert that Philip is plotting against us and all the Greeks, and that we should take precautions against the man, and more to the same effect" (we must admit and acknowledge it; for so we do); "and yet, O ye wretchedest of mankind, though Philip has been ten months away, and by illness and winter and wars prevented from returning home, you have neither liberated Eubœa, nor recovered any of your dominions. He, on the contrary, whilst you were staying at home, at leisure, in health (if men so acting may be called in health), established two rulers in Eubœa, one like a hostile fortress opposite Attica, one threatening Sciathus; [1] and these nuisances you have never got rid of; not even this would ye attempt; you have submitted, left the road open to him clearly, and made it manifest that, if he died a hundred times, you would stir never a step the more.   Then wherefore send embassies and make accusations and give us trouble? " If they asked this, what could we answer or say, men of Athens? I really cannot tell.

There are some persons indeed, who imagine they confute the speaker by asking, What must we do? I can give them a perfectly just and true answer—Do not what you are now doing: however, I will enter into more full detail; and I trust they will be as ready to act as to interrogate. First, men of Athens, you must be satisfied in your minds that Philip is at war with the republic, and has broken the peace (pray cease reproaching one another about this); that he is

[1] Clitarchus was established in Eretria, which is opposite the coast of Athens; Philistides in Oreus, which is in the north of Eubœa. The island of Sciathus is a little above Eubœa, and off the Magnesian coast of Thessaly.   As the group of islands, of which Sciathus was one, belonged to Athens, Oreus was a dangerous position to be occupied by an enemy.

ill-disposed and hostile to all Athens, to her very ground, and (I may say) to all her inhabitants, even those who think they oblige him most. Or let them look at Euthycrates and Lasthenes the Olynthians,[1] who fancied themselves on the most friendly footing with him, but, since they betrayed their country, are sunk to the most abject state. But there is nothing that his wars and his schemes are directed against so much as our constitution; nothing in the world is he so earnest to destroy. And this policy is in some sort natural for him. He knows perfectly that even if he conquer everything else he can hold nothing secure while your democracy subsists; but on the occurrence of any reverse (and many may happen to a man), all who are now under constraint will come and seek refuge with you. For you are not inclined yourselves to encroach and usurp dominion; you are famous for checking the usurper or depriving him of his conquest; ever ready to molest the aspirants for empire, and vindicate the liberties of all people. He likes not that a free spirit should proceed from Athens, to watch the moments of his peril: far otherwise; nor is his reasoning weak or idle. First then, you must assume him for this reason to be an irreconcilable enemy of our constitution and democracy: without such conviction upon your minds you will have no zeal for public duty. Secondly, you must be assured that all his operations and contrivances are planned against our country, and, wherever he is resisted, the resistance will be for our benefit. None of you surely is so foolish as to suppose that Philip covets those miseries in Thrace (for what else can one call Drongilus, and Cabyle, and Mastira, and the places which he is taking and conquering now?) and to get them endures toils and winters and the extreme of danger, but covets not the Athenian harbours, and docks, and galleys, and silver-mines,[2] and revenues of such value; and that he

---

[1] They betrayed Olynthus to Philip, and went to reside afterwards at his court. But they were universally scouted as traitors, and on their complaining to Philip, he said, the Macedonians were a plain-spoken people, who called a spade a spade.

[2] The mines of Laurium in Attica.

will suffer you to keep them, while for the sake of the barley and millet in Thracian caverns he winters in the midst of horrors.[1] Impossible. The object of that and every other enterprise is to become master here. What then is the duty of wise men? With these assurances and convictions, to lay aside an indolence which is becoming outrageous and incurable, to pay contributions and to call upon your allies, see to and provide for the continuance of the present force, that, as Philip has a power ready to injure and enslave all the Greeks, so you may have one ready to save and to succour all. It is not possible with hasty levies to perform any effective service. You must have an army on foot, provide maintenance for it, and paymasters and commissaries, so ordering it that the strictest care shall be taken of your funds, and demand from those officers an account of the expenditure, from your general an account of the campaign. If ye so act and so resolve in earnest, you will compel Philip to observe a just peace and abide in his own country (the greatest of all blessings), or you will fight him on equal terms.

It may be thought, and truly enough, that these are affairs of great expense and toil and trouble: yet only consider what the consequences to us must be, if we decline these measures, and you will find it is our interest to perform our duties cheerfully. Suppose some god would be your surety —for certainly no mortal could guarantee such an event— that, notwithstanding you kept quiet and abandoned everything, Philip would not attack you at last, yet, by Jupiter and all the gods, it were disgraceful, unworthy of yourselves, of the character of Athens and the deeds of your ancestors, for the sake of selfish ease to abandon the rest of Greece to servitude. For my own part, I would rather die than have given such counsel; though, if another man advises it, and you are satisfied, well and good; make no resistance, abandon

---

[1] The original signifies a pit, into which condemned criminals were thrown at Athens. It is pretty much the same as if we were to speak of the black hole: and the horrors of Thrace would convey to an Athenian the same sort of idea as the horrors of Siberia to an Englishman.

all. If, however, no man holds this opinion, if, on the contrary, we all foresee, that the more we let Philip conquer the more ruthless and powerful an enemy we shall find him, what subterfuge remains? what excuse for delay? Or when, O Athenians, shall we be willing to perform our duty? Peradventure, when there is some necessity. But what may be called the necessity of freemen is not only come but past long ago; and surely you must deprecate that of slaves. What is the difference? To a freeman, the greatest necessity is shame for his proceedings; I know not what greater you can suggest: to a slave, stripes and bodily chastisement; abominable things! too shocking to mention!

I would gladly enter into every particular, and show how certain politicians abuse you; but I confine myself to one. When any question about Philip arises, people start up and cry, What a blessing it is to be at peace! what a burden to maintain a large army! certain persons wish to plunder our treasury!—and more to the same effect; by which they amuse you, and leave him at leisure to do what he pleases. The result is to you, Athenians, ease and idleness for the present, which, I fear, you may hereafter think dearly purchased; to these men, popularity and payment for their speeches. Methinks it is not you that need persuading to peace, who sit here pacifically disposed, but the person who commits hostilities: let him be persuaded, and all is ready on your part. Burdensome we should deem, not what we expend for our deliverance, but what we shall suffer in case of our refusal to do so. Plunder of the treasury should be prevented by a plan for its safe keeping, not by abandonment of our interests. But this very thing makes me indignant, that some of you, Athenians, are grieved at the thought of your treasury being robbed, though it depends on yourselves to keep it safe and to chastise the peculator, yet are not grieved at Philip's conduct, seizing thus successively on every country in Greece, and seizing them for his designs upon you.

What then is the reason, men of Athens, that while Philip is thus openly in arms, committing aggressions, capturing cities, none of these persons ever say that he is making war; but they denounce as authors of the war whoever advises you to oppose him and prevent these losses?    I will explain. Their desire is that any anger, which may be naturally excited by your sufferings in the war, may be turned upon your honest counsellors, so that you may try them instead of resisting Philip, and they themselves be accusers instead of paying the penalty of their conduct.    Such is the meaning of their assertion that there is a war-party among you; and such is the object of this present debate.    I am indeed sure, that, before any Athenian moved a declaration of war, Philip had taken many of our possessions, and recently sent succour to Cardia.    If however we choose to assume that he is not at war with us, it were extreme folly in him to convince us of our mistake.    But when he marches to attack us, what shall we say?    He will assure us that he is not making war, as he assured the people of Oreus when his troops were in their country, as he assured the Pheræans before he assaulted their walls, and the Olynthians at first, until he was actually in their territories with his army.    Shall we then declare that men who bid us defend ourselves make war?    If so, we must be slaves: nothing else remains, if we neither resist nor are suffered to be at peace.    And remember, you have more at stake than other people: Philip seeks not to subdue, but to extirpate our city.    He knows for certain you will not submit to servitude; you could not if you would, being accustomed to empire; and if you get the opportunity, you will be able to give him more annoyance than all the rest of the world.

You must therefore be convinced that this is a struggle for existence: these men who have sold themselves to Philip you must execrate and cudgel to death; for it is impossible, impossible to overcome your enemies abroad, until you have punished your enemies (his ministers) at home.    They will be the stumbling-blocks that prevent your reaching the others. Why do you suppose Philip now insults you (for to this, in my opinion, his conduct amounts), and while to other people, though he deceives them, he at least renders services, he is already threatening you? For example, the Thessalians by many benefits he seduced into their present servitude: how he cheated the wretched Olynthians, first giving them Potidæa and divers other things, no man can describe: now he is enticing the Thebans by giving up to them Bœotia, and delivering them from a toilsome and vexatious war. Thus did each of these people grasp a certain advantage, but some of them have suffered what all the world know, others will suffer what may hereafter befall them. From you—all that has been taken I recount not: but in the very making of the peace, how have you been abused! how despoiled! Of Phocis, Thermopylæ, places in Thrace, Doriscus, Serrium, Cersobleptes himself! Does he not now possess the city of Cardia and avow it? Wherefore, I say, deals he thus with other people, and not in the same manner with you? Because yours is the only state in which a privilege is allowed of speaking for the enemy, and an individual taking a bribe may safely address the assembly, though you have been robbed of your dominions. It was not safe at Olynthus to be Philip's advocate, unless the Olynthian commonly had shared the advantage by possession of Potidæa: it was not safe in Thessaly to be Philip's advocate, unless the people of Thessaly had shared the advantage, by Philip's expelling their tyrants and restoring the Pylæan synod: it was not safe in Thebes, until he gave up Bœotia to them and destroyed the Phocians. Yet at Athens, though Philip has deprived you of Amphipolis and the Cardian territory, nay, is even making Eubœa a fortress to curb us, and advancing to attack Byzantium, it is safe to speak on Philip's behalf. Therefore of these men, some, from being poor, have become rapidly rich, from nameless and obscure, have become honoured and distinguished; you have done the reverse, fallen from

honour to obscurity, from wealth to poverty; for I deem
the riches of a state, allies, confidence, attachment, of all
which you are destitute. And from your neglecting these
matters and suffering them to be lost, Philip has grown
prosperous and mighty, formidable to all the Greeks and
barbarians, whilst you are abject and forlorn, magnificent
in the abundance of your market, but in provision for actual
need ridiculous. I observe, however, that some of our orators
take different thought for you and for themselves. You,
they say, should be quiet even under injustice; they cannot
live in quiet among you themselves, though no man injures
them.

Then some one steps forward and says, " Why, you won't
move any resolution, or run any risk; you are cowardly and
faint-hearted." Let me say this: bold, brutal, and impudent
I neither am nor wish to be; yet, methinks, I possess far
more courage than your headstrong politicians. For a man
who, neglecting the interest of the state, tries, confiscates,
bribes, accuses, does not act from any courage, Athenians;
the popularity of his speeches and his measures serves for a
pledge of security, and he is bold without danger. But one
who acting for the best frequently opposes your wishes, who
never speaks to flatter but always to benefit you, and adopts
a line of policy in which more depends on fortune than on
calculations, while he makes himself responsible to you for
both, this is a courageous man, aye, and a useful citizen is he;
not they who for ephemeral pleasure have thrown away the
main resources of the country; whom I am so far from emulat-
ing or esteeming as worthy citizens of Athens, that if I were
asked to declare, what service I had done the state, although,
ye men of Athens, I could mention services as ship-captain
and choir-master, payment of contributions, ransom of
prisoners, and similar acts of liberality, I would mention none
of them; I would say that I espouse a different course of
politics from these, that although I might perhaps, like
others, accuse and bribe and confiscate and do everything

which these men do, I have never engaged myself in such a
task, never been induced either by avarice or ambition; I
continue to offer counsel, by which I sink below others in
your regard; but you, if you followed it, would be exalted.
So perhaps might one speak without offence. I consider it
not the part of an honest citizen to devise measures by which
I shall speedily become the first among you, and you the last
among nations: with the measures of good citizens the
advancement of their country should keep pace; their
counsel should still be the salutary, rather than the agreeable:
to the latter will nature herself incline; to the former a good
citizen must direct by argument and instruction.

I have ere now heard an objection of this kind, that true
it is I always advise for the best, yet my services are only
words, and you want deeds and something practical. Upon
which I will tell you my sentiments without reserve. I do
not think a counsellor has any other business but to give the
best advice: and that this is so I can easily demonstrate.
You are aware, doubtless, that the brave Timotheus once
harangued the people, urging them to send troops and save
the Eubœans, when the Thebans were attempting their conquest; and to this effect he spake:—" What? do you deliberate," said he, " when you have Thebans in the island, how to
deal with them, how to proceed? Will you not cover the
sea, Athenians, with your galleys? Will you not start up
and march to Piræus? will you not launch your vessels?
Thus Timotheus spake and you acted,[1] and through both
together success was obtained. But had his advice been ever
so good, as it was, and you shrunk from exertion and disregarded it, would any of those results have accrued to
Athens? Impossible. Then do likewise in regard to my

[1] Diocles and Chares conducted this expedition, which took place
B.C. 357, and which, after various combats in the island of Eubœa,
ended in the expulsion of the Thebans. Just at that time the finances
of the Athenians were exceedingly low, and the generosity of the
wealthier citizens was largely taxed to provide necessaries for the
armament. Demosthenes himself came forward as a liberal con-
tributor.

counsels or any other man's; for action look to yourselves, to the orator for the best instruction in his power.

I will sum up my advice, and quit the platform. I say, you must contribute money, maintain the existing troops, rectifying what abuses you may discover, but not on the first accusation disbanding the force. Send out ambassadors everywhere, to instruct, to warn, to effect what they can for Athens. Yet further I say, punish your corrupt statesmen, execrate them at all times and places to prove that men of virtue and honourable conduct have consulted wisely both for others and themselves. If you thus attend to your affairs, and cease entirely neglecting them, perhaps, perhaps even yet, they may improve. But while ye sit here, zealous as far as clamour and applause, laggards when any action is required, I see not how any talking, unaided by your needful exertions, can possibly save the country.

# THE THIRD PHILIPPIC

## ARGUMENT

THIS speech was delivered about three months after the last, while
Philip was advancing into Thrace, and threatening both the Chersonese and the Propontine coast. No new event had happened, which
called for any special consultation; but Demosthenes, alarmed by the
formidable character of Philip's enterprise and vast military preparations, felt the necessity of rousing the Athenians to exertion. He
repeats in substance the arguments which he had used in the Oration
on the Chersonese; points out the danger to be apprehended from the
disunion among the Greek states, from their general apathy and lack
of patriotism, which he contrasts with the high and noble spirit of
ancient times. From the past conduct of Philip he shows what is to
be expected in future; explains the difference between Philip's new
method of warfare and that adopted in the Peloponnesian war, and
urges the necessity of corresponding measures for defence. The peace-
ful professions of Philip were not to be trusted; he was never more
dangerous than when he made overtures of peace and friendship.
The most powerful instruments that he employed for gaining ascendancy were the venal orators, who were to be found in every Grecian
city, and on whom it was necessary to inflict signal punishment before
they had a chance of opposing foreign enemies. The advice of Demosthenes now is, to despatch reinforcements to the Chersonese, to stir
up the people of Greece, and even to solicit the assistance of the Persian
king, who had no less reason than themselves to dread the ambition of
Philip.
    The events of the following year, when Philip attacked the Pro-
pontine cities, fully justified the warnings of Demosthenes. And the
extraordinary activity which the Athenians displayed in resisting him
shows that the exertions of the orator had their due effect.

MANY speeches, men of Athens, are made in almost every
assembly about the hostilities of Philip, hostilities which
ever since the treaty of peace he has been committing as well
against you as against the rest of the Greeks; and all (I am
sure) are ready to avow, though they forbear to do so, that
our counsels and our measures should be directed to his
humiliation and chastisement: nevertheless, so low have our
affairs been brought by inattention and negligence, I fear it
is a harsh truth to say, that if all the orators had sought to
suggest, and you to pass resolutions for the utter ruining of

the commonwealth, we could not, methinks, be worse off than we are. A variety of circumstances may have brought us to this state; our affairs have not declined from one or two causes only: but, if you rightly examine, you will find it chiefly owing to the orators, who study to please you rather than advise for the best. Some of whom, Athenians, seeking to maintain the basis of their own power and repute, have no forethought for the future, and therefore think you also ought to have none; others, accusing and calumniating practical statesmen, labour only to make Athens punish Athens, and in such occupation to engage her, that Philip may have liberty to say and do what he pleases. Politics of this kind are common here, but are the causes of your failures and embarrassment. I beg, Athenians, that you will not resent my plain speaking of the truth. Only consider. You hold liberty of speech in other matters to be the general right of all residents in Athens, insomuch that you allow a measure of it even to foreigners and slaves, and many servants may be seen among you speaking their thoughts more freely than citizens in some other states; and yet you have altogether banished it from your councils. The result has been that in the assembly you give yourselves airs and are flattered at hearing nothing but compliments, in your measures and proceedings you are brought to the utmost peril. If such be your disposition now, I must be silent: if you will listen to good advice without flattery, I am ready to speak. For though our affairs are in a deplorable condition, though many sacrifices have been made, still, if you will choose to perform your duty, it is possible to repair it all. A paradox, and yet a truth, am I about to state. That which is the most lamentable in the past is best for the future. How is this? Because you performed no part of your duty, great or small, and therefore you fared ill: had you done all that became you, and your situation were the same, there would be no hope of amendment. Philip has indeed prevailed over your sloth and negligence, but not over the country:

you have not been worsted; you have not even bestirred yourselves.

If now we were all agreed that Philip is at war with Athens and infringing the peace, nothing would a speaker need to urge or advise but the safest and easiest way of resisting him. But since, at the very time when Philip is capturing cities and retaining divers of our dominions and assailing all people, there are men so unreasonable as to listen to repeated declarations in the assembly, that some of us are kindling war, one must be cautious and set this matter right: for whoever moves or advises a measure of defence is in danger of being accused afterwards as author of the war.

I will first then examine and determine this point, whether it be in our power to deliberate on peace or war. If the country may be at peace, if it depends on us (to begin with this), I say we ought to maintain peace, and I call upon the affirmant to move a resolution, to take some measure, and not to palter with us. But if another, having arms in his hand and a large force around him, amuses you with the name of peace, while he carries on the operations of war, what is left but to defend yourselves? You may profess to be at peace, if you like, as he does; I quarrel not with that. But if any man supposes this to be a peace, which will enable Philip to master all else and attack you last, he is a madman, or he talks of a peace observed towards him by you, not towards you by him. This it is that Philip purchases by all his expenditure, the privilege of assailing you without being assailed in turn.

If we really wait until he avows that he is at war with us, we are the simplest of mortals: for he would not declare that, though he marched even against Attica and Piræus, at least if we may judge from his conduct to others. For example, to the Olynthians he declared, when he was forty furlongs from their city, that there was no alternative, but either they must quit Olynthus or he Macedonia; though before that time, whenever he was accused of such an intent, he took it ill and sent ambassadors to justify himself. Again, he marched towards the Phocians as if they were allies, and there were Phocian envoys who accompanied his march, and many among you contended that his advance would not benefit the Thebans. And he came into Thessaly of late as a friend and ally, yet he has taken possession of Pheræ: and lastly he told these wretched people of Oreus,[1] that he had sent his soldiers out of good-will to visit them, as he heard they were in trouble and dissension, and it was the part of allies and true friends to lend assistance on such occasions. People who would never have harmed him, though they might have adopted measures of defence, he chose to deceive rather than warn them of his attack; and think ye he would declare war against you before he began it, and that while you are willing to be deceived? Impossible. He would be the silliest of mankind, if, whilst you the injured parties make no complaint against him, but are accusing your own countrymen, he should terminate your intestine strife and jealousies, warn you to turn against him, and remove the pretexts of his hirelings for asserting, to amuse you, that he makes no war upon Athens. O heavens! would any rational being judge by words rather than by actions, who is at peace with him and who at war? Surely none. Well then; Philip immediately after the peace, before Diopithes was in command or the settlers in the Chersonese had been sent out, took Serrium and Doriscus, and expelled from Serrium and the Sacred Mount the troops whom your general had stationed there.[2] What do you call such conduct? He

---

[1] When he established his creature Philistides in the government of Oreus, as mentioned in the last oration and at the end of this.

[2] This general was Chares, to whom Cersobleptes had entrusted the defence of those places. The Sacred Mount was a fortified position on the northern coast of the Hellespont. It was here that Miltocythes intrenched himself, when he rebelled against Cotys; and Philip took possession of it just before the peace with Athens was concluded, as being important to his operations against Cersobleptes. The statement of Demosthenes, that the oaths had then been taken, is incorrect, for they were sworn afterwards in Thessaly. But the argument is substantially the same; for the peace had been agreed to, and the ratification was purposely delayed by Philip, to gain time for the completion of his designs.

had sworn the peace. Don't say—what does it signify? how is the state concerned?—Whether it be a trifling matter, or of no concernment to you, is a different question: religion and justice have the same obligation, be the subject of the offence great or small. Tell me now; when he sends mercenaries into Chersonesus, which the king and all the Greeks have acknowledged to be yours, when he avows himself an auxiliary and writes us word so, what are such proceedings? He says he is not at war; I cannot however admit such conduct to be an observance of the peace; far otherwise: I say, by his attempt on Megara,[1] by his setting up despotism in Eubœa, by his present advance into Thrace, by his intrigues in Peloponnesus, by the whole course of operations with his army, he has been breaking the peace and making war upon you; unless indeed you will say that those who establish batteries are not at war until they apply them to the walls. But that you will not say: for whoever contrives and prepares the means for my conquest is at war with me before he darts or draws the bow. What, if anything should happen, is the risk you run? The alienation of the Hellespont, the subjection of Megara and Eubœa to your enemy, the siding of the Peloponnesians with him. Then can I allow that one who sets such an engine at work against Athens is at peace with her? Quite the contrary. From the day that he destroyed the Phocians I date his commencement of hostilities. Defend yourselves instantly, and I say you will be wise: delay it, and you may wish in vain to do so hereafter. So much do I dissent from your other counsellors, men of Athens, that I deem any discussion about Chersonesus or Byzantium out of place. Succour them—I advise that—watch that no harm befalls them, send all necessary supplies to your troops in that quarter; but let your deliberations be for the safety of all Greece, as being in the utmost peril. I must tell you why I am so alarmed at the state of our affairs: that, if my

---

[1] Not long before this oration was delivered, Philip was suspected of a design to seize Megara.

reasonings are correct, you may share them, and make some
provision at least for yourselves, however disinclined to do
so for others: but if, in your judgment, I talk nonsense and
absurdity, you may treat me as crazed, and not listen to me,
either now or in future.

That Philip from a mean and humble origin has grown
mighty, that the Greeks are jealous and quarrelling among
themselves, that it was far more wonderful for him to rise
from that insignificance than it would now be, after so many
acquisitions, to conquer what is left; these and similar
matters, which I might dwell upon, I pass over. But I
observe that all people, beginning with you, have conceded to
him a right, which in former times has been the subject of
contest in every Grecian war. And what is this? The right
of doing what he pleases, openly fleecing and pillaging the
Greeks, one after another, attacking and enslaving their
cities. You were at the head of the Greeks for seventy-three
years,[1] the Lacedæmonians for twenty-nine;[2] and the
Thebans had some power in these latter times after the
battle of Leuctra. Yet neither you, my countrymen, nor
Thebans, nor Lacedæmonians, were ever licensed by the
Greeks to act as you pleased; far otherwise. When you, or
rather the Athenians of that time, appeared to be dealing
harshly with certain people, all the rest, even such as had
no complaint against Athens, thought proper to side with
the injured parties in a war against her. So, when the
Lacedæmonians became masters and succeeded to your
empire, on their attempting to encroach and make oppressive
innovations,[3] a general war was declared against them, even

---

[1] This would be from about the end of the Persian war to the end of
the Peloponnesian, B.C. 405.
[2] From the end of the Peloponnesian war to the battle of Naxos,
B.C. 376.
[3] The Spartans, whose severe military discipline rendered them far
the best soldiers of Greece, were totally unfit to manage the empire, at
the head of which they found themselves after the humiliation of
Athens. Their attempt to force an oligarchy upon every dependent
state was an unwise policy, which made them generally odious. The
decemvirates of Lysander, and the governors established in various

by such as had no cause of complaint. But wherefore mention other people? We ourselves and the Lacedæmonians, although at the outset we could not allege any mutual injuries, thought proper to make war for the injustice that we saw done to our neighbours. Yet all the faults committed by the Spartans in those thirty years, and by our ancestors in the seventy, are less, men of Athens, than the wrongs which, in thirteen incomplete years that Philip has been uppermost, he has inflicted on the Greeks: nay they are scarcely a fraction of these, as may easily be shown in a few words. Olynthus and Methone and Apollonia, and thirty-two cities[1] on the borders of Thrace, I pass over; all which he has so cruelly destroyed that a visitor could hardly tell if they were ever inhabited: and of the Phocians, so considerable a people exterminated, I say nothing. But what is the condition of Thessaly? Has he not taken away her constitutions and her cities, and established tetrarchies, to parcel her out, not only by cities, but also by provinces, for subjection? Are not the Eubœan states governed now by despots, and that in an island near to Thebes and Athens? Does he not expressly write in his epistles, " I am at peace with those who are willing to obey me? " Nor does he write so and not act accordingly. He is gone to the Hellespont; he marched formerly against Ambracia; Elis, such an important city in Peloponnesus, he possesses; he plotted lately to get Megara: neither Hellenic nor Barbaric land contains the man's ambition. And we, the Greek community, seeing and hearing this, instead of sending embassies to one another about it and expressing indignation, are in such a miserable state, so intrenched in our separate towns, that to

Greek cities to maintain Lacedæmonian influence, were regarded as instruments of tyranny. It was found that Spartan governors and generals, when away from home, gave loose to their vicious inclinations, as if to indemnify themselves for the strictness of domestic discipline. It became a maxim in their politics that the end justified the means. The most flagrant proof was given by the seizure of the Cadmea at Thebes; a measure which led to a formidable confederacy against Sparta, and brought her to the verge of destruction.

[1] The Chalcidian cities.

this day we can attempt nothing that interest or necessity requires; we cannot combine, or form any association for succour and alliance; we look unconcernedly on the man's growing power, each resolving (methinks) to enjoy the interval that another is destroyed in, not caring or striving for the salvation of Greece: for none can be ignorant that Philip, like some course or attack of fever or other disease, is coming even on those that yet seem very far removed. And you must be sensible that whatever wrong the Greeks sustained from Lacedæmonians or from us, was at least inflicted by genuine people of Greece; and it might be felt in the same manner as if a lawful son, born to a large fortune, committed some fault or error in the management of it; on that ground one would consider him open to censure and reproach, yet it could not be said that he was an alien, and not heir to the property which he so dealt with. But if a slave or a spurious child wasted and spoiled what he had no interest in—Heavens! how much more heinous and hateful would all have pronounced it! And yet in regard to Philip and his conduct they feel not this, although he is not only no Greek and noway akin to Greeks, but not even a barbarian of a place honourable to mention; in fact, a vile fellow of Macedon, from which a respectable slave could not be purchased formerly.

What is wanting to make his insolence complete? Besides his destruction of Grecian cities, does he not hold the Pythian games, the common festival of Greece, and, if he comes not himself, send his vassals to preside? Is he not master of Thermopylæ and the passes into Greece, and holds he not those places by garrisons and mercenaries? Has he not thrust aside Thessalians, ourselves, Dorians, the whole Amphictyonic body, and got preaudience of the oracle,[1] to

---

[1] This privilege, which had belonged to the Phocians, was transferred to Philip. It was considered an advantage as well as an honour in ancient times, for there were only certain days appointed in every month when the oracle could be consulted, and the order of consultation was determined by lot in common cases. The Delphians used to confer the right of pre-consultation on particular states or persons as a

which even the Greeks do not all pretend? Does he not write to the Thessalians what form of government to adopt? send mercenaries to Porthmus,[1] to expel the Eretrian commonalty; others to Oreus, to set up Philistides as ruler? Yet the Greeks endure to see all this; methinks they view it as they would a hailstorm, each praying that it may not fall on himself, none trying to prevent it. And not only are the outrages which he does to Greece submitted to, but even the private wrongs of every people: nothing can go beyond this! Has he not wronged the Corinthians by attacking Ambracia[2] and Leucas? the Achaians, by swearing to give Naupactus[3] to the Ætolians? from the Thebans taken Echinus?[4] Is he not marching against the Byzantines his allies? From us—I omit the rest—but keeps he not Cardia, the greatest city of the Chersonese? Still under these indignities we are all slack and disheartened, and look towards our neighbours, distrusting one another, instead of the common enemy. And how think ye a man, who behaves so insolently to all, how will he act when he gets each separately under his control?

But what has caused the mischief? There must be some cause, some good reason, why the Greeks were so eager for liberty then, and now are eager for servitude. There was

reward for some service or act of piety. Thus the Spartans received it; and Crœsus, king of Lydia, for the magnificent presents which he sent to the temple.

[1] Porthmus was the port of Eretria, on the strait, opposite Athens. The circumstances are stated by Demosthenes at the latter end of the speech.

[2] Divers colonies were planted on the north-western coast of Greece by the Corinthians, and also by the Corcyræans, who were themselves colonists from Corinth. Among them were Leucas, Ambracia, Anactorium, Epidamnus, and Apollonia. Leucas afterwards became insular, by cutting through the isthmus. Philip's meditated attack was in B.C. 343, after the conquest of Cassopia. Leucas, by its insular position, would have been convenient for a descent on Peloponnesus. We have seen that this design of Philip was baffled by the exertions of Demosthenes.

[3] Naupactus, now *Lepanto*, lay on the northern coast of the Corinthian gulf. At the close of the Peloponnesian war it came into the hands of the Achians, from whom it was taken by Epaminondas, but after his death they regained it. The Ætolians got possession of the town some time after, perhaps by Macedonian assistance.

[4] The Echinus here mentioned was a city on the northern coast of the Maliac gulf in Thessaly.

something, men of Athens, something in the hearts of the multitude then, which there is not now, which overcame the wealth of Persia and maintained the freedom of Greece, and quailed not under any battle by land or sea; the loss whereof has ruined all, and thrown the affairs of Greece into confusion. What was this? Nothing subtle or clever: simply that whoever took money from the aspirants for power or the corruptors of Greece were universally detested: it was dreadful to be convicted of bribery; the severest punishment was inflicted on the guilty, and there was no intercession or pardon. The favourable moments for enterprise, which fortune frequently offers to the careless against the vigilant, to them that will do nothing against those that discharge all their duty, could not be bought from orators or generals; no more could mutual concord, nor distrust of tyrants and barbarians, nor anything of the kind. But now all such principles have been sold as in open market, and those imported in exchange, by which Greece is ruined and diseased. What are they? Envy where a man gets a bribe; laughter if he confesses it; mercy to the convicted; hatred of those that denounce the crime: all the usual attendants upon corruption.[1] For as to ships and men and revenues and abundance of other materials, all that may be reckoned as constituting national strength—assuredly the Greeks of our day are more fully and perfectly supplied with such advantages than Greeks of the olden time. But they are all rendered useless, unavailable, unprofitable, by the agency of these traffickers.

That such is the present state of things, you must see, without requiring my testimony: that it was different in former times I will demonstrate, not by speaking my own words, but by showing an inscription of your ancestors, which they graved on a brazen column and deposited in the citadel, not for their own benefit (they were right-minded enough without such records), but for a memorial and ex-

[1] He glances more particularly at Philocrates, Demades, and Æschines.

ample to instruct you, how seriously such conduct should be taken up. What says the inscription then? It says: " Let Arthmius, son of Pythonax the Zelite,[1] be declared an outlaw and an enemy of the Athenian people and their allies, him and his family." Then the cause is written why this was done: because he brought the Median gold into Peloponnesus. That is the inscription. By the gods! only consider and reflect among yourselves, what must have been the spirit, what the dignity of those Athenians who acted so. One Arthmius a Zelite, subject of the king (for Zelea is in Asia), because in his master's service he brought gold into Peloponnesus, not to Athens, they proclaimed an enemy of the Athenians and their allies, him and his family, and outlawed. That is, not the outlawry commonly spoken of: for what would a Zelite care, to be excluded from Athenian franchises? It means not that; but in the statutes of homicide it is written, in cases where a prosecution for murder is not allowed, but killing is sanctioned, " and let him die an outlaw," says the legislator: by which he means, that whoever kills such a person shall be unpolluted. Therefore they considered that the preservation of all Greece was their own concern (but for such opinion, they would not have cared, whether people in Peloponnesus were bought and corrupted), and whomsoever they discovered taking bribes, they chastised and punished so severely as to record their names in brass. The natural result was that Greece was formidable to the Barbarian, not the Barbarian to Greece. 'Tis not so now: since neither in this nor in other respects are your sentiments the same. But what are they? You know yourselves: why am I to upbraid you with everything? The Greeks in general are alike and no better than you. Therefore I say, our present affairs demand earnest attention and wholesome counsel. Shall I say what? Do you bid me, and won't you be angry?

[1] Zelea is a town in Mysia. Arthmius was sent by Artaxerxes into Peloponnesus, to stir up a war against the Athenians, who had irritated him by the assistance which they lent to Egypt.

*[Here is read the public document which Demosthenes produces, after which he resumes his address [1]]*

There is a foolish saying of persons who wish to make us easy, that Philip is not yet as powerful as the Lacedæmonians were formerly, who ruled everywhere by land and sea, and had the king for their ally, and nothing withstood them; yet Athens resisted even that nation, and was not destroyed. I myself believe that, while everything has received great improvement, and the present bears no resemblance to the past, nothing has been so changed and improved as the practice of war. For anciently, as I am informed, the Lacedæmonians and all Grecian people would for four or five months, during the season [2] only, invade and ravage the land of their enemies with heavy-armed and national troops, and return home again: and their ideas were so old-fashioned, or rather national, they never purchased an advantage from any; theirs was a legitimate and open warfare. But now you doubtless perceive that the majority of disasters have been effected by treason; nothing is done in fair field or combat. You hear of Philip marching where he pleases, not because he commands troops of the line, but because he has attached to him a host of skirmishers, cavalry, archers, mercenaries, and the like. When with these he falls upon a people in civil dissension, and none (for mistrust) will march out to defend the country, he applies engines and besieges them. I need not mention that he makes no difference between winter and summer, that he has no stated season of repose. You, knowing these things, reflecting on them, must not let the

[1] The Secretary of the Assembly stood by the side of the orator, and read any public documents, such as statutes, decrees, bills and the like, which the orator desired to refer to or to verify. It does not appear what the document was which Demosthenes caused to be read here. If we may judge from the argument, it was some energetic resolution of the people, such as he would propose for an example on the present occasion.

[2] The campaigning season, during the summer and fine time of the year. The Peloponnesians generally invaded Attica when the corn was ripe, burning and plundering all in their route. Thucydides in his history divides the year into two parts, summer and winter.

war approach your territories, nor get your necks broken,
relying on the simplicity of the old war with the Lacedæmonians, but take the longest time beforehand for defensive
measures and preparations, see that he stirs not from home,
avoid any decisive engagement.  For a war, if we choose,
men of Athens, to pursue a right course, we have many
natural advantages; such as the position of his kingdom,
which we may extensively plunder and ravage, and a thousand
more; but for a battle he is better trained than we are.[1]

Nor is it enough to adopt these resolutions and oppose him
by warlike measures: you must on calculation and on principle abhor his advocates here, remembering that it is impossible to overcome your enemies abroad, until you have
chastised those who are his ministers within the city.  Which,
by Jupiter and all the gods, you cannot and will not do!
You have arrived at such a pitch of folly or madness or—
I know not what to call it: I am tempted often to think, that
some evil genius is driving you to ruin—for the sake of scandal
or envy or jest or any other cause, you command hirelings to
speak (some of whom would not deny themselves to be
hirelings), and laugh when they abuse people.  And this,
bad as it is, is not the worst: you have allowed these persons
more liberty for their political conduct than your faithful
counsellors: and see what evils are caused by listening to such
men with indulgence.  I will mention facts that you will all
remember.

In Olynthus some of the statesmen were in Philip's interest,
doing everything for him; some were on the honest side,
aiming to preserve their fellow-citizens from slavery.  Which
party now destroyed their country? or which betrayed the
cavalry,[2] by whose betrayal Olynthus fell?  The creatures

---

[1] Chæronea proved the wisdom of this advice.  Similar counsel was
given by Pericles in the Peloponnesian war.  Had the Athenians
attempted to meet the invading army in the field, they must inevitably
have been defeated in the early period of the war.
[2] After Olynthus was besieged by Philip, various sallies were made
from the city, some of which were successful.  But the treachery of
Lasthenes and his accomplices ruined all.  A body of five hundred

of Philip; they that, while the city stood, slandered and calumniated the honest counsellors so effectually that the Olynthian people were induced to banish Apollonides.

Nor is it there only, and nowhere else, that such practice has been ruinous. In Eretria, when, after riddance of Plutarch [1] and his mercenaries, the people got possession of their city and of Porthmus, some were for bringing the government over to you, others to Philip. His partisans were generally, rather exclusively, attended to by the wetched and unfortunate Eretrians, who at length were persuaded to expel their faithful advisers. Philip, their ally and friend, sent Hipponicus and a thousand mercenaries, demolished the walls of Porthmus, and established three rulers, Hipparchus, Automedon, Clitarchus. Since that he has driven them out of the country, twice attempting their deliverance: once he sent the troops with Eurylochus, afterwards those of Parmenio.

What need of many words? In Oreus Philip's agents were Philistides, Menippus, Socrates, Thoas, and Agapæus, who now hold the government: that was quite notorious: one Euphræus, a man that formerly dwelt here among you, was labouring for freedom and independence. How this man was in other respects insulted and trampled on by the people of Oreus were long to tell: but a year before the capture, discovering what Philistides and his accomplices were about, he laid an information against them for treason. A multitude then combining, having Philip for their paymaster, and acting under his direction, take Euphræus off to prison as a disturber of the public peace. Seeing which, the people of Oreus, instead of assisting the one and beating the others to death, with them were not angry, but said his punishment was just, and rejoiced at it. So the conspirators, having full liberty of action, laid their schemes and took their measures

horses were led by him into an ambuscade, and captured by the besiegers.

[1] When he was expelled by Phocion after the battle of Tamynæ, B.C. 354.

for the surrender of the city; if any of the people observed it, they were silent and intimidated, remembering the treatment of Euphræus; and so wretched was their condition that on the approach of such a calamity none dared to utter a word, until the enemy drew up before the walls: then some were for defence, others for betrayal. Since the city was thus basely and wickedly taken, the traitors have held despotic rule; people who formerly rescued them, and were ready for any maltreatment of Euphræus, they have either banished or put to death; Euphræus killed himself, proving by deed that he had resisted Philip honestly and purely for the good of his countrymen.

What can be the reason—perhaps you wonder—why the Olynthians and Eretrians and Orites were more indulgent to Philip's advocates than to their own? The same which operates with you. They who advise for the best cannot always gratify their audience, though they would; for the safety of the state must be attended to: their opponents by the very counsel which is agreeable advance Philip's interest. One party required contribution; the other said there was no necessity; one were for war and mistrust; the other for peace, until they were ensnared. And so on for everything else (not to dwell on particulars); the one made speeches to please for the moment, and gave no annoyance; the other offered salutary counsel that was offensive. Many rights did the people surrender at last, not from any such motive of indulgence or ignorance, but submitting in the belief that all was lost. Which, by Jupiter and Apollo, I fear will be your case, when on calculation you see that nothing can be done. I pray, men of Athens, it may never come to this! Better die a thousand deaths than render homage to Philip, or sacrifice any of your faithful counsellors. A fine recompense have the people of Oreus got for trusting themselves to Philip's friends and spurning Euphræus! Finely are the Eretrian commons rewarded, for having driven away your ambassadors and yielded to Clitarchus! Yes; they are slaves, exposed to the lash and the torture. Finely he spared the Olynthians, who appointed Lasthenes to command their horse, and expelled Apollonides! It is folly and cowardice to cherish such hopes, and, while you take evil counsel and shirk every duty, and even listen to those who plead for your enemies, to think you inhabit a city of such magnitude that you cannot suffer any serious misfortune. Yea, and it is disgraceful to exclaim on any occurrence, when it is too late, " Who would have expected it? However—this or that should have been done, the other left undone." Many things could the Olynthians mention now, which, if foreseen at the time, would have prevented their destruction. Many could the Orites mention, many the Phocians, and each of the ruined states. But what would it avail them? As long as the vessel is safe, whether it be great or small, the mariner, the pilot, every man in turn should exert himself, and prevent its being overturned either by accident or design: but when the sea hath rolled over it, their efforts are vain. And we, likewise, O Athenians, whilst we are safe, with a magnificent city, plentiful resources, lofty reputation—what must we do? Many of you, I dare say, have been longing to ask. Well then, I will tell you; I will move a resolution: pass it if you please.

First, let us prepare for our own defence; provide ourselves, I mean, with ships, money, and troops—for surely, though all other people consented to be slaves, we at least ought to struggle for freedom. When we have completed our own preparations and made them apparent to the Greeks, then let us invite the rest, and send our ambassadors everywhere with the intelligence, to Peloponnesus, to Rhodes, to Chios, to the king, I say (for it concerns his interests, not to let Philip make universal conquest); that, if you prevail, you may have partners of your dangers and expenses, in case of necessity, or at all events that you may delay the operations. For, since the war is against an individual, not against the collected power of a state, even this may be useful; as were the embassies last year to Peloponnesus, and the remonstrances with which I and Polyeuctus, that excellent man, and Hegesippus, and Clitomachus, and Lycurgus, and the other envoys went round, and arrested Philip's progress, so that he neither attacked Ambracia nor started for Peloponnesus. I say not, however, that you should invite the rest without adopting measures to protect yourselves: it would be folly, while you sacrifice your own interest, to profess a regard for that of strangers, or to alarm others about the future, whilst for the present you are unconcerned. I advise not this: I bid you send supplies to the troops in Chersonesus, and do what else they require; prepare yourselves and make every effort first, then summon, gather, instruct the rest of the Greeks. That is the duty of a state possessing a dignity such as yours. If you imagine that Chalcidians or Megarians will save Greece, while you run away from the contest, you imagine wrong. Well for any of those people, if they are safe themselves. This work belongs to you: this privilege your ancestors bequeathed to you, the prize of many perilous exertions. But if every one will sit seeking his pleasure, and studying to be idle himself, never will he find others to do his work, and more than this, I fear we shall be under the necessity of doing all that we like not at one time. Were proxies to be had, our inactivity would have found them long ago; but they are not.

Such are the measures which I advise, which I propose: adopt them, and even yet, I believe, our prosperity may be re-established. If any man has better advice to offer, let him communicate it openly. Whatever you determine, I pray to all the gods for a happy result.

# THE FOURTH PHILIPPIC

## ARGUMENT

THE subject of this oration is the same as the last, viz., the necessity of resistance to Philip. The time of its delivery would appear to have been a little later, whilst Philip was yet in Thrace, and before he commenced the siege of the Propontine towns. No new event is alluded to, except the seizure of Hermias by the satrap Mentor, the exact date of which is uncertain. The orator urges here, still more strongly than he had done in the third Philippic, the necessity of applying to Persia for assistance. His advice was followed, and a negotiation was opened with that monarchy which led to the effective relief of Perinthus. There is a remarkable passage in this speech on the importance of general unanimity which seems to imply that disputes had arisen between the richer and poorer classes, chiefly in regard to the application of the public revenue. The view which is here taken on the subject of the Theoric distributions is so different from the argument in the Olynthiacs, that modern critics have generally considered this Oration to be spurious. Another ground for such opinion is, that it contains various passages borrowed from other speeches, and not very skilfully put together. Yet the genuineness seems not to have been doubted by any of the ancient grammarians.

BELIEVING, men of Athens, that the subject of your consultation is serious and momentous to the state, I will endeavour to advise what I think important. Many have been the faults, accumulated for some time past, which have brought us to this wretched condition; but none is under the circumstances so distressing as this, men of Athens; that your minds are alienated from public business; you are attentive just while you sit listening to some news, afterwards you all go away, and, so far from caring for what you heard, you forget it altogether.

Well; of the extent of Philip's arrogance and ambition, as evinced in his dealings with every people, you have been informed. That it is not possible to restrain him in such course by speeches and harangues, no man can be ignorant: or, if other reasons fail to convince you, reflect on this. Whenever we have had to discuss our claims, on no occasion have we been worsted or judged in the wrong; we have still beaten and got the better of all in argument. But do his affairs go badly on this account, or ours well? By no means. For as Philip immediately proceeds, with arms in his hand, to put all he possesses boldly at stake, whilst we with our equities, the speakers as well as the hearers, are sitting still, actions (naturally enough) outstrip words, and people attend not to what we have argued or may argue, but to what we do. And our doings are not likely to protect any of our injured neighbours: I need not say more upon the subject. Therefore, as the states are divided into two parties, one that would neither hold arbitrary government nor submit to it, but live under free and equal laws; another desiring to govern their follow-citizens, and be subject to some third power, by whose assistance they hope to accomplish that object; the partisans of Philip, who desire tyranny and despotism, have everywhere prevailed, and I know not whether there is any state left, besides our own, with a popular constitution firmly established. And those that hold the government through him have prevailed by all the means efficacious in worldly affairs; principally and mainly by having a person to bribe the corruptible; secondly, a point no less important, by having at their command, at whatever season they required, an army to put down their opponents. We, men of Athens, are not only in these respects behindhand; we cannot even be awaked; like men that have drunk mandrake[1] or some other sleeping potion; and methinks—for I judge the truth must be spoken—we are by reason thereof held in such disrepute and contempt, that, among the states in imminent danger, some dispute with us for the lead, some for the place of congress; others have resolved to defend themselves separately rather than in union with us.

Why am I so particular in mentioning these things? I

---

[1] Used for a powerful opiate by the ancients. It is called **Mandragora** also in English.

seek not to give offence; so help me all the powers of heaven!
I wish, men of Athens, to make it clear and manifest to you
all that habitual sloth and indolence, the same in public
matters as in private life, is not immediately felt on every
occasion of neglect, but shows itself in the general result.
Look at Serrium and Doriscus; which were first disregarded
after the peace. Their names perhaps are unknown to many
of you: yet your careless abandonment of these lost Thrace
and Cersobleptes your ally. Again, seeing these places neglected and unsupported by you, he demolished Porthmus, and
raised a tyrant in Eubœa like a fortress against Attica. This
being disregarded, Megara was very nearly taken. You were
insensible, indifferent to all his aggressions; gave no intima-
tion that you would not permit their continuance. He
purchased Antrones,[1] and not long after had got Oreus into
his power. Many transactions I omit; Pheræ, the march
against Ambracia, the massacres at Elis,[2] and numberless
others: for I have not entered upon these details to enume-
rate the people whom Philip has oppressed and wronged, but
to show you that Philip will not desist from wronging all
people and pursuing his conquests, until an effort is made
to prevent him.

There are persons whose custom it is, before they hear any
speech in the debate, to ask immediately—" What must we
do? "—not with the intention of doing what they are told
(or they would be the most serviceable of men), but in order
to get rid of the speaker. Nevertheless you should be
advised what to do. First, O my countrymen, you must be
firmly convinced in your minds that Philip is at war with

---

[1] A town in Thessaly. We do not know all the details of Philip's
proceedings in that country, but we have seen enough to show that
under the guise of a protector he was not far short of being the master
of the Thessalian people. Some of their towns were actually in his
possession, as Pheræ and Pagasæ.

[2] The Elean exiles, having engaged in their service a body of the
Phocian mercenaries, made an irruption into Elis, but were defeated.
A large number of prisoners were taken and put to death. This
happened B.C. 343. The government of Elis was at that time in the
hands of a Macedonian party.

our state, and has broken the peace; that, while he is inimical
and hostile to the whole of Athens, to the ground of Athens,
and I may add, to the gods in Athens (may they exterminate
him!), there is nothing which he strives and plots against so
much as our constitution, nothing in the world that he is so
anxious about, as its destruction. And thereunto he is driven
in some sort by necessity. Consider. He wishes for empire:
he believes you to be his only opponents. He has been a
long time injuring you, as his own conscience best informs
him; for by means of your possessions, which he is able to
enjoy, he secures all the rest of his kingdom: had he given
up Amphipolis and Potidæa, he would not have deemed himself safe even in Macedonia. He knows therefore, both that
he is plotting against you, and that you are aware of it; and,
supposing you to have common sense, he judges that you
detest him as you ought. Besides these important considerations, he is assured that, though he became master of
everything else, nothing can be safe for him while you are
under popular government: should any reverse ever befall
him (and many may happen to a man), all who are now under
constraint will come for refuge to you. For you are not
inclined yourselves to encroach and usurp dominion; but
famous rather for checking the usurper or depriving him of
his conquests, ever ready to molest the aspirants for empire,
and vindicate the liberty of all nations. He would not like
that a free spirit should proceed from Athens, to watch the
occasions of his weakness; nor is such reasoning foolish or
idle. First then you must assume that he is an irreconcile-
able enemy of our constitution and democracy; secondly,
you must be convinced that all his operations and contrivances are designed for the injury of our state. None of you
can be so silly as to suppose that Philip covets those miseries
in Thrace (for what else can one call Drongilus and Cabyle
and Mastira and the places which he is said now to occupy?),
and that to get possession of them he endures hardships and
winters and the utmost peril, but covets not the harbours

of Athens, the docks, the galleys, the silver mines, the revenues of such value, the place and the glory—never may he or any other man obtain these by the conquest of our city! —or that he will suffer you to keep these things, while for the sake of the barley and millet in Thracian caverns he winters in the midst of horrors. Impossible. The object of that and every other enterprise of Philip is to become master here.

So should every man be persuaded and convinced; and therefore, I say, should not call upon your faithful and upright counsellor to move a resolution for war: such were the part of men seeking an enemy to fight with, not men forwarding the interests of the state. Only see. Suppose for the first breach of the treaty by Philip, or for the second or third (for there is a series of breaches), any one had made a motion for war with him, and Philip, just as he has now without such motion, had aided the Cardians, would not the mover have been sacrificed? would not all have imputed Philip's aid of the Cardians to that cause? Don't then look for a person to vent your anger on for Philip's trespasses, to throw to Philip's hirelings to be torn in pieces. Do not, after yourselves voting for war, dispute with each other whether you ought or ought not to have done so. As Philip conducts the war, so resist him: furnish those who are resisting him now [1] with money and what else they demand; pay your contributions, men of Athens, provide an army, swift-sailing galleys, horses, transports, all the materials of war. Our present mode of operation is ridiculous; and by the gods I believe that Philip could not wish our republic to take any other course than what ye now pursue. You miss your time, waste your money, look for a person to manage your affairs, are discontented, accuse one another. How all this comes about I will explain, and how it may cease I will inform you.

Nothing, O men of Athens, have you ever set on foot or contrived rightly in the beginning: you always follow the

---

[1] Referring to Diopithes and his troops in the Chersonese.

event, stop when you are too late, on any new occurrence prepare and bustle again. But that is not the way of proceeding. It is never possible with sudden levies to perform any essential service. You must establish an army, provide maintenance for it, and paymasters, and commissaries, so ordering it that the strictest care be taken of your funds; demand from those officers an account of the expenditure, from your general an account of the campaign; and leave not the general any excuse for sailing elsewhere or prosecuting another enterprise. If ye so act and so resolve in earnest, you will compel Philip to observe a just peace and remain in his own country, or will contend with him on equal terms; and perhaps, Athenians, perhaps, as you now inquire what Philip is doing, and whither marching, so he may be anxious to learn whither the troops of Athens are bound, and where they will make their appearance.

Should any man think that these are affairs of great expense and toil and difficulty, he thinks rightly enough: but let him consider what the consequences to Athens must be, if she refuse so to act, and he will find it is our interest to perform our duties cheerfully. Suppose you had some god for your surety—for certainly no mortal could guarantee a thing so fortunate—that, although you kept quiet and sacrificed everything, Philip would not attack you at last, yet, by Jupiter and all the gods, it would be disgraceful, unworthy of yourselves, of the dignity of your state, and the deeds of your ancestors, for the sake of selfish indolence to abandon the rest of Greece to servitude. For my part, I would rather die than have advised such a course: however, if any other man advises it, and can prevail on you, be it so; make no defence, abandon all. But if no man holds such an opinion, if on the contrary we all foresee that the more we permit Philip to conquer, the more fierce and formidable an enemy we shall find him, what subterfuge remains? what excuse for delay? Or when, O Athenians, shall we be willing to act as becomes us? Peradventure, when there is some necessity.

But what may be called the necessity of freemen is not only come, but past long ago; and that of slaves you must surely deprecate. What is the difference? To a freeman shame for what is occurring is the strongest necessity; I know of none stronger that can be mentioned: to a slave, stripes and bodily chastisement; abominable things! too shocking to name!

To be backward, men of Athens, in performing those services to which the person and property of every one are liable, is wrong, very wrong, and yet it admits of some excuse: but refusing even to hear what is necessary to be heard, and fit to be considered, this calls for the severest censure. Your practice however is neither to attend until the business actually presses, as it does now, nor to deliberate about anything at leisure. When Philip is preparing, you, instead of doing the like and making counter-preparation, remain listless, and, if any one speaks a word, clamour him down: when you receive news that any place is lost or besieged, then you listen and prepare. But the time to have heard and consulted was then when you declined; the time to act and employ your preparations is now that you are hearing. Such being your habits, you are the only people who adopt this singular course: others deliberate usually before action, you deliberate after action.

One thing [1] remains, which should have been done long ago, but even yet is not too late: I will mention it. Nothing in the world does Athens need so much as money for approaching exigencies. Lucky events have occurred, and, if we rightly improve them, perhaps good service may be done. In the first place, those [2] whom the king trusts and regards as his benefactors are at enmity and war with Philip. Secondly, the agent and confidant [3] of all Philip's prepara-

[1] He means negotiation with Persia, to obtain pecuniary assistance.

[2] The Thracians, who had always been regarded as benefactors of the Persian king since they assisted Darius on his invasion of Scythia. Philip was making war in Thrace at this time, and had subjected a considerable part of the country.

[3] Hermias, governor of Atarneus of Mysia, who for his treasonable

tions against the king has been snatched off, and the king will hear all the proceedings, not from Athenian accusers, whom he might consider to be speaking for their own interests, but from the acting minister himself; the charges therefore will be credible, and the only remaining argument for our ambassadors will be, one which the Persian monarch will rejoice to hear, that we should take common vengeance on the injurer of both, and that Philip is much more formidable to the king if he attack us first; for, should we be left in the lurch and suffer any mishap, he will march against the king without fear. On all these matters then I advise that you despatch an embassy to confer with the king, and put aside that nonsense which has so often damaged you—" the barbarian," forsooth, " the common enemy "—and the like. I confess, when I see a man alarmed at a prince in Susa and Ecbatana, and declaring him to be an enemy of Athens, him that formerly assisted in re-establishing her power,[1] and lately made overtures [2]—if you did not accept them, but voted refusal, the fault is not his—while the same man speaks a different language of one who is close at our doors, and growing up in the centre of Greece to be the plunderer of her people; I marvel, I dread this man, whoever he is, because he dreads not Philip.

There is another thing too, the attacking of which by unjust reproach and improper language hurts the state, and affords an excuse to men who are unwilling to perform any public duty: indeed you will find that every failure to discharge the obligation of a citizen is attributable to this. I am really afraid to discuss the matter; however, I will speak out.

practices against Artaxerxes was seized by Mentor and sent in chains to Susa, where he was put to death. He was a friend of Aristotle, who was at his court when he was taken prisoner.

[1] In the confederate war, when the Persian fleet enabled Conon to defeat the Lacedæmonians at Cnidus, B.C. 394.

[2] Artaxerxes had applied both to Athens and Lacedæmon to aid him in the recovery of Egypt, which for many years had been held in a state of revolt. Both these states refused to assist him. He then applied to Thebes and Argos, each of which sent an auxiliary force.

I believe I can suggest, for the advantage of the state, a plea for the poor against the rich, and for men of property against the indigent; could we remove the clamour which some persons unfairly raise about the theatric fund, and the fear that it cannot stand without some signal mischief. No greater help to our affairs could we introduce; none that would more strengthen the whole community. Look at it thus. I will commence on behalf of those who are considered the needy class. There was a time with us, not long ago, when only a hundred and thirty talents came into the state; and among the persons qualified to command ships or pay property-tax, there was not one who claimed exemption from his duty because no surplus existed: galleys sailed, money was forthcoming, everything needful was done. Since that time fortune happily has increased the revenue, and four hundred talents come in instead of one, without loss to any men of property, but with gain to them; for all the wealthy come for their share of the fund, and they are welcome to it. Why then do we reproach one another on this account, and make it an excuse for declining our duties, unless we grudge the relief given by fortune to the poor? I would be sorry to blame them myself, and I think it not right. In private families I never see a young man behaving so to his elders, so unfeeling or so unreasonable, as to refuse to do anything himself, unless all the rest will do what he does. Such a person would certainly be amenable to the laws against undutiful conduct: for I ween there is a tribute assigned to parents both by nature and by law, which ought to be cheerfully offered and amply paid. Accordingly, as each individual among us hath a parent, so should we regard the whole people as parents of the state, and, so far from depriving them of what the state bestows, we ought, in the absence of such bounty, to find other means to keep them from destitution. If the rich will adopt this principle, I think they will act both justly and wisely; for to deprive any class of a necessary provision is to unite them in disaffection to the commonwealth.

To the poor I would recommend that they remove the cause, which makes men of property discontented with the present system, and excites their just complaints. I shall take the same course on behalf of the wealthy as I did just now, and not hesitate to speak the truth. There cannot, I believe, be found a wretch so hard-hearted—I will not say among Athenians, but among any other people—who would be sorry to see poor men, men without the necessaries of life, receiving these bounties. Where then is the pinch of the matter? where the difficulty? When they see certain persons transferring the usage established for the public revenue to private property, and the orator becoming immediately powerful with you, yea (so far as privilege can make him), immortal, and your secret vote contradicting your public clamour. Hence arises mistrust, hence indignation. We ought, O ye men of Athens, to have a just communion of political rights; the opulent holding themselves secure in their fortunes, and without fear of losing them, yet in time of danger imparting their substance freely for the defence of their country; while the rest consider the public revenue as public, and receive their share, but look on private property as belonging to the individual owner. Thus it is that a small commonwealth becomes great, and a great one is preserved. To speak generally then, such are the obligations of each class; to ensure their performance according to law, some regulation should be made.

The causes of our present troubles and embarrassment are many and of ancient date: if you are willing to hear, I will declare them. You have quitted, O Athenians, the position in which your ancestors left you; you have been persuaded by these politicians that to stand foremost of the Greeks, to keep a permanent force and redress injured nations, is all vanity and idle expense; you imagine that to live in quiet, to perform no duty, to abandon one thing after another and let strangers seize on all, brings with it marvellous welfare and abundant security. By such means a stranger has advanced to the post which you ought to have occupied, has become prosperous and great, and made large conquests; naturally enough. A prize there was, noble, great, and glorious, one for which the mightiest states were contending all along; but as the Lacedæmonians were humbled, the Thebans had their hands full through the Phocian war, and we took no regard, he carried it off without competition. The result has been, to others terror, to him a vast alliance and extended power; while difficulties so many and so distressing surround the Greeks that even advice is not easy to be found.

Yet, perilous as I conceive the present crisis to be for all, no people are in such danger as you, men of Athens; not only because Philip's designs are especially aimed at you, but because of all people you are the most remiss. If, seeing the abundance of commodities and cheapness in your market, you are beguiled into a belief that the state is in no danger, your judgment is neither becoming nor correct. A market or a fair one may, from such appearances, judge to be well or ill supplied: but for a state, which every aspirant for the empire of Greece has deemed to be alone capable of opposing him, and defending the liberty of all—for such a state! verily her marketable commodities are not the test of prosperity, but this—whether she can depend on the goodwill of her allies; whether she is puissant in arms. On behalf of such a state these are the things to be considered; and in these respects your condition is wretched and deplorable. You will understand it by a simple reflection. When have the affairs of Greece been in the greatest confusion? No other time could any man point out but the present. In former times Greece was divided into two parties, that of the Lacedæmonians and ours: some of the Greeks were subject to us, some to them. The Persian, on his own account, was mistrusted equally by all, but he used to make friends of the vanquished parties, and retain their confidence, until he put them on an equality with the other side; after which those that he succoured would hate him as much as his original enemies. Now however the king is on friendly terms with all the Greeks though least friendly with us, unless we put matters right. Now too there are protectors [1] springing up in every quarter, and all claim the precedency, though some indeed have abandoned the cause, or envy and distrust each other—more shame for them—and every state is isolated, Argives, Thebans, Lacedæmonians, Corinthians, Arcadians, and ourselves. But, divided as Greece is among so many parties and so many leaderships, if I must speak the truth freely, there is no state whose offices and halls of council appear more deserted by Grecian politics than ours. And no wonder; when neither friendship, nor confidence, nor fear leads any to negotiate with us.

This, ye men of Athens, has come not from any single cause (or you might easily mend it), but from a great variety and long series of errors. I will not stop to recount them, but will mention one, to which all may be referred, beseeching you not to be offended, if I boldly speak the truth.

Your interests are sold on every favourable opportunity: you partake of the idleness and ease, under the charm whereof you resent not your wrongs; while other persons get the reward. Into all these cases I could not enter now: but when any question about Philip arises, some one starts up directly and says, " We must have no trifling, no proposal of war," and then goes on to say, " What a blessing it is to be at peace! what a grievance to maintain a large army! "— and again, " Certain persons wish to plunder the treasury "— and other arguments they urge, no doubt, in the full conviction of their truth. But surely there is no need of persuading you to observe peace, you that sit there persuaded already. It is Philip (who is making war) that needs persuasion: prevail on him, and all is ready on your part. We should consider as grievous, not what we expend for our deliverance, but what we shall suffer in case of refusal. Plunder of the

---

[1] This is said with some irony: many states offer to come forward as protectors, but only on condition of taking the lead: they will not join the common cause on fair terms.

treasury should be prevented by devising a plan for its safe custody, not by abandoning our interests. Yet this very thing makes me indignant, that some of you are pained at the thought of your treasury being robbed, though it depends on yourselves to guard it and to punish the criminal, but are not pained to see Philip plundering Greece, plundering as he does one people after another, to forward his designs upon you.

How comes it, ye men of Athens, that of this flagrant aggressor, this capturer of cities, no one has ever declared that he commits hostility or injustice, while those who counsel against submission and sacrifice are charged as the authors of war? The reason is, that people wish to cast upon your faithful counsellors the blame of any untoward events in the war; for war must necessarily be attended with many misfortunes. They believe that, if you resist Philip with one heart and mind, you will prevail against him, and they can be hirelings no longer; but that if on the first outcry you arraign certain persons and bring them to trial, they by accusing such persons will gain a double advantage, repute among the Athenians and recompense from Philip; and that you will punish your friendly advisers for a cause for which you ought to punish the traitors. Such are the hopes, such the contrivance of these charges, " that certain persons wish to kindle a war." I am sure however, that, without any Athenian moving a declaration of war, Philip has taken many of our possessions, and has recently sent succour to Cardia. If we choose to assume that he is not making war against us, he would be the simplest of mankind to convince us of our mistake: for when the sufferers disclaim the injury, what should the offenders do? But when he marches to attack us, what shall we say then? He will assure us that he is not making war, as he assured the Orites when his troops were in their country, as he assured the Pheræans before he assaulted their walls, and the Olynthians in the first instance, until he was in their territories with his army.

Shall we then say that persons who bid us defend ourselves
kindle a war? If so, we must be slaves; for nothing else
remains.

But remember: you have more at stake than some other
people. Philip desires not to subjugate your city, but to
destroy it utterly. He is convinced you will not submit to
be slaves; if you were inclined, you would not know how,
having been accustomed to command: you will be able,
should occasion offer, to give him more trouble than any
people in the world. For this reason he will show us no
mercy if he get us into his power: and therefore you must
make up your minds that the struggle will be one for life and
death. These persons, who have openly sold themselves to
Philip, you must execrate, you must beat their brains out:
for it is impossible, I say impossible, to vanquish your foreign
enemies, until you have punished your enemies within the
city: these are the stumbling-blocks that must cripple your
efforts against the foreigner.

From what cause, do ye think, Philip insults you now (for
his conduct, in my judgment, amounts to nothing less); and
while he deceives other people by doing them services—
this at least is something—you he threatens already? For
example, the Thessalians by many benefits he seduced into
their present servitude: no man can tell how he cheated the
poor Olynthians, giving them first Potidæa and many other
places: now he is luring the Thebans, having delivered up
Bœotia to them, and freed them from a tedious and harassing
war. Of these people, who each got a certain advantage,
some have suffered what is notorious to all, others have yet
to suffer what may befall them. As to yourselves, the amount
of your losses I do not mention: but in the very making of
the peace how have you been deceived! how plundered!
Lost you not the Phocians, Thermopylæ, country towards
Thrace, Doriscus, Serrium, Cersobleptes himself? Holds
he not Cardia now, and avows it? Why then does he behave
thus to other people, and in a different way to you? Because

our city is the only one where liberty is allowed to speak for the enemy, where a man taking a bribe may safely address the people, though they have been deprived of their possessions.  It was not safe at Olynthus to advocate Philip's cause, without the Olynthian people sharing the benefit by possession of Potidæa.  It was not safe to advocate Philip's cause in Thessaly, without the people of Thessaly sharing the benefit, by Philip's expelling their tyrants and restoring the Pylæan Synod.  It was not safe at Thebes, until he restored Bœotia to them, and destroyed the Phocians.  But at Athens, though Philip has taken from you Amphipolis and the Cardian territory, and is even turning Eubœa into a hostile post, and advancing to attack Byzantium, it is safe to speak on Philip's behalf.  Yea, among these men, some have risen rapidly from poverty to wealth, from meanness and obscurity to repute and honour, whilst you, on the contrary, have fallen from honour to obscurity, from wealth to indigence  For the riches of a state I consider to be allies, confidence, goodwill; of all which you are destitute.  And by your neglecting these things, and suffering your interests thus to be swept away, Philip has grown prosperous and mighty, formidable to all the Greeks and barbarians, whilst you are forlorn and abject, in the abundance of your market magnificent, but in your national defences ridiculous.[1]

Some of our orators, I observe, take not the same thought for you as for themselves.  They say that you should keep quiet, though you are injured; but they cannot themselves keep quiet among you, though no one injures them.  Come, raillery apart, suppose you were thus questioned, Aristodemus,[2]  "Tell me, as you know perfectly well, what every one else knows, that the life of private men is secure and free from trouble and danger, whilst that of statesmen is exposed

[1] The whole of the foregoing passage is taken, with some little variation, from the speech on the Chersonese.
[2] This man was a tragic actor, and charged by Demosthenes with being a partisan of Philip.  He was the first person who proposed peace with Macedonia, shortly before the embassy of ten.  See the Argument to the Oration on the Peace.

to scandal and misfortune, full of trials and hardships every day, how comes it that you prefer, not the quiet and easy life, but the one surrounded with peril? "—what should you say? If we admitted the truth of what would be your best possible answer, namely, that all you do is for honour and renown, I wonder what puts it into your head that you ought from such motives to exert yourself and undergo toil and danger whilst you advise the state to give up exertion and remain idle. You cannot surely allege that Aristodemus ought to be of importance at Athens, and Athens to be of no account among the Greeks. Nor again do I see that for the commonwealth it is safe to mind her own affairs only and hazardous for you not to be a superlative busy-body. On the contrary, to you I see the utmost peril from your meddling and over-meddling, to the commonwealth peril from her inactivity. But I suppose you inherit a reputation from your father and grandfather, which it were disgraceful in your own person to extinguish, whereas the ancestry of the state was ignoble and mean. This again is not so. Your father was a thief, if he resembled you, whereas by the ancestors of the commonwealth, as all men know, the Greeks have twice been rescued from the brink of destruction. Truly the behaviour of some persons, in private and in public, is neither equitable nor constitutional. How is it equitable that certain of these men, returned from prison, should not know themselves, while the state, that once protected all Greece and held the foremost place, is sunk in ignominy and humiliation?

Much could I add on many points, but I will forbear. It is not, I believe, to lack of words that our distresses have been owing either now or heretofore. The mischief is when you, after listening to sound arguments, and all agreeing in their justice, sit to hear with equal favour those who try to defeat and pervert them; not that you are ignorant of the men (you are certain, at the first glance, who speak for hire and are Philip's political agents, and who speak sincerely for your good); your object is to find fault with these, turn the thing into laughter and raillery, and escape the performance of your duty.

Such is the truth, spoken with perfect freedom, purely from goodwill and for the best: not a speech fraught with flattery and mischief and deceit, to earn money for the speaker, and to put the commonwealth into the hands of our enemies. I say, you must either desist from these practices, or blame none but yourselves for the wretched condition of your affairs.

# THE ORATION ON THE LETTER

## ARGUMENT

THE Athenians had been persuaded by the advice of Demosthenes to
solicit the aid of Persia. This was accorded, and events had happened
on the Propontine coast which made it peculiarly needful. Towards
the close of the year B.C. 342 Philip commenced the siege of Selymbria,
and early in the following year, that city having been taken, laid siege
to Perinthus. But here he met with an obstinate resistance: Perinthus
was strong by nature and well fortified. The satraps of Western Asia
had supplied it with a stock of provisions and ammunition, and a
large body of Greek mercenaries. Byzantium also had sent assistance. Philip, after making great efforts to take Perinthus by storm
turned the siege into a blockade, and marched northward against
Byzantium. Here he was no more successful than he had been at
Perinthus. The Byzantines had well prepared themselves to resist
his attack, and received powerful aid not only from their old allies of
Cos, Chios, and Rhodes, but also from other parts of Greece, and
especially from Athens. In order to reconcile the Byzantines to his
countrymen, with whom they had been at variance ever since the
Social war, Demosthenes himself undertook a voyage to the Bosphorus.
By his exertions an alliance was concluded, and an Athenian fleet was
sent under the command of Chares; but Chares being feared and dis-
liked by the Byzantines, they refused to admit him into the town;
and afterwards Phocion was despatched with a hundred and twenty
ships and a considerable body of troops. The result of these effective
measures was, that Philip was baffled in his attempts on both cities,
and compelled to raise the siege.

In the meantime important operations had taken place elsewhere.
An expedition had been sent under the command of Phocion to Eubœa,
of which we have no detailed account, but the result was, that the
Macedonian party was overpowered, and Citarchus and Philistides,
the partisans of Philip, were expelled from the island. A fleet was
then sent by the Athenians into the Pagasæan bay, which took some
Thessalian towns, and seized Macedonian merchant-men on the coast.
The island of Halonnesus was recovered from Philip by a sudden
incursion of the Peparethians. This was revenged by Philip, who
ravaged Peparethus, and compelled the islanders to restore their
conquest.

Philip saw that peace with Athens could no longer be preserved even
in name. Under this conviction, and not, as Mitford says, in alarm at
the fourth Philippic, he wrote a letter to the Athenians (the letter
which precedes this Oration), in which he reproaches them with the
various acts of hostility which they had committed, and concludes
with a virtual declaration of war. An assembly was held, at which
this letter was read, and Demosthenes is supposed to have delivered
the following speech in reply to it. The exact time when the letter
was received is uncertain; but it would appear from the internal
evidence to have been after the siege of Perinthus had commenced,
and before that of Byzantium. The arguments of Philip produced
no effect; things had gone too far for reconciliation; and it was not
difficult for Demosthenes to obtain a decree for the vigorous prosecution of the war.

223

It will be seen on a perusal of the letter and answer, that the orator does not attempt to meet the specific charges and complaints of Philip. We have nothing but the old arguments, showing the necessity of succouring Perinthus and Byzantium, as formerly of succouring Olynthus; the real weakness of Philip's empire, and the good chance that by vigorous measures it might be overturned. Mitford considers that it was impossible to confute the reasoning of Philip, and therefore that bold invective was the only thing that remained for the orator. And even Leland says, it would have been difficult to answer the letter particularly, because, though Athens had the better cause, she had committed many irregularities. I cannot agree with this view of the question. If Philip had been the good-natured easy person that Mitford represents, who was raised to the surface of Greek affairs by the merest accidents, and rather had greatness thrust upon him by the opposition of the Athenians, than either sought or desired it himself, then indeed the acts of hostility which Philip complains of might justly be regarded as breaches of good faith, and violations by Athens of the law of nations. But I read the history of the times very differently. Philip had been for many years pursuing his career of conquest steadily and successfully. The Chersonese, Eubœa, all the possessions of the Athenians, their commerce and their corn-trade, were at this time in imminent danger. War between Athens and Macedonia, if not open, was understood: argument was out of the question.

But why should Philip address a letter of complaint to a people so bent on hostilities? Why did the wolf complain of the lamb? An aggressive power has never lacked a pretext for making war in either ancient times or modern. It was a part of Philip's system, not only in his dealings with Athens, but with other states, to make friendly overtures and pacific professions, when he meditated some decisive blow. By this means he gained credit for moderation with neutral states, and he created a party for himself within the state which he had designs upon. He put colourable arguments into the mouths of his adherents, distracted the efforts of the people, and at all events gained time for the prosecution of his schemes. It is argued with much force and justice in the exordium of the Oration on Halonnesus, that the tendency of such correspondence was to deter the adversaries of Philip from expressing their opinions freely.

But for motives of this kind, Philip would hardly have adopted the strain of remonstrance which we read in the Letter. He could never seriously believe that the Athenians would resign their claims on Amphipolis, because it belonged to Macedonia in very early times, or would give up the Persian alliance because it was a disgraceful connection. It should be observed, however, that the Athenians afforded him a handle for using such arguments, by declaiming in the same style themselves when it suited them; and Philip perhaps was pleased at the idea of beating them with their own weapons. The language of the epistle is simple and dignified, and may be regarded as a good specimen of a diplomatic paper. The pith lies in the last clause, which contains a threat of war.

For these reasons it could scarcely have been worth while for the orator to answer every particular charge contained in the Letter. Nor can such omission be deemed an argument against the genuineness of the Oration. This, however, has been doubted by many critics; and it may be allowed that a good part of the speech is not very suitable to the occasion upon which it purports to have been spoken.

## THE LETTER OF PHILIP

PHILIP to the senate and people of Athens greeting:—

Whereas I have frequently sent ambassadors, that we may abide by our oaths and agreements, and you paid them no regard, I thought proper to write to you concerning the matters in which I consider myself aggrieved. Marvel not at the length of this epistle; for, there being many articles of complaint, it is necessary to explain myself clearly upon all.

First then; after Nicias the herald was snatched from my dominions, you chastised not the culprits, but imprisoned the injured party for ten months; and my letters, of which he was the bearer, you read on the hustings.[1]

Secondly, when the Thasians were receiving in their port the Byzantine galleys and all pirates that chose to enter, you took no notice, although the treaty expressly declares that whoever act thus shall be enemies.

Again, about the same time Diopithes made an irruption into my territory, carried off the inhabitants of Crobyle and Tiristasis[2] for slaves, and ravaged the adjacent parts of Thrace; proceeding to such lawless extremities that he seized Amphilochus who came to negotiate about the prisoners, and, after putting on him the hardest durance, took from him a ransom of nine talents. And this he did with the approbation of the people. Howbeit, to offer violence to a herald and ambassadors is considered impious by all nations, and especially by you. Certain it is, when the

---

[1] It is mentioned by Plutarch that a letter from Philip to his Queen Olympias, which fell into the hands of the Athenians, was returned unopened. But whether it was on this or another occasion, does not appear.

[2] Crobyle must have been in Thrace. Tiristasis is mentioned by Pliny as a place in the Chersonese. Probably then it was near Cardia, not far from the isthmus.

Megarians killed Anthemocritus,[1] your people went so far as to exclude them from the mysteries, and erect a statue before their gates for a monument of the crime.    Then is it not shameful that you are seen committing the same offence, for which, when you were the sufferers, you so detested the authors?

Further, Callias [2] your general took all the towns situate in the Pagasæan bay, towns under treaty with you and in alliance with me; and sold all people bound for Macedonia, adjudging them enemies; and on this account you praised him in your decrees.    So that I am puzzled to think what worse could happen if you were confessedly at war with me: for when we were in open hostility, you used to send out privateers and sell people sailing to our coast, you assisted my enemies, infested my country.

Yet more; you have carried your animosity and violence so far that you have even sent ambassadors to the Persian, to persuade him to make war against me: a thing which is most surprising: for before he gained Egypt and Phœnicia, you resolved,[3] in case of any aggression on his part, to invite me as well as the other Greeks to oppose him; but now you have such an overflow of malice against me, as to negotiate with him for an offensive alliance.    Anciently, as I am informed, your ancestors condemned the Pisistratids for bringing the Persian to invade Greece: yet you are not

[1] The Athenians, having charged the people of Megara with profaning a piece of consecrated ground, sent Anthemocritus to admonish them to desist from the sacrilege.    The Megarians put him to death, and drew upon themselves the wrath of their powerful neighbours, who passed the decree of excommunication here referred to.    The monument which recorded their impiety was to be seen in the time of Pausanias on the sacred road leading from Athens to Eleusis.

[2] This is the same Callias, ruler of Chalcis, whom we have seen opposing the Athenians at the time when Phocion was sent to assist Plutarch of Eretria.

[3] The time referred to is B.C. 354, when there was a rumour of a Persian invasion, and a proposal at Athens to declare war against Artaxerxes, upon which Demosthenes made the speech *de Symmoriis*. Phœnicia and Egypt were recovered some years after that.    The argument of Philip is, that since the recovery of those provinces Persia was more dangerous than before, and therefore it was more disgraceful for a Greek state to be connected with that monarchy.

ashamed of doing the same thing, for which you continue to reproach the tyrants.

In addition to other matters, you write in your decrees, commanding me to let Teres [1] and Cersobleptes rule in Thrace, because they are Athenians. I know nothing of them as being included in the treaty of peace with you, or as inscribed on the pillars, or as being Athenians; I know however that Teres took arms with me against you, and that Cersobleptes was anxious to take the oaths separately to my ambassadors, but was prevented by your generals pronouncing him an enemy of Athens. How can it be equitable or just, when it suits your purpose, to call him an enemy of the state, and when you desire to calumniate me, to declare the same person your citizen—and on the death of Sitalces,[2] to whom you imparted the freedom of your city, to make friendship immediately with his murderer, but on behalf of Cersobleptes to espouse a war with me?—knowing too as you must, that, of the persons who receive such gifts, none have the least regard for your laws or decrees? However—to omit all else and be concise—you bestowed citizenship on Evagoras of Cyprus,[3] and Dionysius of Syracuse,[4] and their descendants. If you can persuade the people who expelled each of those

[1] Of Teres nothing is known but from this passage: he must have been a prince in the interior of Thrace.

[2] It is impossible that this can refer to the Sitalces, King of the Odrysæ, and ally of the Athenians, whose wars and death are related by Thucydides. He fell in a battle with the Triballi, and was succeeded by his nephew Seuthes. It was his son Sadocus, and not he, that was made a citizen of Athens.

[3] Evagoras, the friend of Conon, who assisted the Athenians in the re-establishment of their independence, was made a citizen of Athens, and statues of him and of Conon were placed side by side in the Ceramicus. He aimed at becoming absolute master of Cyprus, and was engaged in a long war against the Persian king, in which he was ultimately overpowered, but, on submission to Artaxerxes, was permitted to rule in Salamis. On his death, B.C. 374, he was succeeded by his son Nicocles, who was father of the Evagoras here referred to.

[4] This refers to the younger Dionysius, twice expelled from Syracuse, first by Dion, B.C. 356, afterwards by Timoleon, B.C. 343. He was in alliance with Sparta, and sent troops to her assistance against Epaminondas. His connection with Athens began after she had made common cause with Sparta; from that time many Athenians resorted to his court, and (among others) Plato is said to have visited him.

princes to reinstate them in their government, then recover Thrace from me, all that Teres and Cersobleptes reigned over. But if against the parties, who mastered Evagoras and Dionysius, you will not utter a word of complaint, and yet continue to annoy me, how can I be wrong in resisting you?

On this head I have many arguments yet remaining, which I purposely omit. But as to the Cardians, I avow myself their auxiliary; for I was allied to them before the peace, and you refused to come to an arbitration, although I made many offers, and they not a few. Surely I should be the basest of men, if, deserting my allies, I paid more regard to you, who have harassed me all along, than to those who have always been my steadfast friends.

Another thing I must not leave unnoticed. You have arrived at such a pitch of arrogance, that, while formerly you did but remonstrate with me on the matters aforesaid, in the recent case, where the Peparethians complained of harsh treatment, you ordered your general to obtain satisfaction from me on their account.[1]  Yet I punished them less severely than they deserved. For they in time of peace seized Halonnesus, and would restore neither the place nor the garrison, though I sent many times about them. You objected not to the injury which the Peparethians had done me, but only to their punishment, well knowing that I took the island neither from them nor from you, but from the pirate Sostratus. If now you declare that you gave it up to Sostratus, you acknowledge to having commissioned pirates; but if he got possession against your will, what hardship have you suffered by my taking it and rendering the coast safe for navigators? I had such regard for your state that I offered you the island; yet your orators would not let you accept it, but counselled you to obtain restitution, in order that, if I submitted to your command, I might confess my occupation

[1] Peparethus is in the same group of islands with Halonnesus. Philip's ravaging of Peparethus is spoken of in the Oration for the Crown.

to be unlawful, if I refused to abandon the place, your commonalty might suspect me. Perceiving which, I challenged you to a reference of the question, so that, if it were decided to be mine, the place should be given by me to you, if it were adjudged yours, then I should restore it to the people. This I frequently urged; you would not listen; and the Peparethians seized the island. What then became it me to do? Not to punish the violators of their oaths? not to avenge myself on the perpetrators of these gross outrages? If the island belonged to the Peparethians, what business had Athenians to demand it? If it was yours, why resent you not their unlawful seizure?

To such a degree of enmity have we advanced, that, wishing to pass with my ships into the Hellespont, I was compelled to escort them along the coast through the Chersonese with my army, as your colonists according to the resolution of Polycrates were making war against me, and you were sanctioning it by your decrees, and your general was inviting the Byzantines to join him, and proclaiming everywhere that he had your instructions to commence war on the first opportunity. Notwithstanding these injuries, I refrained from attacking either your fleet or your territory, though I was in a condition to take the greater part, if not all; and I have persisted in offering to submit our mutual complaints to arbitration. Consider now, whether it is fairer to decide by arms or by argument, to pronounce the award yourselves or persuade others to do so: reflect also, how unreasonable it is that Athens should compel Thasians and Maronites to a judicial settlement of their claims to Stryme,[1] yet refuse to determine her disputes with me in the same manner, especially when you know that, if beaten, you will lose nothing, if successful, you will get what is in my possession.

The most unaccountable thing of all, in my opinion, is this

---

[1] Maronea and Stryme were neighbouring towns, on the coast of Thrace, north-east of the island of Thasos. Stryme was founded by the Thasians, whom the Maronites endeavoured to deprive of their colony.

—when I sent ambassadors from the whole confederacy,[1] that they might be witnesses, and desired to make a just arrangement with you on behalf of the Greeks, you would not even hear what the deputies had to propose on the subject, though it was in your power, either to secure against all danger the parties mistrustful of me, or plainly to prove me the basest of mankind. That was the interest of the people, but it suited not the orators. To them—as persons acquainted with your government say—peace is war, and war is peace: for they always get something from the generals, either by supporting or calumniating them, and also, by railing on your hustings at the most eminent citizens and most illustrious foreigners, they acquire credit with the multitude for being friends of the constitution.

Easy were it for me, at a very small expense, to silence their invectives, and make them pronounce my panegyric.[2] But I should be ashamed to purchase your goodwill from these men, who—besides other things—have reached such a point of assurance as to contest Amphipolis with me, to which I conceive I have a far juster title than the claimants. For if it belongs to the earliest conquerors, how can my right be questioned, when Alexander my ancestor first occupied the place, from which, as the first fruits of the captive Medes, he brought the offering of a golden statue to Delphi? Or, should this be disputed, and the argument be that it belongs to the last possessors, so likewise I have the best title; for I besieged and took the place from a people who expelled you and were planted by the Lacedæmonians.[3] But we all

---

[1] This seems to have been the embassy that led to the second Philippic. See the argument to that Oration. By " the whole confederacy," he means the Amphictyonic union, and affects to treat the Athenians as belonging to it.

[2] This observation laid Philip open to a severe retort. What experience had he of the facility of bribing orators at Athens or elsewhere? If he had none, it was a gratuitous piece of slander, and an insult to the Athenians, to suppose their leading statesmen so corruptible. If he spoke from experience, he proved the justice of what Demosthenes asserted of him, and the danger to be apprehended from his intrigues.

[3] After the death of Brasidas, the Amphipolitans paid divine honours to his memory, and treated him as their founder, destroying every

hold cities either by inheritance from our ancestors, or by conquest in war. You claim this city, not being either the first occupants or the present possessors, having abode for a very short period in the district, and after having yourselves given the strongest testimony in my favour. For I have frequently written in letters concerning it, and you have acknowledged the justice of my tenure, first by making the peace whilst I held the city, and next by concluding alliance on the same terms. How can any property stand on a firmer title than this, which was left to me originally by my fore-fathers, has again become mine in war, and thirdly has been conceded by you, who are accustomed to claim what you have not the least pretensions to?

Such are the complaints which I prefer. As you are the aggressors, as by reason of my forbearance you are making new encroachments, and doing me all the mischief you can, I will in a just cause defend myself, and, calling the gods to witness, bring the quarrel between us to an issue.

## THE ORATION IN REPLY

ATHENIANS! that Philip, instead of concluding peace with us, only deferred the war, has now become manifest to you all. Ever since he gave Halus to the Pharsalians,[1] and settled the Phocian business, and subdued all Thrace, making fictitious charges and inventing unjust pretexts, he has been actually carrying on war against Athens; and now in the letter which he has sent he avowedly declares it. That it becomes you neither to fear his power nor to withstand him ignobly, but with men and money and ships, in short, with

vestige of Hagnon the Athenian. Therefore they are spoken of as being a Lacedæmonian colony.

[1] Parmenio was besieging Halus in Thessaly during the first embassy of the Athenians for peace. Philip told the ambassadors, he desired their meditation between the people of Halus and Pharsalus. He afterwards took the former city, and gave it up to the Pharsalians, who were his devoted allies.

all you have unsparingly to prosecute the war, I will endeavour to show.

In the first place, O Athenians, you may expect that the gods are your greatest allies and defenders, when Philip, violating his faith and disregarding his oaths to them, has perfidiously broken the peace. In the second place, he has exhausted all the tricks by which he once rose to greatness, continually deceiving some people and promising them signal benefits. It is understood by the Perinthians and Byzantines and their allies, that he wishes to deal with them in the same manner that he dealt with the Olynthians formerly: it escapes not the Thessalians that he designs to be the master of his allies and not their chief: he is suspected by the Thebans, for holding Nicæa [1] with a garrison, for having crept into the Amphictyonic council, for drawing to himself the embassies from Peloponnesus,[2] and stealing their confederacy from them: so that of his former friends some are at war with him irreconcilably, some are no longer hearty auxiliaries, all are jealous and complaining of him. Besides— what is of no small moment—the satraps of Asia have just thrown in mercenary troops for the relief of Perinthus, and now that hostility has begun between them, and the peril is imminent if Byzantium should be reduced, not only will they assist us with alacrity themselves, but they will urge the Persian king to supply us with money; and he possesses greater wealth than all nations put together; he has such influence over proceedings here, that in our former wars with Lacedæmon, whichsoever side he joined he caused them to vanquish their opponents, and now siding with us he will easily beat down the power of Philip.

With these advantages, I will not deny that Philip has by favour of the peace snatched from us many fortresses and

[1] On account of its neighbourhood to the pass of Thermopylæ.
[2] The Messenians and Arcadians. See the Argument to the second Philippic. Those people had been the allies of the Thebans since the time of Epaminondas, but were now more inclined to Philip, as being better able to protect them.

harbours and other like conveniences for war; yet I observe
that if an alliance is consolidated by goodwill and all who
take part in the wars have a common interest, the union is
firm and lasting; whereas, if it be kept up by deceit and
violence, with insidious and ambitious views (as this of
Philip is), any slight pretence, any accidental failure, shakes
to pieces and destroys it all in a moment.[1]   And by much
consideration, men of Athens, I find, not only that the allies
of Philip have come to distrust and dislike him, but that
even his own subjects are not well-disposed or loyal, or what
people imagine.   Generally speaking, the Macedonian power,
as an auxiliary, is important and useful, but by itself it
is feeble, and ridiculously disproportioned to these gigantic
enterprises.   Moreover this very man by his wars, his expeditions, and all the proceedings which may seem to establish
his greatness, has rendered it more precarious for himself.
Don't suppose, men of Athens, that Philip and his subjects
delight in the same things.   Bear in mind that he desires
glory, they security; he cannot gain his object without
hazard; they want not to leave parents, wives, and children
at home, to wear themselves out and risk their lives for him
every day.[2]

Hence one may judge what the feelings of the Macedonian
people towards Philip are.   As to his guards and the leaders
of his mercenaries, you will find they have a reputation for
courage, yet live in greater terror than men of no repute.
For those are in danger only from the enemy; these fear
flatterers and calumniators more than battles: those together
with the whole army fight their opponents in the field;
these have their full share in the hardships of war, and it is
also their peculiar lot to dread the humours of the king.
Besides, if any common soldier does wrong, he is punished
according to his desert; but with these men, it is when they

[1] Compare the second Olynthiac, p. 128, where this same passage
occurs with some variation.
[2] Many of these observations are applicable to France, harassed and
worn out by conscriptions in the latter part of Napoleon's reign.

have achieved the most signal success that they are most outrageously vilified and abused. No reasonabe man can disbelieve this statement; for he is reported by those who have lived with him to be so covetous of honour, that, wishing all the noblest exploits to be considered his own, he is more offended with the generals and officers who have achieved anything praiseworthy than with those who have altogether miscarried.

How then, under such circumstances, have they for a long time faithfully adhered to him? Because for the present, men of Athens, success throws a shade over all this: good fortune covers the faults of men, screens them wonderfully: but let him fail in something, and all will be fully revealed. It is the same as in the human body. When a man is healthy, he has no feeling of local disorders; but when he falls ill, every sore is felt, whether he has a rupture, or a sprain, or any member not perfectly sound. Just so with monarchies or other states: whilst they are successful in war, their weaknesses are imperceptible to most men; but when they have suffered a reverse (which Philip very likely will, having taken on him a burden beyond his strength) all their difficulties become manifest to the world.

Yet if any Athenian, seeing that Philip has been fortunate, therefore thinks it hard and terrible to contend with him, such person, I grant, exercises a prudent forethought. For indeed fortune is the prime—nay, the sole mover in all the business of mankind. Nevertheless in many respects might our good fortune be preferred to Philip's. The leadership that we have received from our ancestors takes its date, not before Philip only, but (let me say roundly) before all the kings that ever reigned in Macedonia. They have paid tribute to the Athenians, but Athens has never paid tribute to any nation. We have more title than Philip to the favour of the gods, inasmuch as we have invariably shown more regard to religion and justice.

How comes it then that Philip has obtained more successes

than you in the former war? Because, O men of Athens (I will tell you candidly), he takes the field himself, he toils, he faces the danger, letting slip no opportunity, omitting no season of the year: whilst we—the truth must be spoken—sit idling here, delaying always and voting, and asking in the market-place if there is any news. But what greater news could there be, than a man of Macedonia contemning Athenians, and daring to send such an epistle as you have just heard? Again; he keeps soldiers in his pay, aye, and some of our orators besides, who, imagining they carry his presents home, are not ashamed to live for Philip, and perceive not that they are selling for petty lucre all that belongs to their country and themselves. We neither attempt to disturb any of his proceedings, not like to maintain mercenaries, nor dare to take the field in person. It is no wonder then that he has gained advantages over us in the former war: it is rather strange that we, doing nothing that becomes a people at war, expect to vanquish one who pursues all the measures necessary to conquest.

You must reflect on all this, men of Athens, consider that we have not even the power of saying we are at peace—since Philip has now declared war and commenced it in earnest—spare not any treasures, public or private; march eagerly all to battle, wherever occasion calls; and employ better generals than before. Let none of you suppose that by the same proceedings which have damaged the commonwealth it can again recover and improve. Imagine not that while you are as remiss as you have been, others will strive zealously for your welfare. Bear in mind how disgraceful it is that your fathers underwent numerous hardships and fearful dangers warring with the Lacedæmonians, whilst you will not courageously defend even the well-earned honours which they bequeathed you; and that a man springing from Macedonia is so enamoured of danger, that, to enlarge his empire, he has been wounded all over his body fighting with the enemy, whilst Athenians, whose birthright it is to submit to none, but to conquer all in war, through slackness or effeminacy desert the conduct of their ancestors and the interests of their country.

Not to be tedious, I say we must all prepare ourselves for war; the Greeks we must invite, not by words but by deeds, to espouse our alliance. All speech is idle, unattended by action; and Athenian speech the more so on this account, that we are reputed more dexterous in the use of it than any of the Greeks.

# THE ORATION ON THE DUTIES OF THE STATE

## ARGUMENT

The object of this Oration is to show the necessity of making a proper application of the public revenue, and compelling every citizen to perform service to the state. With respect to the first point, the advice given in the first and third Olynthiacs is in substance repeated, viz., that the Theoric distributions should be put on a different footing; that the fund should either not be distributed at all, or that every man should accept his share as a remuneration for service in the army and navy, or the discharge of some other duty. This was but a circuitous way of proposing that the law of Eubulus should be repealed. (See the Argument to the first Olynthiac.) It is here further recommended that the duties required by the state should be systematically divided among all classes, and performed with regularity. No specific plan, however, is pointed out.

At what time or on what occasion this speech was delivered, we cannot determine. It is mentioned in the exordium that an assembly of the people was held to consider how certain public moneys should be disposed of. But this gives us no clue to the circumstances. There is no mention of Philip, or of any historical event in connection with the subject. It is stated by the orator that he had discussed the same question before; and perhaps it may be inferred from hence that the present speech was later than the Olynthiacs. Again, it may be presumed to have been earlier than the fourth Philippic, in which Demosthenes appears to have changed or modified his views on the subject of the theoric fund.

In consequence of this uncertainty, commentators are not agreed as to the date of the Oration before us. Pabst and some others think it was spoken soon after the Olynthiacs. Mitford, following Ulpian, places it before all the Philippics. Leland and Francis place it after the Philippics; but there is very little ground for their opinion.

Dionysius makes no mention of this speech in his letter to Ammæus; and some critics have thought it spurious.

With respect to the present money and the purpose for which you hold the assembly, men of Athens, it appears to me that two courses are equally easy; either to condemn those who distribute and give away the public funds, to gain their esteem who think the commonwealth is injured by such means or to advocate and recommend the system of allowances, to gratify those who are pressingly in need of them. Both parties praise or blame the practice, not out of regard

237

to the public interest, but according to their several conditions of indigence or affluence. For my part, I would neither propose that the allowances be discontinued, nor speak against them; yet I advise you to consider and reflect in your minds that this money about which you are deliberating is a trifle, but the usage that grows up with it is important. If you will ordain it so, that your allowances be associated with the performance of duty, so far from injuring you will signally benefit the commonwealth and yourselves. But if for your allowances a festival or any excuse be sufficient, while about your further obligations you will not even hear a word, beware lest, what you now consider a right practice, you may hereafter deem a grievous error.

My opinion is—don't clamour at what I am going to say, but hear and judge—that, as we appointed an assembly for the receiving of money, so should we appoint an assembly for the regulation of duties and the making provision for war; and every man should exhibit not only a willingness to hear the discussion, but a readiness to act, that you may derive your hopes of advantage from yourselves, Athenians, and not be inquiring what this or that person is about. All the revenue of the state, what you now expend out of your private fortunes to no purpose, and what is obtained from your allies, I say you ought to receive, every man his share, those of the military age as pay, those exempt from the roll [1] as inspection-money,[2] or what you please to call it; but you must take the field yourselves, yield that privilege to none; the force of the state must be native, and provided from these resources; that you may want for nothing while you perform your obligations. And the general should command that force so that you, Athenians, may experience not the same

---

[1] The roll in which were inscribed the names of all citizens qualified to serve in the cavalry or heavy-armed infantry. Men past the military age were exempt.

[2] It would be the duty of these persons who received such fees to inspect the militia roll, see that it was complete, that all the qualified citizens took their turns of service, were properly armed and equipped, etc.

results as at present—you try the generals, and the issue of your affairs is, " Such a one, the son of such a one, impeached such a one; " nothing else—but what results?—first, that your allies may be attached to you not by garrisons, but by community of interest; secondly, that your generals may not have mercenaries to plunder the allies, without even seeing the enemy (a course from which the emoluments are theirs in private, while the odium and reproach fall upon the whole country), but have citizens to follow them, and do unto the enemy what they now do unto your friends. Besides, many operations require your presence, and (not to mention the advantage of employing our own army for our own wars) it is necessary also for other purposes. If indeed you were content to be quiet, and not to meddle with the politics of Greece, it would be a different matter: but you assume to take the lead and determine the rights of others, and yet have not provided, nor endeavour to provide for yourselves, a force to guard and maintain that superiority. Whilst you never stirred, whilst you kept entirely aloof, the people of Mitylene have lost their constitution; whilst you never stirred, the Rhodians have lost theirs—our enemies, it may be said—true, men of Athens; but a strife with oligarchies for the principle of government should be considered more deadly than a strife with popular states on any account whatsoever.

But let me return to the point—I say, your duties must be marshalled; there must be the same rule for receiving money and performing what service is required. I have discussed this question with you before, and shown the method of arranging you all, you of the heavy-armed, you of the cavalry, and you that are neither, and how to make a common provision for all. But what has caused me the greatest despondency, I will tell you without reserve. Amid such a number of important and noble objects, no man remembers any of the rest, but all remember the two obols.[1] Yet two

---

[1] The sum distributed as the price of admittance to the the theatres.

obols can never be worth more than two obols; whilst, what I proposed in connection therewith, is worth the treasures of the Persian king—that a state possessing such a force of infantry, such a navy, cavalry, and revenue, should be put in order and preparation.

Why, it may be asked, do I mention these things now? For this reason. There are men shocked at the idea of enlisting all the citizens on hire, whilst the advantage of order and preparation is universally acknowledged. Here then, I say, you should begin, and permit any person that pleases to deliver his opinion upon the subject. For thus it is. If you can be persuaded to believe that now is the time for making arrangements, when you come to want them they will be ready: but if you neglect the present time as unseasonable, you will be compelled to make preparations when you have occasion for their use.

It has been said before now, I believe, Athenians, not by you the multitude, but by persons who would burst if these measures were carried into effect—" What benefit have we got from the harangues of Demosthenes? He comes forward when he likes, he stuffs our ears with declamation, he abuses the present state of things, he praises our forefathers, he excites and puffs up our imaginations, and then sits down." I can only say, could I persuade you to follow some of my counsels, I should confer upon the state such important benefits, as, if I now attempted to describe them, would appear incredible to many, as exceeding possibility. Yet even this I conceive to be no small advantage, if I accustom you to hear the best advice. For it is necessary, O men of Athens, that whosoever desires to render your commonwealth a service, should begin by curing your ears. They are corrupted: so many falsehoods have you been accustomed to hear, anything indeed rather than what is salutary. For instance—let me not be interrupted by clamour, before I have finished—certain persons lately, you know, broke open the treasury: and all the orators cried out that the

democracy was overthrown, the laws were annihilated; or
to that effect. Now, ye men of Athens—only see whether
I speak truly—the guilty parties committed a crime worthy
of death; but the democracy is not overthrown by such
means. Again, some oars were stolen: and people clamoured
for stripes and torture, saying the democracy was in danger.
But what do I say? I agree with them, that the thief merits
death; but I deny that the constitution is by such means
overturned. How indeed it is in danger of subversion, no
man is bold enough to tell you; but I will declare. It is
when you, men of Athens, are under bad leading, a helpless
multitude, without arms, without order, without unanimity!
when neither general nor any other person pays regard to your
resolutions, no one will inform you of your errors, or correct
them, or endeavour to effect a change. This it is that happens
now.

And by Jupiter, O Athenians, another sort of language is
current among you, false and most injurious to the constitution; such as this, that your safety lies in the courts of
justice, and you must guard the constitution by your votes.
It is true, these courts are public tribunals for the decision of
your mutual rights; but by arms must your enemies be vanquished, by arms the safety of the constitution must be maintained. Voting will not make your soldiers victorious, but
they who by soldiership have overcome the enemy provide
you with liberty and security for voting and doing what
you please. In arms you should be terrible, in courts of
justice humane.

If any one thinks I talk a language above my position, this
very quality of the speech is laudable. An oration to be
spoken for a state so illustrious, and on affairs so important,
should transcend the character of the speaker, whoever he
be; it should approximate to your dignity rather than his.
Why none of your favourites speak in such a style I will
explain to you. The candidates for office and employment
go about and cringe to the voting interest, each ambitious to

be created general, not to perform any manlike deed.  Or if there be a man capable of noble enterprise, he thinks now that starting with the name and reputation of the state, profiting by the absence of opponents, holding out hopes to you, and nothing else, he shall himself inherit your advantages—which really happens—whereas, if you did everything by yourselves, you would share with the rest, not in the actions only, but also in their results.  Your politicians and that class of men, neglecting to give you honest advice, ally themselves to the former class: and as you once had boards for taxes, so now you have boards for politics; an orator presiding, a general under him, and three hundred men to shout on either side; while the rest of you are attached some to one party, some to the other.  Accordingly—this is what you get by the system—such and such a person has a brazen statue; here and there is an individual more thriving than the commonwealth: you, the people, sit as witnesses of their good fortune, abandoning to them for an ephemeral indolence your great and glorious heritage of prosperity.

But see how it was in the time of your ancestors; for by domestic (not foreign) examples you may learn your lesson of duty.  Themistocles who commanded in the sea-fight at Salamis, and Miltiades who led at Marathon, and many others, who performed services unlike the generals of the present day—assuredly they were not set up in brass nor overvalued by your forefathers, who honoured them, but only as persons on a level with themselves.  Your forefathers, O my countrymen, surrendered not their part in any of those glories.  There is no man who will attribute the victory of Salamis to Themistocles, but to the Athenians; nor the battle of Marathon to Miltiades, but to the republic.  But now people say that Timotheus took Corcyra,[1] and Iphicrates cut off the Spartan division,[2] and Chabrias won the naval

---

[1] Timotheus brought back Corcyra to the Athenian alliance, B.C. 376. The Lacedæmonians attempted to recover it three years after, but were defeated.

[2] At Lechæum near Corinth.  See the first Philippic, p. 148, note 1.

victory at Naxos: [1] for you seem to resign the merit of these actions, by the extravagance of the honours which you have bestowed on their account upon each of the commanders.

So wisely did the Athenians of that day confer political rewards; so improperly do you. But how the rewards of foreigners? To Menon the Pharsalian, who gave twelve talents in money for the war at Eion [2] by Amphipolis, and assisted them with two hundred horsemen of his own retainers, the Athenians then voted not the freedom of their city, but only granted immunity from imposts. And in earlier times to Perdiccas,[3] who reigned in Macedonia during the invasion of the Barbarian—when he had destroyed the Persians who retreated from Platæa after their defeat, and completed the disaster of the king—they voted not the freedom of their city, but only granted immunity from imposts; doubtless esteeming their country to be of high value, honour, and dignity, surpassing all possible obligation. But now, ye men of Athens, ye adopt the vilest of mankind, menials and the sons of menials, to be your citizens, receiving a price as for any other saleable commodity. And you have fallen into such a practice, not because your natures are inferior to your ancestors, but because they were in a condition to think highly of themselves, while from you, men of Athens, this power is taken away. It can never be, methinks, that your spirit is generous and noble while you are engaged

The division of the Lacedæmonian army which Iphicrates defeated, was little more than four hundred men. The fame of the exploit, so disproportioned to the numbers engaged, was owing partly to the great renown of the Spartan infantry, which had not been defeated in a pitched battle for a long period before, and partly to the new kind of troops employed by the Athenian general.

[1] Which annihilated the Spartan navy, B.C. 376. In this battle Phocion first distinguished himself.

[2] Eion is a city on the Strymon below Amphipolis. In the eighth year of the Peloponnesian war, when Brasidas had taken Amphipolis, he sailed down the Strymon to attack Eion, but the town had been put in a posture of defence by Thucydides the historian, who came to its relief with some ships from Thasos. There is no mention in Thucydides of Menon the Pharsalian.

[3] It was Alexander who reigned in Macedonia at this time. This then is either a mistake of the orator, or we may suppose with Lucchesini, that Perdiccas, the son of Alexander, was governor of a principality, and therefore dignified with the kingly title.

in petty and mean employments; no more than you can be abject and mean-spirited while your actions are honourable and glorious. Whatever be the pursuits of men, their sentiments must necessarily be similar.

Mark what a summary view may be taken of the deeds performed by your ancestors and by you. Possibly from such comparison you may rise superior to yourselves. They for a period of five-and-forty years took the lead of the Greeks by general consent, and carried up more than ten thousand talents into the citadel; and many glorious trophies they erected for victories by land and sea, wherein even yet we take a pride. And remember, they erected these not merely that we may survey them with admiration, but also that we may emulate the virtues of the dedicators.[1] Such was their conduct: but for ours—fallen as we have on a solitude manifest to you all—look if it bears any resemblance. Have not more than fifteen hundred talents been lavished ineffec- tually on the distressed people of Greece? Have not all private fortunes, the revenues of the state, the contributions from our allies, been squandered? Have not the allies whom we gained in the war been lost recently in the peace? But, forsooth, in these respects only was it better anciently than now, in other respects worse. Very far from that! Let us examine what instances you please. The edifices which they left, the ornaments of the city in temples, harbours, and the like, were so magnificent and beautiful, that room is not left for any succeeding generation to surpass them: yonder gate- way,[2] the Parthenon, docks, porticoes, and other structures,

---

[1] The trophy, which consisted of armour and spoils taken from the enemy, was hung up, usually on a tree, near the field of battle, and consecrated to some god, with an inscription showing the names of the conquerors and the conquered. But sometimes pillars of brass and stone were erected as lasting memorials of important victories.

[2] The Propylæa, which could be seen from the Pnyx, where the people assembled, and were pointed to by the orator. This was an ornamental fortification in front of the Acropolis, considered the most beautiful structure in Athens. It was constructed of white marble, at an immense expense, in the time of Pericles, and took five years in building. Particular descriptions of it may be found in Thirlwall's and Grote's Histories of Greece.

which they adorned the city withal and bequeathed to us. The private houses of the men in power were so modest and in accordance with the name of the constitution, that if any one knows the style of house which Themistocles occupied, or Cimon, or Aristides, or Miltiades, and the illustrious of that day, he perceives it to be no grander than that of the neighbours. But now, ye men of Athens—as regards public measures—our government is content to furnish roads, fountains, white-washing, and trumpery; not that I blame the authors of these works; far otherwise; I blame you, if you suppose that such measures are all you have to execute. As regards individual conduct—your men in office have (some of them) made their private houses, not only more ostentatious than the multitude, but more splendid than the public buildings; others are farming land which they have purchased of such an extent, as once they never hoped for in a dream.

The cause of this difference is, that formerly the people were lords and masters of all; any individual citizen was glad to receive from them his share of honour, office, or profit. Now, on the contrary, these persons are the disposers of emoluments; everything is done by their agency; the people are treated as underlings and dependents, and you are happy to take what these men allow you for your portion.

Accordingly the affairs of the republic are in such a state, that, if any one read your decrees and recounted your actions directly afterwards, no man would believe that both came from the same persons. Take for example the decrees that you passed against the accursed Megarians, when they were cultivating the sacred ground; that you would sally forth and prevent and not allow it: your decrees in regard to the Phliasians,[1] when they were driven lately into exile; that you would assist, and not abandon them to the murderers,

[1] The Phliasians had for some time been at enmity with their neighbours the Argives, partly in consequence of their attachment to Sparta. When the Thebans invaded Peloponnesus, B.C. 366, Chares was sent from Athens to assist the Phliasians, whose city was threatened by the confederates. The events referred to must have been of a much later date, though we cannot exactly determine it. We learn from

and invite the Peloponnesians who were inclined to join you. All these were honourable, men of Athens, and just and worthy of the country: but the deeds that followed them, utterly worthless. Thus by decrees you manifest your hostility, yet cannot execute a single undertaking: for your decrees are proportioned to the dignity of the state, while your power corresponds not with them. I would advise you—and let no man be angry with me—to lower your pride and be content with minding your own business, or to provide yourselves with a greater force. If I knew you to be Siphnians or Cythnians [1] or any other people of that sort, I would have advised you to lower your pride; but, as you are Athenians, I recommend the providing a force. It were disgraceful, men of Athens, disgraceful, to desert that post of magnanimity, which your ancestors bequeathed to you. Besides, even should you desire to withdraw from Grecian affairs, it is not in your power. For many feats have been performed by you from the earliest time; and your established friends it were disgraceful to abandon, your enemies you cannot trust and suffer to become great. In short, the position which your statesmen hold relative to you—they cannot retire when they choose—is precisely that which you have arrived at: for you have interfered in the politics of Greece.

I can sum up all that has been spoken, men of Athens. Your orators never make you either vicious or good, but you make them whichever you please: for you aim not at what they desire, but they at what they suppose to be your objects. You therefore must begin by having noble purposes, and all will be well. Either men will abstain from unworthy counsels, or gain nothing by them, having none to follow their advice.

Diodorus, that as early as B.C. 374 some Phliasian exiles made an ineffectual attempt to betray their city to the Argives. It seems this attempt was afterwards repeated with more success. Whether Philip had anything to do with it, or whether the Argives alone, or in conjunction with their Peloponnesian allies, effected the reduction of Phlius, we cannot ascertain. The exiled party implored the assistance of Athens, and obtained the promises which the orator refers to.

[1] Siphnos and Cythnos are small islands in the Ægean sea.

# THE ORATION ON THE NAVY BOARDS

## ARGUMENT

THIS was (according to Dionysius) the first speech delivered by
Demosthenes before the popular assembly.   The date of it was B.C. 354;
the occasion as follows :
  In the second year of the Social war Chares, who commanded the
Athenian fleet, either from inability to maintain his troops, or from
motives of selfish avarice, or both causes combined, went into the
service of Artabazus, the Ionian satrap, then in revolt against Artaxerxes.   To him Chares rendered important assistance, and received
a rich recompense in money.   At first this measure was approved of
at Athens; but in the beginning of the next year an embassy was sent
by Artaxerxes, to prefer a formal complaint against Chares for his
violation of the peace between Athens and Persia.   Chares was immediately ordered to quit the service of Artabazus; but the Athenians
soon received intelligence that the Persian king was making vast
naval preparations, and they conjectured, not without reason, that
these were intended to support their revolted allies.   Accordingly
they hastened to put an end to the Social war, in which they had met
with nothing but disasters, and the same year a negotiation was opened
with the allies, and a peace concluded, by which their independence
was acknowledged.
  Meanwhile the Persian armament was still talked of at Athens, and
there were rumours of a threatened invasion, which excited alarm in
some, and stirred up the patriotism of others.   Statesmen of the old
school recalled to mind the glorious days of their ancestors, and
imagined the time was come for taking vengeance on the common
enemy of Greece.   Isocrates was a patriot of that class, as we learn
from his extant orations.   Others less honest than Isocrates took
advantage of the general agitation, and would, for selfish purposes,
have precipitated their country into a useless and unseasonable war.
An assembly was held to consider what measures should be adopted.
A proposal was actually made to declare war against Persia, and
invite the other states of Greece to join in the common cause.   Orators
who supported this motion declaimed about the older times, boasted
of Marathon and Salamis, flattered the vanity of their countrymen,
and appealed to the national prejudices.   What the temper of the
assembly was, may partly be gathered from the following Oration.
Demosthenes rose (then in his thirty-first year of age, according to
others, in his twenty-eighth), and in a calm and temperate speech
dissuaded the Athenians from adopting any such absurd resolution.
He pointed out the folly of commencing hostilities, which they had not
sufficient means to carry on: that the project of uniting the Greeks
for such a purpose was chimerical; they were too jealous of one another
and especially of Athens to join in any aggressive war, though they
might possibly combine to resist a Persian invasion if it were really
attempted.   At present there was no cause for alarm: if Athens would
keep quiet the Persian king would leave her alone; but if she attacked
him without provocation, he would in all probability get some of the

Greek people on his own side. The true way of averting the supposed danger was, not to begin the attack but to put the country in a posture of defence, so that, whether menaced with war from Persia or from any other quarter, they might not be taken unprepared. How to make their defensive preparations was the chief thing to be considered; and to this question Demosthenes addressed himself in so masterly and practical a style that in the youthful orator might already be discerned the future statesman.

In this speech there is no effort to make a display of eloquence: it is confined to the giving of useful and simple advice. A definite plan is proposed for the regulation of the Athenian navy, by which the number of ships might be increased to three hundred, and a provision made for their speedy and punctual equipment. To effect this object, Demosthenes proposes a reform, from which the Oration takes its title, in the system of *Symmoriæ*, or *Boards for the Management of the Trierarchy*. The details of the proposed scheme are plainly set forth in the Oration itself, and will easily be understood by the reader.

It is pleasing to see Demosthenes, at the outset of his political career, coming forward to moderate the intemperate zeal of the people, to allay the ferment excited by factious demagogues and foolish dreamers —showing himself at the same time attached to the government of his country, and even to the form of her institutions, while he is desirous of adapting them to circumstances, and correcting the abuses by which their proper working was impeded. Here indeed is struck the key-note of that which for many years continued to be the policy of this great man: viz., to uphold the dignity of Athens on the basis of wise laws, to maintain her independence by the spirit and exertions of her own people, to rally round her, for empire and for safety, a host of willing confederates, united by the bonds of common interest, mutual confidence and esteem.

It appears to me, O Athenians, that the men who praise your ancestors adopt a flattering language, not a course beneficial to the people whom they eulogise. For attempting to speak on subjects, which no man can fully reach by words, they carry away the reputation of clever speakers themselves, but cause the glory of those ancients to fall below its estimation in the minds of the hearers. For my part, I consider the highest praise of our ancestors to be the length of time which has elapsed, during which no other men have been able to excel the pattern of their deeds. I will myself endeavour to show, in what way, according to my judgment, your preparations may most conveniently be made. For thus it is. Though all of us who intend to speak should prove ourselves capital orators, your affairs, I am certain, would prosper none the more: but if any person whomsoever [1] came forward,

---

[1] This is a modest allusion to himself.

and could show and convince you what kind and what amount of force will be serviceable to the state, and from what resources it should be provided, all our present apprehensions would be removed. This will I endeavour to do, as far as I am able, first briefly informing you what my opinion is concerning our relations with the king.

I hold the king to be the common enemy of all the Greeks; yet not on this account would I advise you, without the rest, to undertake a war against him. For I do not observe that the Greeks themselves are common friends to one another; on the contrary, some have more confidence in him than in certain of their own people. Such being the case, I deem it expedient for you to look that the cause of war be equitable and just, that all necessary preparations should be made, and that this should be the groundwork of your resolution. For I think, men of Athens, if there were any clear and manifest proof that the Persian king was about to attack the Greeks, they would join alliance and be exceedingly grateful to those who sided with and defended them against him: but if we rush into a quarrel before his intentions are declared, I fear, men of Athens, we shall be driven to a war with both the king and the people whom we are anxious to protect. He will suspend his designs—if he really has resolved to attack the Greeks— will give money to some of them and promise friendship: they, desiring to carry on their private wars with better success, and intent on projects of that kind, will disregard the common safety of all.

I beseech you not to betray our country into such embarrassment and folly. For you, I see, cannot adopt the same principles of action in reference to the king as the other Greeks can. It is open, I conceive, to many of them, to prosecute their selfish interests and neglect the body of the nation: it would be dishonourable in you, though you had suffered wrong, to punish the offenders in such a way as to let any of them fall under the power of the barbarian.

Under these circumstances, we must take care that we

ourselves engage not in the war upon unequal terms, and that he, whom we suppose to entertain designs upon the Greeks, do not gain the credit of appearing their friend.    How can it be managed?    By giving proof to the world that the forces of our state are mustered and prepared, and that possessing such forces we espouse sentiments of justice.    To the over-daring, who are vehement in urging you to war, I have this to say: It is not difficult in the season for deliberation to earn the repute of courage, or, when danger is nigh, to be exceeding eloquent:    it is, however, both difficult and becoming in the hour of danger to exhibit courage, in counsel to find better advice than other men.

It is my opinion, men of Athens, that a war with the king would distress our republic, though any action in the course of the war would be an easy affair.    Why so?    Because, methinks, every war necessarily requires a fleet and money and posts; and of all these things I perceive that he has a greater abundance than ourselves: but for action, I observe, nothing is so much needed as brave soldiers, and of these, I imagine, we and our confederates have the greater number. My advice therefore is, that we should by no means begin the war, though for action we ought to be fully prepared.    If indeed there were one description of force wherewith bar- barians could be resisted, and another wherewith Greeks, we might reasonably perhaps be regarded as arraying our- selves against Persia:    but since all arming is of the same character; and your force must amount to the same thing, namely, the means of resisting your enemies, of succouring your allies, of preserving your valuable possessions; why, when we have professed enemies,[1] do we look out for others?

---

[1] This refers principally to the Thebans, between whom and the Athenians an enmity had subsisted ever since the severance of their alliance, when the Athenians, jealous of the growing power of Thebes under Epaminondas, went over to the side of Sparta.    This enmity was increased by the events of the Sacred war, which had now been raging for two years, and in which the Thebans were engaged as prin- cipals on one side, while the Phocians received assistance from Athens and Lacedæmon.    The Locrians and most of the tribes of Thessaly, then in alliance with Thebes, are to be reckoned among the enemies

why do we not rather prepare ourselves against the former, and be ready to resist the king also, if he attempt to injure us?

And now you invite the Greeks to join you. But if you will not act as they desire, some of them having no goodwill towards you, how can you expect they will obey your call? Because, forsooth, they will hear from you that the Persian has designs against them. And pray, do you imagine they don't foresee it themselves? I believe they do: but at present this fear outweighs not the enmity which some of them bear towards you and towards each other. Your ambassadors then will only travel round and rhapsodise. But when the time comes, if what we now expect be really brought to pass, I fancy none of the Greek community rate themselves so high that, when they see you possessed of a thousand horse, as many infantry soldiers as one could desire, and three hundred ships, they would not come with entreaties, and regard such aid as their surest means of deliverance. The consequences then are—by inviting them now, you are suppliants, and, if your petition be not granted, you fail: whereas, by waiting your time and completing your preparations, you save men at their own request, and are sure they will all come over to you.

Swayed by these and the like considerations, men of Athens, I sought not to compose a bold harangue of tedious length: but have taken exceeding pains in devising a plan, the best and the speediest, for getting your forces ready. It will be for you to hear it, and, if it meet your approval, to vote for its adoption.

The first and most essential part of preparation, men of Athens, is to be so disposed in your minds that every citizen is willing and earnest to perform his duty. For you see, O Athenians, whenever you have had a common wish, and every man has thought afterwards that the accomplishment belonged to himself, nothing has ever escaped you; but when

whom Demosthenes refers to: perhaps also the Olynthians and the revolted subjects of Athens.

*I 546

you have wished only, and then looked to one another, each expecting to be idle while his neighbour did the work, none of your designs have been executed.

You being so animated and determined, I advise that we fill up the twelve hundred and make two thousand, adding eight hundred to them: for if you appoint that number, I reckon that, after deducting the heiresses and wards, and holders of allotments and partnership property,[1] and persons in reduced circumstances, you will still have your twelve hundred members. Of them I think you should make twenty boards, as at present, each having sixty members. Each of these boards I would have you divide into five sections of twelve men, putting always with the wealthiest person some of the least wealth, to preserve equality. And thus I say the members ought to be arranged: the reason you will understand when you have heard the whole scheme of arrangement. But how about the ships? I recommend you to fix the whole number at three hundred, and form twenty divisions of fifteen vessels each, giving five of the first hundred and five of the second hundred and five of the third hundred to each division; then allot one division of fifteen ships to every board of men, and let the board assign three ships to each of their own sections.

When these regulations have been made, I propose—as the rateable capital of the country is six thousand talents—in order that your supplies may be apportioned, you should

---

[1] The persons here enumerated were exempt from service of the *Trierarchia*. Heiresses and wards were exempt, because, although they might have property enough to defray the contingent expense, yet the service was connected with a personal trust, which by reason of sex and age they were incapable of performing. The colonial allottees were exempt, by reason of their absence. The operation of the law would be as follows. The state in the first instance looks to the visible property of the citizens, such as land, houses, stock in trade, or agriculture. A register is formed of the twelve hundred owners of property most competent to serve the office of *trierarch*. This register continues the same, until circumstances have happened which call for an alteration; and, practically speaking, the same families continue for a long period in the register. But (says Demosthenes) the thing worked so, that at any given time, when there was a call for service, the register could not be depended on for the whole number.

divide this capital and make a hundred parts of sixty talents each; then allot five of these hundredth parts to each of the twenty larger boards, and let the board assign one hundredth part to each of their own sections; so that, if you have need of a hundred ships, sixty talents may be applied to the expense, and there may be twelve to serve as commanders; [1] if of two hundred, there may be thirty talents applied to the expense, and six persons to serve; if of three hundred, there may be twenty talents defraying the expense, and four persons to serve.

In the same manner, O Athenians, I advise that all the furniture of the ships which is out on loan [2] should be valued according to the register, and divided into twenty parts; that you then allot one good portion to every large board; that every board distribute equal shares among their own sections; that the twelve in each section call their implements in, and get the ships which are severally allotted to them in readiness. Thus do I think the supplies, the vessels, the commanders, and the collection of implements, may be most effecutally provided and arranged. How the manning may be made sure and easy, I proceed to explain.

I say the generals should divide the dockyards into ten departments, taking care that there be thirty docks in each as near as possible to one another; and when they have done this, let them attach two boards and thirty ships to each of these departments, then allot the tribes and the several commanders to each dockyard, so that there may be two boards, thirty ships, one tribe. And whichever department be allotted to a tribe, let them divide in it three and the ships likewise, and then allot the third of a tribe to each, so that of the whole dockyards there may be one division belong-

---

[1] *Trierarchs.* The name was kept up, when it had become a matter of contribution and civil trust, rather than of naval service. So, the Lord High Admiral of our own government might never have seen the sea.

[2] It was customary for individuals to borrow the naval implements and stores from the public arsenal, when the state had no occasion for them.

ing to every tribe, and the third of a tribe may have the third part of every division, and you may know, in case of necessity, first, where the tribe is stationed, next, where the third of the tribe, next, who are the commanders and how many ships there are; and the tribe may have thirty ships, and every third of a tribe have ten. Let the system be only put in train, and though we should forget something now—for it is difficult to make all the details perfect—it will be ascertained in the working; and there will be one arrangement for all the ships and every division.

In regard to money and real supplies, I know that I am about to make an extraordinary statement, yet still it shall be made; for I am persuaded that, on a correct view, I alone shall be found to have declared and predicted the truth. I say, we ought not at present to speak of money: a supply there is, if occasion require it, ample, honourable, and just: if we look for it immediately, we shall not think we have it even in reserve; so far shall we be from providing it now; but if we leave it alone, we shall have it. What then is this supply, which hath no being now, but will exist hereafter?— for certainly it is like a riddle. I will explain.

You see the extent of this city, men of Athens. It contains treasures equal, I may almost say, to the rest of the states put together. But the owners are so minded, that—if all your orators alarmed them with intelligence that the king was coming, that he was at hand, that the danger was inevitable—if, besides the orators, an equal number of persons gave oracular warning—so far from contributing, they would not even discover their wealth or acknowledge the possession. Yet if they knew that these proceedings, so terrible in report, were actually begun, there is not a man so foolish who would not be ready to give and foremost to contribute. For who would rather perish with all his possessions than contribute a part of his possessions to preserve himself and the remainder? Thus, I say, we have money against the time of actual need, but not before. And therefore I advise you not to search for it now. Indeed what you would raise, if you determined to raise it, would be more ridiculous than nothing at all. For example:—Let a tax be proposed of one per cent. — there are sixty talents. Let twice as much, namely two per cent., be proposed—there are a hundred and twenty. But what is this to the twelve hundred camels, which, these men say, carry the king's gold? Let me suppose, however, that we contributed the twelfth of our property, five hundred talents. This you would not submit to; but if you did pay it, the sum would be insufficient for the war. Your proper course then is to complete your other preparations; let the owners retain their money for the present (it cannot be in better keeping for the state), and should the occasion ever arrive, then take it from them in voluntary contributions.

These, O my countrymen, are practicable measures, these are honourable and advantageous, fit to be reported as your proceedings to the king; and by them no little terror would be excited in him. He knows right well that by three hundred galleys, whereof we furnished a hundred, his ancestors lost a thousand ships; and he will hear that we ourselves have now equipped three hundred; so that, were he ever so mad, he could hardly deem it a light matter to provoke the hostility of our republic. Should he, however, entertain an overweening confidence in his wealth, even this he will find to be a weaker support than yours. He is coming, they say, with gold. But if he give it away, he will lack supplies: for even wells and fountains are apt to fail if you draw from them constantly and by wholesale. He will hear that the valuation of our land is a capital of six thousand talents. That we shall defend it against invaders from that quarter his ancestors who were at Marathon would know best: and certainly, as long as we are victorious, money can never fail us.

Nor is there, as it appears to me, any ground for what some persons fear, that, having money, he will collect a large

body of mercenaries. I do indeed believe, that against
Egypt [1] and Orontes,[2] and any other barbarians, many of the
Greeks would be willing to serve in his pay, not that he may
subdue any of those adversaries, but in order to obtain
supplies for themselves to relieve their several necessities.
Against Greece, however, I do not believe that any Grecian
would march. For whither could he betake himself afterwards? Go to Phrygia and be a slave?—Remember, a war
with the barbarian can be for no other stake than for country
and life and customs and freedom and everything of the kind.
Who then is so wretched that he would sacrifice himself,
parents, sepulchres, fatherland, for the sake of a paltry
pittance? I believe, no man. But further—it is not even
the king's interest that mercenaries should conquer the
Greeks. For they that conquer us must have been his
masters already: and he desires, not to subdue us and then
be dependent on others, but to rule, if possible, over all; if
that be not possible, at least over his present subjects.

Should any one think the Thebans will be on his side—I
know it is difficult to speak to you about that people: you
hate them so, you will not like to hear even the truth or anything favourable of them—however men who are considering
important questions must not omit any useful argument on
any pretext. My opinion then is, the Thebans, so far from
being likely to join him in any attack upon Greece, would
give a large sum of money, if they had it, for the opportunity
of repairing their former offences against her.[3]    But supposing

[1] Egypt had been in a state of revolt from Persia ever since the
reign of Darius Nothus.

[2] Orontes was satrap of Mysia in the reign of Artaxerxes Mnemon.
He joined the great conspiracy of the satraps and the king of Egypt in
the year B.C. 362. He was chosen to command their forces, and entrusted with a large fund which had been collected to carry on the war.
He was induced, however, to change sides; and the trust which had
been reposed in him enabled him to betray his party to the king most
effectually. Other rebels followed his example; and this confederacy
which at one time had threatened the very existence of the Persian
monarchy, was suddenly dissolved. What became of Orontes afterwards is unknown.

[3] The Thebans had always been reproached for siding with Xerxes
against the Greeks. (See the second Philippic, p. 83.) After the

the Thebans to be so utterly wrongheaded, of this at least you
are all aware, that, if the Thebans are in his interest, their
enemies must necessarily be in the interest of the Greeks.

I believe then, that our cause (the cause of justice) and its
adherents will be better armed against all adversaries than
the traitors and the barbarian can be. And therefore my
advice is—be not over-alarmed at the war; neither be led on
to commence it. I do not see, indeed, that any other people
of Greece have reason to fear this war. For which of them is
ignorant that whilst, looking on the Persian as a common
enemy, they were in concord among themselves they enjoyed
many advantages; but since they have regarded him as a
friend and quarrelled about private disputes with each other,
they have suffered greater calamities than could have been
wished in pronouncing a curse upon them? Then should we
fear a man, whom fortune and heaven declare to be unprofitable as a friend, and useful as an enemy? Let us do no
such thing! Yet do him no injustice either, having regard
to ourselves, and to the disturbances and jealousies among
the other people of Greece. If it were possible with one heart
and with combined forces to attack him alone, such an injury
I would not have pronounced an injustice. But since this
cannot be, I say we must be cautious, and not afford the
king a pretence for vindicating the rights of the other Greeks.
As long as we remain quiet, any such attempt on his part
would awaken suspicion; but if we are the first to commence

capture of Thebes by Alexander, this old charge was (not very fairly)
revived against them by their enemies. The penalty which had been
denounced against them ever since the Persian war was then inflicted,
and Thebes was razed to the ground. Here we find Demosthenes
speaking more liberally of the Thebans than his countrymen were
wont to do. The Athenians, besides their recent grounds of quarrel,
had a long standing enmity with that people, arising out of various
causes. The Thebans had been their most bitter opponents in the
Peloponnesian war, and at its termination had proposed to destroy
Athens altogether. Their merciless treatment of the Platæans, both
in that war, and afterwards B.C. 373, when they destroyed the city,
could never be forgotten by the Athenians, between whom and the
Platæans the closest friendship had subsisted ever since the battle of
Marathon.

hostilities it will naturally be thought that he courts their friendship because of his enmity with us.

Do not expose the melancholy condition of Greece by convoking her people when you cannot persuade them, and making war when you cannot carry it on.  Only keep quiet, fear nothing, and prepare yourselves.  Let it be reported of you to the king—not (for heaven's sake) that all the Greeks and the Athenians are in distress and alarm and confusion which is very far from the truth—but that, if falsehood and perjury were not considered as disgraceful by the Greeks as by him they are considered honourable, you would have marched against him long ago; that you will forbear to do this for your own sakes, but you pray unto all the gods that he may be inspired with the same madness that his ancestors were formerly.  Should he come to reflect on these matters, he will find that your resolutions are taken with prudence. He knows assuredly that Athens by her wars with his ancestors became prosperous and great, whilst by the repose, which she enjoyed before, she was not raised above any Grecian state so much as she is at present.  And as to the Greeks, he perceives that they stand in need of some mediator, either a voluntary or an involuntary one; and he knows that he should himself step in as such a mediator if he stirred up war.  Therefore the accounts that he will receive from his informants will be intelligible and credible.

Not to trouble you, men of Athens, with over many words, I will give a summary of my advice and retire.  I bid you prepare yourselves against existing enemies, and I declare that with this same force you should resist the king and all other people, if they attempt to injure you; but never commence an injustice either in word or deed.  Let us look that our actions, and not our speeches on the platform, be worthy of our ancestors.  If you pursue this course you will do service, not only to yourselves, but also to them who give the opposite counsel, since you will not be angry with them afterwards for your errors committed now.

# THE ORATION ON THE LIBERTY OF THE
# RHODIANS

## ARGUMENT

THIS Oration was delivered B.C. 351 on the following occasion:

In the island of Rhodes, as in divers other of the Grecian states, there had been many contests between the democratical party and the oligarchical. At the close of the Peloponnesian war it was in the hands of an oligarchy, under the protection of Lacedæmon. About the year 396 Conon, being at the head of a considerable fleet in that part of the Ægean, drove the Peloponnesians from the port of Rhodes, and compelled the islanders to renew their connection with Athens. Democracy was then re-established; but four years afterwards the opposite faction again prevailed, a Spartan fleet made its appearance, the popular leaders and the friends of Athens were banished or put to death. For the next thirty years or more following that event little is known of the Rhodian history. After the destruction of the Spartan navy, Rhodes with most of the Ægean isles returned to the Athenian confederacy, and we may fairly presume that a new democratical revolution was effected in the island during that period. But in the year 358 a rupture of a most serious kind took place between Rhodes and Athens, pregnant with disastrous consequences to both. This was the breaking out of the Social war, the immediate causes of which are obscurely reported to us, though there is sufficient evidence to show that the provocation to revolt proceeded from the misconduct, or at least the imprudence of the Athenians themselves.

We learn from various parts of Demosthenes, especially from the Oration on the Chersonese (p. 178), how the Athenian commanders at this period, sent out with inadequate forces and supplies, were tempted or driven to commit irregularities, amounting often to acts of plunder and violence, in order to maintain their armaments or carry on their wars. Not confining their aggressions to the enemies of Athens, or even to neutrals, they harassed the allies, by extorting from them loans and contributions, and thus brought the name of their country into general odium and discredit. It seems that Chares, having the command of a fleet destined to act against Amphipolis, and conceiving himself to hold large discretionary powers, sailed to Rhodes, and by his vexatious and arbitrary proceedings so irritated the people, that they were ready on the first opportunity to throw off their connection with Athens. The islands of Cos and Chios had been alienated from the Athenians by similar causes, and desired to recover their independence. These three states entered into a league with Byzantium, which in fact had been meditated some years before, and raising a fleet powerful enough to set the Athenians at defiance, commenced the Social war, which, after a three years' continuance, was terminated (as we have seen) by a peace humiliating to Athens, B.C. 355.

In the course of this war the allies received assistance from Mausolus,

259

king of Caria. He had formed the design of annexing Rhodes to his own dominions, to which it was so conveniently adjacent; but there was little hope of accomplishing this purpose unless he could sever it from the Athenian alliance. The oligarchical party in Rhodes, still watching for a new revolution, were easily brought over to his views; and at the close of the war a Carian garrison was introduced into the island, which established the oligarchy, and in effect brought the island in subjection to a foreign yoke. The Rhodians had no hopes of recovering their liberty; they had lost the protection of a powerful state; while Mausolus could obtain effectual aid from the Persian king, whose vassal he was, and to whom it was important to acquire any of the islands near Asia Minor. Mausolus died in the year B.C. 353, and was succeeded by his queen Artemisia. In her reign the government of Rhodes became oppressive to the people; who at length resolving to throw off their yoke, sent a deputation to Athens, to implore her assistance. These petitioners, who were not very favourably received at Athens, found an advocate in Demosthenes.

It was natural to expect that there would be a strong feeling at Athens against a people who had deeply injured her. A very few years had elapsed since the Social war, and the events were fresh in the memory of all. To overcome this feeling of resentment was the principal difficulty which an advocate of the Rhodian people had to encounter. Demosthenes appeals to the higher and nobler feelings of his countrymen. Motives of honour, generosity and compassion should influence Athenians: it was not worth while to remember the wrongs done them by so insignificant a people as the Rhodian; they should consider only what was due from them to Athens and to Greece. It was their duty as well as their interest to vindicate the liberties of a Greek people under oppression, and more especially to defend the cause of popular government against oligarchs and tyrants. Unless they did so, their own constitution might soon be in danger; for there was a perpetual strife going on between oligarchy and democracy, and, if all other democracies were put down, the Athenian must be assailed at last. It was urged on the other side, that interference with Rhodes might provoke the hostility of the Persian king. Demosthenes contends that the loss of Rhodes, which did not properly belong to him, was not likely to provoke the king; that in the present state of the Persian empire both he and Artemisia would probably remain neutral; but that at all events the Athenians ought to espouse the cause of the Rhodian people, even at the risk of Persian hostility.

I THINK, men of Athens, that on a consultation of such moment you ought to grant liberty of speech to every one of your advisers. For my own part, I have never thought it difficult to make you understand right counsel—for to speak plainly, you seem all to possess the knowledge yourselves—but to persuade you to follow it I have found difficult; for when any measure has been voted and resolved, you are then as far from the performance as you were from the resolution before.

One of the events for which I consider you should be

thankful to the Gods is, that a people, who, to gratify their own insolence, went to war with you not long ago, now place their hopes of safety in you alone. Well may we be rejoiced at the present crisis: for if your measures thereupon be wisely taken, the result will be that the calumnies of those who traduce our country you will practically and with credit and honour refute. The Chians, Byzantines, and Rhodians accused us of a design to oppress them, and therefore combined to make the last war against us. It will turn out that Mausolus, who contrived and instigated these proceedings, pretending to be a friend of the Rhodians, has deprived them of their liberty; the Chians and Byzantines, who called them allies, have not aided them in misfortune; whilst you, whom they dreaded, are the only people who have wrought their deliverance. And, this being seen by all the world, you will cause the people in every state to regard your friendship as the token of their security: nor can there be a greater blessing for you than thus to obtain from all men a voluntary attachment and confidence.

I marvel to see the same persons advising you to oppose the king on behalf of the Egyptians, and afraid of him in the matter of the Rhodian people. All men know that the latter are Greeks, the former a portion of his subjects. And I think some of you remember that, when you were debating about the king's business, I first came forward and advised—nay, I was the only one, or one of two, that gave such counsel—that your prudent course in my opinion was, not to allege your quarrel with the king as the excuse for your arming, but to arm against your existing enemies, and defend yourselves against him also, if he attempted to injure you. Nor did I offer this advice without obtaining your approval; for you agreed with me. Well then: my reasoning of to-day is consistent with the argument on that occasion. For, would the king take me to his counsels, I should advise him as I advise you, in defence of his own possessions, to make war upon any Greeks that opposed him, but not to think of claiming dominions to which he had no manner of title. If now it be your general determination, Athenians, to surrender to the king all places that he gets possession of, whether by surprise or by deluding certain of the inhabitants, you have determined, in my judgment, unwisely: but if in the cause of justice you esteem it your duty, either to make war, if needful, or to suffer any extremity; in the first place, there will be the less necessity for such trials, in proportion as you are resolved to meet them; and secondly, you will manifest a spirit that becomes you.

That I suggest nothing new, in urging you to liberate the Rhodians—that you will do nothing new, in following my counsel—will appear, if I remind you of certain measures that succeeded. Once, O Athenians, you sent Timotheus out to assist Ariobarzanes,[1] annexing to the decree, "that he was not to infringe your treaty with the king." Timotheus, seeing that Ariobarzanes had openly revolted from the king, and that Samos was garrisoned by Cyprothemis, under the appointment of Tigranes, the king's deputy, renounced the intention of assisting Ariobarzanes, but invested the island with his forces and delivered it. And to this day there has been no war against you on that account. Men will not

---

[1] Ariobarzanes, satrap of Phrygia, was concerned in the rebellion of B.C. 362. It seems that, in soliciting Athenian aid, which he obtained the more easily on account of his connection with the state—he having received the honour of citizenship—Ariobarzanes had concealed the object of his preparations; and therefore the Athenians, in sending Timotheus, took the precaution of restricting his powers in the way mentioned by the orator. Timotheus, in return for some service which he had done, was helped by the satrap to get possession of Sestus and Crithote in the Chersonese. Cornelius Nepos praises the Athenian general, because, instead of getting any private recompense from Ariobarzanes, he had looked only to the advantage of his country; while Agesilaus, who had gone out in the same service, took a pecuniary reward for himself. Timotheus then proceeded to besiege Samos, which was occupied by a Persian garrison, and took it in the course of the following year. Isocrates the orator, who acted as the secretary of Timotheus, was at the siege of Samos, and praises the general for having taken it with little or no cost to Athens.

The occupation of Samos by the Persians was an infringement of the peace of Antalcidas, by the terms of which the Greek islands were to be independent. Therefore the conduct of Timotheus, in wresting Samos from Persia, afforded an apt illustration for the argument of Demosthenes.

fight for aggressive purposes so readily as for defensive. To resist spoliation they strive with all their might; not so to gratify ambition: this they will attempt, if there be none to hinder them; but, if prevented, they regard not their opponents as having done them an injury.

My belief is, that Artemisia would not even oppose this enterprise now if our state were embarked in the measure. Attend a moment and see whether my calculation be right or wrong. I consider—were the king succeeding in all his designs in Egypt, Artemisia would make a strenuous effort to get Rhodes into his power, not from affection to the king, but from a desire, while he tarried in her neighbourhood, to confer an important obligation upon him, so that he might give her the most friendly reception: but since he fares as they report, having miscarried in his attempts, she judges that this island—and so the fact is—would be of no further use to the king at present, but only a fortress to overawe her kingdom and prevent disturbances. Therefore, it seems to me, she would rather you had the island, without her appearing to have surrendered it, than that he should obtain possession. I think, indeed, she will send no succours at all, but, if she do, they will be scanty and feeble. As to the king—what he will do I cannot pretend to know; but this I will maintain, that it is expedient for Athens to have it immediately understood whether he means to claim the Rhodian city or not: for, if he should, you will have to deliberate not on the concerns of Rhodes only, but on those of Athens and all Greece.

Even if the Rhodians, who are now in the government, had held it by themselves, I would not have advised you to espouse their cause; not though they promised to do everything for you. But I see that in the beginning, in order to put down the democracy, they gained over a certain number of citizens, and afterwards banished those very men, when they had accomplished their purpose. I think, therefore, that people who have been false to two parties, would be no steadier allies to you. And never would I have proffered this counsel had I thought it would benefit the Rhodian people only; for I am not their state-friend, nor is any one of them connected with me by ties of private hospitality. And even if both these causes had existed, I would not have spoken, unless I had considered it for your advantage. Indeed, as far as the Rhodians are concerned, if the advocate for their deliverance may be allowed to say so, I am rejoiced at what has happened—that, after grudging to you the recovery of your rights, they have lost their own liberty; and, when they might have had an alliance on equal terms with Greeks and their betters, they are under subjection to barbarians and slaves, whom they have admitted into their fortresses.[1] I would almost say, that, if you determine to assist them, these events have turned out for their good. For, during prosperity, I doubt whether they would have learned discretion, being Rhodians; but since they are taught by experience that folly is mightily injurious to men, they may possibly perhaps become wiser for the future; and this I think would be no small advantage to them. I say, therefore, you should endeavour to rescue these people, and not harbour resentment, considering that you too have often been deceived by miscreants, but for no such deceit would you allow that you merited punishment yourselves.

Observe also, men of Athens, that you have waged many

[1] Vitruvius relates a stratagem by which Artemisia got complete dominion of Rhodes. The Rhodians had plotted with a party in Halicarnassus to overthrow the Carian government, and sent a fleet with troops to assist in the execution of their design. The troops landed and advanced to the city, where the inhabitants were ranged under the walls as if to give them a friendly reception. But this was done by order of Artemisia, who had discovered the plot and laid an ambush for the Rhodians. They were surrounded and slain. Artemisia took their ships, and put a Carian force on board, which sailing to Rhodes, and being mistaken by the people for their own armament returning, got possession of the Rhodian capital. If the story be well founded the occurrence was probably later than this Oration, which refers to no act of hostility between the Rhodians and the ruler of Caria. It should be noticed that besides the capital city of Rhodes there were other considerable and much more ancient towns in the island, Lindus, Ialysus, and Camirus.

wars both against democracies and against oligarchies—this indeed you know without my telling—but for what cause you have been at war with either, perhaps not one of you considers. What are the causes? Against democratical states your wars have been either for private grievances, when you could not make public satisfaction, or for territory, or boundaries, or a point of honour, or the leadership: against oligarchies, for none of these matters, but for your constitution and freedom. Therefore I would not hesitate to say, I think it better that all the Greeks should be your enemies with a popular government, than your friends under oligarchal. For with freemen I consider you would have no difficulty in making peace when you chose; but with people under an oligarchy even friendship I hold to be insecure. It is impossible that the few can be attached to the many, the seekers of power to the lovers of constitutional equality.

I marvel none of you conceive—when the Chians and Mitylenæans are governed by oligarchies, when the Rhodians and nearly all people are about being drawn into this slavery —that our constitution is in the same peril: and none consider, it is impossible if all establishments are on the principle of oligarchy, that they will let your democracy alone. They know too well that no other people will bring things back to the state of liberty: therefore they will wish to destroy a government from which they apprehend mischief to themselves. Ordinary doers of wrong you may regard as enemies to the sufferers only; they that subvert constitutions and transform them into oligarchies must be looked upon, I say, as the common enemies to all lovers of freedom. And besides, men of Athens, it is right that you, living under self-government, should show the same feeling for a free people in misfortune that you would expect others to have for you in case of a similar calamity; which I trust may never befall! Though indeed it may be said that the Rhodians have had their deserts, the occasion is not a fit one for triumph: the fortunate should always be seen to interest themselves for the benefit of the unfortunate, since the future is uncertain to all men.[1]

I often hear it said before this assembly, that, when our commonwealth was in misfortune, certain people were solicitous for its preservation; among whom—I will here mention a little circumstance of the Argives alone.[2] I would not have you, famous as you have ever been for succouring the distressed, appear in a matter of this kind inferior to the Argives: who, inhabiting a country adjacent to the Lacedæmonians, seeing them to have dominion over land and sea, did not fear or hesitate to show their attachment to you, but even passed a vote—when ambassadors had come from Lacedæmon (as we are told) to demand certain Athenian refugees—that, unless they departed before sunset, they should be adjudged enemies. Would it not be disgraceful, my countrymen, if, when the commons of Argos dreaded not the power and empire of the Lacedæmonians in those times, you who are Athenians, should be frightened at a person of barbarian origin, and a woman too? They indeed might allege that they have often been defeated by the Lacedæmonians: whereas you have often vanquished the king, and not once been defeated either by the king himself or by his subjects; for, if ever the king has obtained an advantage over our state, he has obtained it in this way—and in no other—by bribing the betrayers of Greece and the basest of her people. And even such advantage has not benefited him. At the very time when he had enfeebled Athens by aid of the Lacedæmonians, you will find him struggling for his kingdom with Clearchus and Cyrus.[3] Thus he has neither beaten us

[1] The Melian orator, in the debate written by Thucydides, warns the Athenians not to be cruel and oppressive to others, for fear of retaliation at some future time; lest, rendering no mercy, they should find none. Demosthenes recommends a still higher policy, to succour the unfortunate; to win golden opinions in the hour of prosperity, and secure friends against the day of misfortune.

[2] This occurred soon after the Peloponnesian war, when Athens was under the dominion of the thirty tyrants, and a large number of Athenian citizens were compelled to seek safety in exile.

[3] It was to the pecuniary assistance of Persia, obtained by the management of Lysander, that the Spartans were mainly indebted for

openly, nor done himself any good by his intrigues. There are some, I observe, who are used to slight Philip [1] as a person of no account, but dread the king as an enemy terrible to any that he chooses. However, if we are not to oppose the one, because he is contemptible, and yield everything to the other, because he is formidable, against whom shall we take the field, O Athenians?

There are persons here, men of Athens, famous for advocating the rights of others against you; to whom I would give one little piece of advice—to undertake the defence of your rights against others, that they may set an example of dutiful conduct. It is absurd for any one to instruct you in the principles of justice, without acting justly himself: and it is not just, that a citizen should have considered the arguments against you, and not the arguments in your favour. Look you, I pray! How happens it there is none in Byzantium who will admonish them not to take possession of Chalcedon,[2] which belongs to the king, and you held it once,

their success in the Peloponnesian war. A few years afterwards Cyrus, who had been most active in the Spartan cause, marched from his province in Asia Minor to contend for the crown with his brother Atraxerxes. Clearchus commanded the Greek mercenaries in his service. The death of Cyrus, who was slain charging at the head of his troops in the battle of Cunaxa, delivered Artaxerxes and his kingdom from further danger. This expedition is the subject of Xenophon's *Anabasis*. The retreat of the ten thousand Greeks (after the treacherous murder of their generals), under the skilful conduct of Xenophon himself, is one of the most interesting pieces of Grecian history.

[1] About a year only had elapsed since the speaking of the first Philippic. Whatever effect that speech may have produced at the time, it seems to have made no lasting impression. The inaction of Philip in the two following years relieved the Athenians from any immediate apprehension of danger. They were roused to new alarm by the rupture of Philip with Olynthus.

[2] Chalcedon, founded by the Megarians on the Asiatic coast of the Bosphorus, was called the city of the blind, because the settlers had overlooked the more beautiful spot on the European coast, where afterwards Byzantium (site of the modern Constantinople) was built. The fate of Chalcedon, like many other towns similarly situated, was to fall alternately under the dominion of Persia, Athens, and Lacedæmon. It was taken from the Lacedæmonians by Alcibiades, but surrendered to Lysander after the decisive battle of Ægos-Potamos. The peace of Antalcidas restored it to Persia. At this time the Byzantines, who had acquired considerable power since the Social war, were endeavouring to draw it over to their alliance.

and by no manner of title is it theirs?—also that they are
not to make Selymbria,[1] a city formerly in your alliance,
tributary to themselves, and that Byzantium is not to determine the limits of the Selymbrian territory contrary to the
oaths and the treaties, by which it is declared that the cities
shall be independent?   And none has there been to advise
Mausolus in his lifetime, none since his death to advise
Artemisia, not to seize upon Cos[2] and Rhodes and other
Grecian cities, which the king their master ceded by his
treaty to the Greeks, and for which the Greeks of that period
sustained numerous perils and honourable contests.   Or, if
they have both of them[3] such a monitor, yet seemingly there
are none to follow his advice.

I esteem it a just measure to restore the Rhodian democracy:   yet, granting it were not just, when I look at the
conduct of these people, I conceive it right to advise the
measure.   And why?   Because, O Athenians, if all men
were inclined to observe justice, it would be disgraceful for
us alone to refuse;   but, when all the rest are seeking the
power to do wrong, for us to profess high principle and
undertake no enterprise, would in my opinion be not justice,
but cowardice.   I see that men have their rights allowed
them in proportion to their power:   of which I can produce
an example familiar to you all.   There are two treaties
between the Greeks and the king;   that which our republic
made, which is universally praised, and this latter one, concluded by the Lacedæmonians, which is the subject of complaint.[4]   And the definition of rights in both the treaties is

[1] Selymbria is on the Propontine coast, between Byzantium and
Perinthus.
[2] The island of Cos, celebrated as the birthplace of Hippocrates the
physician and Apelles the painter, lies a little off the coast of Caria, not
far from Halicarnassus.   It is mentioned in the Oration on the Peace
that Cos, Chios, and Rhodes were seized upon by the Carian government.   Shortly before this time the city of Cos had been rebuilt on a
scale of great splendour, and had become one of the richest and most
beautiful in Greece.
[3] I.e. the Byzantines and Artemisia.
[4] The first of these treaties is supposed to be the peace of Cimon,
according to which the Greek cities on the coast of Asia Minor were

not the same. For, although private political rights are granted by the laws impartially to all, the same for the weak as for the strong; the rule of Hellenic right is prescribed by the greater powers to the less.

Since then it is your fixed resolution to pursue a just policy, you must look that you have the means to carry it out. Such means you will possess if you are supposed to be the common protectors of Grecian liberty. It is, doubtless, very difficult for you to adopt proper measures. The rest of mankind have one battle to fight, namely, against their avowed enemies: if they conquer those, nothing hinders them accomplishing their desires. You, Athenians, have a double contest; that which the rest have, and also another, prior to that, and more arduous: for you must in council overcome a faction who act among you in systematic opposition to the state. Since therefore through these men it is impossible for any good measure to be affected without a struggle, the natural consequence is that you lose many advantages. Perhaps the chief cause why so many adopt this line of politics without scruple, is the support afforded them by their hirers: at the same time you are yourselves chargeable with blame. You ought, O Athenians, to hold the same opinion concerning the post of civil duty as you hold concerning the military. What is that? You consider that one who deserts the post assigned by his general should be degraded and deprived of constitutional privileges. It is right, therefore, that men who desert the political post

made independent, the Persian king was precluded from approaching the coast within the distance of a day's journey on horseback, and from sending any ship of war between the Cyanean islands at the mouth of the Bosphorus and the Chelidonian islands off the Lycian coast. The second of the treaties here referred to is the peace of Antalcidas, negotiated by the Lacedæmonians B.C. 387; according to which the Greek cities were to be independent, Sparta retaining her dominions in Peloponnesus, and Athens keeping only Lemnos, Imbrus, and Scyrus; the Greek cities of Asia, and the islands of Cyprus and Clazomenæ were acknowledged to belong to the Persian empire. The Lacedæmonians, by sacrificing the Asiatic Greeks to Persia, detached that monarchy from the Athenian alliance, and were enabled to maintain their own ascendancy over the Grecian states.

received from their ancestors, and support oligarchial measures, should be disabled to act as your counsellors. Among your allies you regard those to be the most attached who have sworn to have the same friends and enemies with yourselves; and yet of your statesmen you esteem those the most faithful who to your certain knowledge have sided with the enemies of Athens.

However—matter of accusation against these men, matter of censure against the people, is not hard to discover: the difficulty is to know by what counsels or what conduct our present evils may be repaired. This perhaps is not the occasion to speak of all: could you only give effect to your policy by some useful effort, things in general, perhaps, one after another, would go on improving. My opinion is that you should take this enterprise vigorously in hand, and act worthily of the state, remembering that you love to hear men praise your ancestors and recount their exploits and speak of their trophies. Consider then, your forefathers erected these, not that you may view and admire them only but that you may imitate also the virtues of the dedicators.[1]

---

[1] The speech of Demosthenes produced no effect. Athens abstained from interference; the Rhodians continued under the government of an oligarchy, and subjection to Caria. Artemisia died soon after the delivery of this Oration, having reigned two years. She is said to have been inconsolable for the death of her husband Mausolus, whose ashes she drank dissolved in scented water, and to whose memory she paid the most extravagant honours. The monument which she erected was so magnificent as to be considered one of the wonders of the world; and from this the name of *Mausoleum* has been applied to all sepulchres built on a grand scale. She invited the most eminent literary men to her court, and offered a reward for the best funeral panegyric. Theopompus the historian, a native of Chios, and pupil of Isocrates, gained the prize. Artemisia was succeeded on the throne by her brother Idrieus, who reigned seven years.

# THE ORATION FOR THE MEGALOPOLITANS

## ARGUMENT

MEGALOPOLIS was an Arcadian city near the frontiers of Laconia. It was founded in the year B.C. 371, and, being designed for the metropolis of the whole Arcadian people, who then united themselves into one body, it was built on a scale of magnitude corresponding with that purpose, having a circumference of more than six miles, and received the name of the *great city*. Next to Athens, it is said to have been the most beautiful city in Greece. The population was obtained by migration from the existing Arcadian towns, no less than forty of which were required to contribute to it. Most of these were entirely deserted by their inhabitants, others were reduced to the condition of villages dependent on Megalopolis. A supreme council of ten thousand, taken from the whole Arcadian body, held their public deliberations in the capital. About half a century afterwards, when it was besieged by Polysperchon, there were found to be fifteen thousand citizens capable of bearing arms in its defence.

The chief object of building this metropolis was to establish a permanent union among the Arcadians and preserve their national independence. Before that time, the Arcadians as a body had very little influence in the affairs of Peloponnesus, though they occupied a large portion of its territory. They had generally been in the alliance of Sparta, whose armies they strengthened by a brave and hardy race of soldiers. It was therefore the policy of Sparta to keep them feeble and divided among themselves. In the time of the Peloponnesian war Mantinea, then the principal city of Arcadia, formed a small confederacy among her neighbours, renounced her connection with the Lacedæmonians, and joined an offensive alliance with Athens and Argos. But this was soon put an end to. The Mantineans were compelled, by the success of the Lacedæmonian arms, to abandon their confederacy; and at a later period, B.C. 387, paid dearly for their disaffection to Sparta, by having their city dismantled and being dispersed into villages.

The defeat of the Spartans at Leuctra changed the aspect of affairs in Greece. The prestige of ancient victory was gone; and it was soon found that the vast alliance, of which Sparta had been the head, and which had enabled her for many years to give the law to Greece, would crumble almost entirely away. One of the first effects of this change in Peloponnesus was the rebuilding of Mantinea, which was soon followed by the establishment of Megalopolis. But the heaviest blow to the pride and power of Lacedæmon was the loss of her ancient province of Messenia, which for more than three centuries had been the fairest portion of her domain. Whether the Arcadians could have maintained their independence against Sparta without foreign aid may perhaps be doubted; but this last revolution was wholly due to the arms of Thebes and the genius of Epaminondas.

That general, having assembled a large army in Bœotia, marched across the isthmus and was joined in Arcadia by his Peloponnesian allies. At the head of an overpowering force he invaded and ravaged Laconia. Troops of divers people—who not many years before had followed the Lacedæmonians in their wars, or would hardly have dared to face them in the field—Thebans, Phocians, Locrians, Eubœans, Thessalians, Acarnanians, Argives, Arcadians, Eleans, marched now almost without opposition to the gates of Sparta; and nothing but the shadow of the Spartan name preserved that haughty capital from destruction. Epaminondas did not venture to make a general assault upon the town, but, after continuing his ravages for some time longer, proceeded to execute his well-laid scheme, which he rightly judged would reduce Sparta to the condition of a second or third-rate power in Greece.

The Messenian population had long been, like the Laconian helots, in a state of vassalage to Sparta, but were ripe for insurrection at any favourable opportunity, as they had proved during the Athenian occupation of Pylus. The march of Epaminondas into Laconia was the signal for a universal rising of that people, who were now again to form a nation, and to build a capital city under the protection of the Theban general. But it was not only the existing inhabitants of the country, by whom this task of reconstituting the nation was to be accomplished; for which, after their long servitude, they might not have been so well fitted by themselves. Messenian exiles from every quarter, and especially those of Naupactus, who had been expelled after the Peloponnesian war, and migrated to Sicily and Africa, were invited to return to their ancient home, and assist in the glorious restoration. It has been mentioned as a remarkable example of the love of country that these exiles, during so long an absence, had jealously preserved their ancestral usages and the purity of their original language. They returned in great numbers and formed the nucleus of a Messenian government. The new city was founded on the site of the ancient Ithome, Epaminondas laying the first stone, and received the name of Messene. This was B.C. 369.

The humiliation of Sparta was now complete. She had no power to disturb the new settlement. She was hemmed in by a chain of enemies, who cut off her communication with Peloponnesus; by the Messenians on the west, the Arcadians and Argives on the north. Her war with Thebes continued for eight more years. The succour of Athens and her few remaining allies saved her from further disasters; and the death of her great enemy, Epaminondas, brought on a general peace, B.C. 361.

From the negotiations of this peace the Lacedæmonians kept aloof, refusing to acknowledge the independence of Messenia, which they regarded as a deep disgrace to themselves. Their spirit, though depressed, was not extinguished; and they only awaited for an opportunity of recovering their lost dominion. Archidamus, son of Agesilaus, who had acquired honour in the late war by the *tearless victory* (in which he defeated the Arcadians and Argives without losing a single Spartan life), kept alive the ambitious hopes of his countrymen, and continually stimulated them to fresh exertions. He was a man of ardent character, to recover Messenia was the principal object of his desire; in which he had even been encouraged by a pamphlet of Isocrates, entitled Archidamus, and still extant. In the course of seven or eight years events occurred which favoured the views of this prince. There had been disturbances in Arcadia. The Sacred war had broken out, in which the principal parties were Phocis and Thebes. An obstinate struggle was yet going on; neither party had gained any decisive advantage, and both were greatly weakened. The Phocian generals had carried the war into the enemy's country; some of the Bœotian towns had been taken; and the Thebans, distressed at home, and burdened with heavy expenses, seemed no longer in a condition to assist their Peloponnesian allies.

Under these circumstances, about the year 353, Archidamus thought the time had arrived to effect a counter-revolution, which should restore the influence of his country. His real aim was the destruction of Megalopolis and Messene. But to avow this purpose, or attempt to execute it without further pretext than the desire to satisfy Spartan ambition, might have drawn on him the hostility of those states which were unconnected with the Theban alliance. Accordingly, he conceived the idea of announcing a principle, which would secure certain advantages to the states hostile to Thebes, and induce them to concur in his own scheme of aggrandisement. He gave it out that ancient rights ought to be resumed; that Athens should have Oropus, the towns of Thespiæ, Platæa, and Orchomenus should be restored; Elis and Phlius should have certain claims conceded to them. While he published these declarations, he kept in the background that portion of the scheme in which Sparta was interested, viz., the recovery of Messenia and the dissolution of the Arcadian union.

Notwithstanding all the care which Archidamus took to conceal his views, they could not fail to be apparent; and it was soon understood that the warlike preparations in Laconia were designed against Megalopolis. Two embassies were sent at the same time to Athens, one by the Spartans, and one by the Megalopolitans, each to solicit assistance in the approaching war. The Spartan ambassadors reminded the Athenians of their former alliance, and showed what advantage would accrue to them from the plan of Archidamus, by which Thebes their old enemy would be depressed. The Megalopolitan deputies urged the justice of their own cause, and the danger that would result from the revival of Spartan supremacy.

There were many speakers on both sides in the Athenian assembly. Demosthenes espoused the cause of the Megalopolitans, and delivered what Auger pronounces to be one of the most subtle of his orations. He begins by condemning the warmth with which both parties had assailed their adversaries. It became them (he argues), without any feeling or prejudice for or against either of the contending states, to decide the question by reference to justice and the good of Athens. Justice required that no people should be oppressed by another. Their alliance with Sparta had been based on that principle, and they had saved her from ruin; but if Sparta commenced ambitious enterprises inconsistent with the spirit of their alliance, they were justified in breaking it off. It was the interest of Athens that neither Sparta nor Thebes should be too powerful. The dissolution of Megalopolis would lead to the re-conquest of Messenia, and that would destroy the balance of power in Peloponnesus. The advantage offered to Athens might be obtained in a more honourable manner, without sacrificing the Peloponnesians; and as to Thebes, it was better to weaken her by conferring an obligation upon her allies, and attaching them to Athens, than by allowing them to suffer injustice.

It appears to me, O Athenians, that both are in fault, they who have spoken for the Arcadians and they who have spoken for the Lacedæmonians.   For as if they were deputies from either people, not citizens of Athens, to which both direct their embassies, they accuse and attack one another.   This might be the duty of the envoys; but to speak independently on the question, and consider your interests dispassionately, was the part of men who presume to offer counsel here.   I really think—setting aside the knowledge of their persons and their Attic tongue—many would take them for either Arcadians or Laconians.

I see how vexatious a thing it is to advise for the best. For when you are carried away by delusion, some taking one view and some another, if any man attempts to advise a middle course, and you are too impatient to listen, he will please neither party and fall into disgrace with both.   However, if this be my case, I will rather myself be thought a babbler than leave you to be misled by certain people, contrary to my notion of Athenian interests.   On other points I will speak, with your permission, afterwards; but will begin with principles admitted by all, and explain what I consider your wisest course.

Well then:   no man will deny it to be good for Athens, that both the Lacedæmonians and our Theban neighbours should be weak.   But things are in this sort of position, if we may form a conjecture from the statements repeatedly made in our assembly—the Thebans will be weakened by the re-establishment of Orchomenus,[1] Thespiæ, and Platæa; the

---

[1] The Bœotian cities were at an early period connected by a federal union, each having an independent government.   Thebes was at their head, and received a council of deputies from the league.   Every state appointed a Bœotarch, who took his share of military command and some other executive duties.   In process of time Thebes asserted an imperial authority over the federal cities, and most of them were compelled to submit.   Platæa espoused the alliance of Athens, and for a long time enjoyed her protection, but in the Peloponnesian war fell a victim to Theban revenge.   The exiles returned and rebuilt the city after the peace of Antalcidas, but it was again destroyed by the Thebans B.C. 373.   Thespiæ was destroyed about the same time, having long been suspected of disaffection to Thebes and favour to Athens.   The Thebans had dismantled its walls in the Peloponnesian war, though the flower of the Thespian youth had fallen in their cause at the battle of Delium.   Orchomenus was taken and depopulated by the Thebans

Lacedæmonians will grow powerful again if they subdue Arcadia and take Megalopolis. We must mind, therefore, that we suffer not the one people to wax mighty and formidable, before the other has become weak; that the power of Lacedæmon do not increase (unremarked by us) in a greater degree than it is well for that of Thebes to be reduced. For we shall hardly say this, that we should like to have Lacedæmonians instead of Thebans for our rivals. It is not this we are anxious for, but that neither may have the means of injuring us: so shall we enjoy the best security.

But granting this ought to be so—it were scandalous, forsooth, to take those men for allies, against whom we were arrayed at Mantinea, and then to assist them against the people, with whom we shared the peril of that day. I think so too, but with one addition—" provided the others are willing to act justly." If all will choose to observe peace, we shall not help the Megalopolitans; for there will be no necessity; and thus we shall be in no opposition to our fellows in arms: one people are, as they profess, our allies already, the other will become so now. And what more could we desire? But should they [1] attempt injustice and determine on war—then—if this be the only question, whether we ought or ought not to abandon Megalopolis to the Lacedæmonians, although it would be unjust, I concede the point; let things take their course, don't oppose your former partners in danger: but if you all know, that after taking that city they will march to attack Messene, let any of the speakers who are now so hard upon the Megalopolitans tell me what in that case he will

B.C. 368. They had resolved on that measure some years before, but were induced by Epaminondas to change their intention. Afterwards, being alarmed by a conspiracy of certain Orchomenian exiles, they fell upon the city, massacred the adult citizens, and sold the women and children for slaves. During the Phocian war, and shortly before or after the date of this Oration, Orchomenus was seized upon by the Phocian general, Onomarchus, and occupied as a fortified post. At the close of that war it was delivered by Philip to the Thebans, who razed it to the ground. After the battle of Chæronea Philip caused all these three cities, Platæa, Thespiæ, and Orchomenus, to be restored.

[1] *I.e.* the Lacedæmonians; whom the orator does not expressly name, because they are uppermost in his mind.

advise us to do. None will declare. However, you all know that you would be obliged to support them, whether these men recommend it or not, both by the oaths that we have sworn to the Messenians,[1] and because it is expedient that their city should be preserved. Reflect therefore in your minds, whether it would be more noble and generous to begin your resistance to Lacedæmonian aggression with the defence of Megalopolis, or with that of Messene. You will now be considered as protectors of the Arcadians, and striving for the maintenance of that peace, for which you exposed yourselves in the battle-field: whereas then it will be manifest to the world that you desire Messene to stand not so much for the sake of justice as for fear of Lacedæmon. Our purposes and our actions should always be just; but we must also be careful that they are attended with advantage.

There is an argument of this kind urged by my opponents, that we should attempt to recover Oropus,[2] and, if we now

---

[1] This engagement was probably entered into at the general peace, which was concluded after the battle of Mantinea, and by which the Athenians, as well as other states of Greece, recognised the independence of Messenia. Pausanias mentions that at this time, when the assistance of Athens was prayed for by the Messenians, it was promised in the event of a Spartan invasion.

It is quite clear from the argument of Demosthenes, that the claims of Megalopolis upon the Athenians stood upon a different footing from those of Messene, not being grounded upon any former alliance. Yet in the narrative of Diodorus, XV. 94, we read that the Athenians sent a body of troops under Pammenes to quell an insurrection in Arcadia, which broke out in about a year's time after the peace, and threatened to dissolve the Megalopolitan community; that Pammenes reduced the malcontents to submission, and compelled those who had seceded from Megalopolis, and gone back to their ancient homes, to return to the capital.

[2] Oropus was on the confines of Attica and Bœotia, on the coast opposite Eretria in Eubœa. It anciently belonged to Athens, but frequently changed masters. In the twentieth year of the Peloponnesian war it was betrayed to the Bœotians and Eretrians. It became independent at the close of the war; but a few years after, the Thebans took advantage of some internal disturbances to seize upon the city, which they removed nearly a mile from the coast, and annexed to the Bœotian confederacy. A new revolution some time after restored it to Athens. But in the year B.C. 366, Themison, ruler of Eretria, got possession of it by the aid of some exiles. The Athenians marched against him, but, the Thebans also making their appearance with an army, they were induced to leave Oropus under Theban protection, until the dispute could be amicably settled. The Thebans, however, kept it in their own

make enemies of the men who would assist us to gain it, we
shall have no allies. I also say, we should try to recover
Oropus: but, that Lacedæmon will be our enemy, if we join
alliance with the Arcadians who wish to be our friends, they
of all men, I consider, are not at liberty to assert, who persuaded you to assist the Lacedæmonians in their hour of
danger. The men who argue thus actually persuaded you—
when all the Peloponnesians came to Athens and desired to
march with you against the Lacedæmonians—to reject their
overtures (on which account, as a last resource, they applied
to Thebes) and to contribute money and risk your lives for
the safety of Lacedæmon. You would hardly, I think, have
been disposed to save them, had they told you, that after their
deliverance, unless you suffered them to have their own way
and commit injustice again, they should owe you no thanks
for your protection. And indeed, however repugnant it may
be to the designs of the Spartans that we should adopt the
Arcadian alliance, surely their gratitude, for having been
saved by us in a crisis of extreme peril, ought to outweigh
their resentment for being checked in their aggression now.
How then can they avoid assisting you to gain Oropus, or
being thought the basest of mankind? By the gods I cannot see.

I wonder also to hear it argued, that, if we espouse the
Arcadian alliance and adopt these measures, our state will be
chargeable with inconstancy and bad faith. It seems to me,
O Athenians, the reverse. Why? Because no man, I apprehend, will question that, in defending the Lacedæmonians,
and the Thebans [1] before them, and lastly the Eubœans,[2] and
making them afterwards her allies, our republic has always
had one and the same object. What is that? To protect
the injured. If this be so, the inconstancy will not be ours,

hands; and so it remained until after the battle of Chæronea, when
Philip gave it up to the Athenians.

[1] He alludes to the war that followed the seizure of the Cadmea,
commenced by the invasion of Cleombrotus B.C. 378.

[2] When the Thebans attempted to get possession of the island.

but theirs who refuse to adhere to justice; and it will appear that while circumstances change, through people continually encroaching, Athens changes not.

It seems to me, the Lacedæmonians are acting the part of very crafty men. For now they say that the Eleans ought to recover a certain part of Triphylia,[1] the Phliasians Tricaranum,[2] certain other Arcadians their territory, and we Oropus: not from a desire to see us each possessing our own —far from this—it would be late for them to have become generous—but to make it appear as if they helped all to recover their claims, so that, when they march themselves to attack Messene, all these people may readily join and assist them, or be deemed ungrateful, after having obtained their concurrence in the question of their own several claims, for not returning the obligation. My opinion is, first, that our state, even without sacrificing any Arcadian people to the Lacedæmonians, may recover Oropus, both with their aid, if they are willing to be just, and that of others who hold that Theban usurpation ought not to be tolerated. Secondly, supposing it were evident to us that, unless we permit the Lacedæmonians to reduce the Peloponnese, we cannot obtain possession of Oropus, allow me to say I deem it more advisable to let Oropus alone than to abandon Messene and Peloponnesus to the Lacedæmonians. I imagine the question between us and them would soon be about other matters.

---

[1] Triphylia was a small province on the Cyparissian bay, between Elis and Messenia. Concerning this there had been many disputes between the Eleans and the Arcadians.

[2] Tricaranum was a fortress in the Phliasian territory. The city of Phlius was on the confines of Argolis, Achaia, and Arcadia. During the Theban war, when most of their allies had deserted the Lacedæmonians, Phlius continued faithful, and was exposed to the attacks of her neighbours. The Argives fortified Tricaranum, and kept it as a hostile post, making incursions to plunder the Phliasian country, and attack the city, which at one time was nearly surprised by an Argive-Arcadian force assisted by some exiles. The Phliasians, whose constancy is praised by Xenophon, baffled all the attempts of their enemies. In the year 366 Chares the Athenian was sent to their assistance, and took Thyamia, another hostile fortress occupied by the Sicyonians. Tricaranum, it seems, remained in possession of the Argives.

However—I will forbear to say what occurs to me—only I think we should in many respects be endangered.

As to what the Megalopolitans have done against you (as they say) under the influence of Thebes, it is absurd to bring that now as a charge against them, and yet, when they proffer their friendship, with an intention of doing you good instead of harm, to mistrust and look for an excuse to reject them, without considering that the more zealous they prove this people to have been in the Theban cause, the more will they themselves deserve your anger, for having deprived Athens of such allies, when they applied to her before they applied to Thebes. It looks, indeed, as if they wished a second time to turn these people to another alliance.

I am sure—to judge from rational observation—and I think most Athenians will agree with me, that, if the Lacedæmonians take Megalopolis, Messene will be in danger; and, if they take that also, I predict that you and the Thebans will be allies. Then it is much better and more honourable for us to receive the Theban confederacy as our friends, and resist Lacedæmonian ambition, than, out of reluctance to preserve the allies of Thebes, to abandon them now, and have afterwards to preserve Thebes herself, and be in fear also for our own safety. I cannot but regard it as perilous to our state, should the Lacedæmonians take Megalopolis, and again become strong. For I see they have undertaken this war, not to defend themselves, but to recover their ancient power: what were their designs, when they possessed that power, you perhaps know better than I, and therefore may have reason to be alarmed.

I would fain ask the men who tell us and say they detest the Thebans and the Lacedæmonians, whether they detest whom they detest respectively out of regard to you and your interests, or detest Thebans for the sake of Lacedæmonians, and Lacedæmonians for the sake of Thebans. If for their sakes, to neither as rational beings ought you to listen: if they say for your sake, wherefore do they exalt either people unduly? It is possible, surely possible, to humble Thebes without increasing the power of Lacedæmon. Aye; and it is much easier too. I will endeavour to show you how.

It is well known that up to a certain point all men (however disinclined) are ashamed not to observe justice, and that they openly oppose the transgressors, especially where any people suffer damage: it will be found, moreover, that what mars everything, and originates every mischief, is the unwillingness to observe justice uniformly. Therefore, that no such obstacle may arise to the depression of Thebes, let us declare that Thespiæ and Orchomenus and Platæa ought to be re-established, and let us co-operate with their people and call on others to assist us—just and honourable were this, not to regard with indifference the extermination of ancient cities —but let us not abandon Megalopolis and Messene to the aggressors, not, on the pretence of Thespiæ and Platæa, suffer existing and flourishing cities to be annihilated. If such be your declared policy, every one will desire that Thebes should no longer hold her neighbour's dominion. If not—in the first place, we may expect to find these men oppose the other scheme, when they see that the establishment of those towns would be their own ruin: secondly, we shall have an interminable business of it ourselves, for where indeed can it end, if we continually allow existing cities to be destroyed, and require those which are in ruins to be restored?

It is urged by the most plausible speakers, that the pillars [1] of their treaty with Thebes must be taken down, if they mean to be our steadfast allies. These people say that with them it is not pillars but interest that binds friendship, and they consider those who assist them to be allies. Granting such to be their views, my notion is this. I say, we should both require of them the destruction of the pillars, and of the

---

[1] It was the practice among Grecian states to inscribe their treaties on pillars of stone or brass, which, so long as the treaties remained in force, were religiously preserved, and exposed to view in temples and other public places. And it was frequently provided in the treaty itself where the pillars recording it should be deposited.

Lacedæmonians the observance of peace; if either party
refuse to comply, whichever it be, we should side immediately
with those that will. Should the Megalopolitans, notwithstanding the maintenance of peace, adhere to the Theban
alliance, it will surely be evident to all that they favour the
ambition of the Thebans instead of justice. On the other
hand, if the Megalopolitans in good faith espouse our alliance,
and the Lacedæmonians do not choose to observe peace, they
will surely prove to the world that they are striving not only
for the restoration of Thespiæ, but for an opportunity of
conquering Peloponnesus while the Thebans are entangled in
this war. One thing in certain men surprises me; that they
dread the enemies of Lacedæmon becoming allies of Thebes,
and yet see no danger in the Lacedæmonians conquering them;
although we have actual experience furnished by the past
that the Thebans always use these allies against Lacedæmon,
whereas the Lacedæmonians, whilst they had the same people,
used them against us.

I think further, you ought to consider this. If you reject
the Megalopolitans—should their city be destroyed and themselves dispersed, the Lacedæmonians at once become powerful: should they chance to escape (as unhoped-for events
do happen) they will in justice be steadfast allies of the
Thebans.[1] If you accept them for allies, the immediate consequence to them will be deliverance by your means; but
passing from their case, let us consider what may be looked for

[1] The event proved the justice of this remark. Demosthenes could
not prevail on the Athenians to follow his counsel. They joined the
alliance of neither party. Archidamus commenced war against the
Arcadians, who were assisted by Argos, Sicyon, and Messene. In the
course of the same year, Philip having defeated Onomarchus in the
great battle of Pagasæ, the Thebans were enabled to send forces to
the succour of their old allies. On the other hand, the Lacedæmonians
were reinforced by some Phocian mercenaries; and the war was carried
on for two years with various success, and at length terminated by a
truce. The Arcadian confederacy, however, were alienated from
Athens, and the bad effects of this were discovered some time after,
when, alarmed at the designs of Sparta, they applied not to Athens
but to Philip for assistance, and thus caused Macedonian influence to
extend itself in Peloponnesus. (See the Argument to the second
Philippic.)

and apprehended with reference to Thebes and Lacedæmon.
Well then: if the Thebans be vanquished in war, as they
ought to be, the Lacedæmonians will not be unduly great,
having these Arcadians for their rivals, living near them.   If
the Thebans chance to recover and come off safe, they will
at all events be the weaker for these men having become our
allies and been preserved through us.   So that in every point
of view it is expedient that we should not abandon the
Arcadians, and that they should not appear (in case they do
escape) to have owed their deliverance to themselves, or to
any other people but you.

I have spoken, O Athenians (Heaven is my witness), not
from private affection or malice towards either party, but
what I consider advantageous for you: and I exhort you not
to abandon the Megalopolitans, nor indeed any other of the
weaker states to the stronger.

# APPENDIX

# APPENDIX

## ATHENIAN MONEY AND MINES

PHIDON, an ancient king of Argos, said to have lived in the eighth century before Christ, was the first person in Greece who established a system of weights and measures, and also a coinage in silver and copper. It acquired the name of the Æginetan, because the people of Ægina, by their commercial intercourse with other parts of Greece, brought it into general use. There was another system called the Euboic, introduced to the Greeks by the people of Chalcis and Eretria, who at an early period were celebrated for their commercial activity, and who worked mines of silver and copper in their own island.

In fact, however, both these systems were derived from the East, having been invented in very ancient times by the Chaldees of Babylon, and brought into Greece by the commerce of the Phœnicians. The standard of weights, which became known as the Euboic, was one used in Asia for gold. Herodotus expressly informs us that in the reign of Darius I. the silver tribute collected from the satrapies of the Persian empire was estimated by the Babylonian talent, the gold tribute by the Euboic. Whether Herodotus means that the term *Euboic* was adopted by the Persian government, or only the weight so called by the Greeks, does not appear.

The denominations under both these systems were the same, although the scales were different; viz., the talent, the mina, the drachm, and the obol; which bore the following invariable relation to each other:—

|  |  |  |
|---|---|---|
| A talent | = | 60 minas. |
| A mina | = | 100 drachms. |
| A drachm | = | 6 obols. |

The word *talent* originally signified *weight*, that is, any weight, or weight in general; and was also used to signify a pair of scales. In such sense it is used by Homer. Afterwards the term was applied to a specific weight, and became the principal standard in the Greek systems. *Mina* was a term of oriental origin. *Drachm* and *obol* are Greek words. Drachm is said by the lexicographers to signify *a handful*, that is, as much coin as could be held in the clenched hand. Obol takes its name from *a spit*, which it somewhat resembled in figure.

The weights under each system were as follows:—

Æginetan talent    about    96 lb.
Euboic talent        „        80 lb.

The denominations of money in Greece were the same as those of weight, and the proportions the same likewise. Money (as is well known) has always been founded on a system of weight. In process of time the coinage ceases to represent the original standard, although the name is preserved. For example *a pound*, in our own country, formerly represented a pound weight of metal; now it signifies a sum of twenty shillings. So in Greece an Euboic talent (in a pecuniary sense) anciently denoted eighty pounds of silver— that being the metal generally current in Greece—afterwards its value would be measured by the number of drachms that were paid for it; and if the drachm-piece had fallen below the ancient standard of weight so would the talent.

The Æginetan system was adopted in Peloponnesus and most of the Dorian states. The Euboic prevailed in the Ionian settlements and in Attica. Solon, however, for certain political reasons which will be noticed elsewhere, lowered the standard of money, and the Attic talent, according to his regulation, was reduced about twenty-seven per cent. The money computed on the Solonian scale is that which we have generally to deal with in perusing the Attic writers. Judging from the ancient coins which have been preserved, the value of the Attic money has been thus estimated in English:—

|  |  | £ | s. | d. |
|---|---|---|---|---|
| An obol | = | 0 | 0 | 1½ |
| A drachm | = | 0 | 0 | 9 |
| A mina | = | 3 | 15 | 0 |
| A talent | = | 225 | 0 | 0 |

The value, however, has been put by others both higher and lower.

It must be observed that the talent and the mina are sums only, the drachm and the obol are coins also. And it will be found in perusing the orators, that the Athenians generally made their computations in drachms, so that, when no specific sum is mentioned, drachms are understood.

The coinage at Athens was principally silver, consisting of drachms and obols, with fractions and multiples of those pieces. The obol and half-obol were small coins, like our silver penny. There were also copper coins, as the quarter-obol, the chalcus. The following is a table of Attic coins:—

| | s. | d. | | | | s. | d. |
|---|---|---|---|---|---|---|---|
| The four-drachm piece (value) | 3 | 0 | The obol . (value) . | | . | 0 | 1½ |
| The two-drachm piece ,, | 1 | 6 | The half-obol ,, | 3 | | | |
| The drachm . . . ,, | 0 | 9 | The quarter- | | | | |
| The four-obol piece . ,, | 0 | 6 | obol . ,, | 1½ | farthings. | | |
| The three-obol piece ,, | 0 | 4½ | The chalcus ,, | ¾ | | | |
| The two-obol piece . ,, | 0 | 3 | The lepton ,, | ⅜ | | | |

Thus the lowest Attic coin was pretty nearly equal to the French centime.

There was no gold coined at Athens before the time of the Macedonian empire. But there was gold in circulation, the coinage of other countries, chiefly the stater and the daric.

The gold stater was equal in value to twenty drachms, or fifteen shillings. It was first coined by Crœsus king of Lydia, or at least first became known to the Greeks as a Lydian coin. There were various other staters brought into Greece from Asia Minor and the islands; for example, from Smyrna, Cyzicus, Phocæa, Samos, Siphnos, Thasos.

The daric, named after the first Darius, who reformed the

Persian currency, was of the same value as the stater. This coin, which had an extensive circulation, was retained by the Macedonian kings, who melted down all the gold coinage of Greece, and had their own image stamped upon it.

There were also half-staters and half-darics in circulation, which are mentioned by Greek writers.

The daric was stamped on one side with the figure of an archer, which gave rise to a good saying of Agesilaus, related by Plutarch. While the Spartan king was overrunning the provinces of Asia Minor, Tithraustes the satrap, to get rid of so formidable an enemy, sent Timocrates of Rhodes with fifty talents of gold into Greece to stir up war against Lacedæmon. This money was distributed in Thebes, Argos, and Corinth—Xenophon says the Athenians had no share of it—and the effects were quickly seen. The Spartans, alarmed at the confederacy against them, recalled Agesilaus; whereupon he declared "that a thousand Persian archers had driven him out of Asia."

There was but a scanty supply of the precious metals in Greece at an early period, while the eastern monarchs collected the treasures of Cholcis, Lydia, Phrygia, Armenia, and India. The wars of Xerxes opened a more extensive intercourse with Asia, and enriched the Greeks by commerce and by plunder. Thus, and by an increase in the produce of their native mines, money became more plentiful among them; and in the time of Demosthenes its value was five times less than in the days of Solon. The relative value of gold to silver in the time of Herodotus was thirteen to one, in the time of Demosthenes, ten to one.

The Greek islands that most abounded in precious metals were Samos, Siphnos, and Thasos, in which there was both gold and silver. The mines of Thasos were anciently worked by the Phœnicians, to whom the Greeks were at an early period indebted for their supply of metal in general. They brought the common metals from Spain and Arabia, tin from Britain, and probably taught the art of mining to the Greeks.

The Thasians found gold and silver on the adjacent continent of Thrace. But when the island was conquered by Cimon, their settlements also fell into the hands of the Athenians, who worked the mines until the close of the Peloponnesian war. The gold which they obtained from this district they used not for coinage but for commercial purposes. Philip afterwards took possession of these mines, and worked them, as we have already seen, with great advantage.

There were silver mines also in Thessaly. But the most valuable in Greece were those of Laurium in Attica, to which Xenophon has devoted a long chapter of his treatise on the Athenian revenues, and on which in modern times a dissertation has been written by Böckh, the celebrated author of the *Staatshaushaltung der Athener*, or Public Economy of Athens, from whom English scholars have derived most of their information upon these subjects.

The mines of Laurium were the property of the Athenian people, but were worked by private speculators, to whom the state granted allotments, receiving a certain sum by way of premium or purchase-money, and receiving a perpetual rent of a twenty-fourth part of the produce. These persons were thus in point of law tenants of the state; but for most purposes might be regarded as the absolute owners. Many wealthy citizens embarked their capital in the mining business, which they carried on by means of agents or sub-tenants. Nicias had several mines, with a thousand slaves at work in them, for each of whom he received from his lessee a clear rent of an obol a day. Thus was Laurium an important source of revenue to Athens. When Deceleia was occupied by the Lacedæmonian army, she suffered greatly by losing the profit of the mines. They had yielded a considerable income in the time of Themistocles, who persuaded his countrymen to apply the money to shipbuilding instead of distributing it among themselves. In the time of Demosthenes, though he speaks in high terms of the value of this property, the quantity of silver obtained was diminished;

and Strabo tells us that in the first century of the Christian era the Laurian mines were exhausted.

Foreigners in Attica were allowed equal privileges with citizens in the renting of the mines, so anxious was the state that they should be let.   To prevent frauds on the revenue, every mine in work was required to be registered, and an indictment lay against any person who evaded this regulation.

Xenophon, who seems to have thought that the riches of Laurium were inexhaustible, recommended that his country-men should improve their finances by abolishing the middle-men, and letting the mines, together with mining-slaves, to the working tenants, in the same way that other revenues were let to farm.   He advised that they should buy slaves gradually, until they had got three slaves to every citizen; and he calculated that the mines would afford profitable employment for all, and the revenue would be immensely increased.

The trade of Athens was much promoted by the purity of her silver coin, which was everywhere exchanged with advantage, while that of other states would only pass at home.   One instance only is recorded of her issuing a debased gold coinage; but this was in a time of distress, at the close of the Peloponnesian war.   The right of coining money was (no doubt) vested in the state, and forgery was a capital crime.

The Attic coins were generally stamped with a head of Pallas on one side, and an owl (her sacred bird) on the other. Hence the point of the story told by Plutarch, in his life of Lysander—That general sent Gylippus with a bag of money to Sparta.   Gylippus unsewed the bottom of the bag, took out a portion of the money, and sewed it up again.   But unfortunately for him, the bag contained a paper which gave an account of the sum sent home.   The magistrates, find-ing the money short, were surprised, and made inquiries. Gylippus had concealed the stolen coins, which were Athenian with the owl-stamp, under the tiles of his house; but his

servant, who was in the secret, betrayed him by declaring
that he had observed a great many owls roost in the Ceramicus. The theft was thus discovered, and Gylippus tarnished
the good name which he had acquired by his victories at
Syracuse.

Although the Attic money has been reduced into terms of
our own, to give the reader some notion of its value, it is
plain enough that the relative values of Attic and English
money could only be fully determined by a comparison of
the quantities of the precious metals, the different modes of
living in the two countries, and many other considerations
of the same kind. For these reasons, besides the awkward-
ness of making Demosthenes talk of pounds shillings and
pence, I have, in the translation, adhered to the Attic terms
for money. The following particulars will help to throw
some light on the subject.

An Athenian could live respectably on the interest of a
talent,—that is, on seven or eight minas a year. In the
speech written by Demosthenes against Bœotus, the plaintiff
says he had been supported and educated out of such an
income. Isæus speaks of an estate of fifty minas as sufficient
to live comfortably, but not to perform public services. The
expenses of Demosthenes, his mother and sister, during his
minority, amounted to seven minas annually, exclusive of
house rent. His father, who was a merchant, left to his
family an estate of fourteen talents, and is represented as
a person of considerable property. But we read of larger
fortunes than his at Athens. Conon possessed 40 talents;
Nicias 100; Alcibiades still more. One of the richest men
was Callias son of Hipponicus, whose property was valued at
200 talents, partly acquired by the plunder of the Persian
war. He had a son Hipponicus (who was killed at the battle
of Delium) who gave his daughter in marriage to Alcibiades,
with a portion of 10 talents, and a promise of 10 more after
the birth of a son; the largest portion ever given by a Greek.

I have spoken of seven or eight minas as being the interest

of a talent; that is, about twelve or thirteen per cent. per annum. Such in fact was a common rate of interest at Athens, but it was considered low; eighteen per cent. being frequently paid for loans on good security. There were no laws against usury; and although usurious money-lenders were regarded, as they have been in all ages, with an evil eye by the people, much higher rates than those above mentioned were exacted from needy borrowers, and wherever the risk was considerable. Thus, we read of thirty per cent. being paid on a bottomry contract for one summer. The lowness of personal credit, frequency of wars, instability of governments, and imperfection of national law, besides other causes of risk, would render all mercantile adventures perilous. The chief money-lenders at Athens were bankers; who kept the cash of their customers pretty much in the same manner as bankers of the present day, and made a profit by lending it out to others. They were serviceable to their customers in various ways; as the depositaries of important documents; as referees; as witnesses to payments and other transactions between them and third persons; and generally by extending their credit. They were usually men of high repute in the commercial world. Isocrates tells us that money was lent to them without witnesses; and this need not surprise us, when we consider that writing materials were not so plentiful or easy to be had, and men were obliged to place more reliance on their agents.

The interest above referred to has been calculated, after the English fashion, by the year: but it must be remembered that it was usually reserved at Athens by the month, which makes it really higher.

# EVERYMAN'S LIBRARY

## *A Selected List*

In each of the thirteen classifications in this list (except BIO-
GRAPHY) the volumes are arranged alphabetically under the authors'
names, but Anthologies, etc., are listed under titles. Where
authors appear in more than one section, a cross-reference is
given. The number at the end of each item is the number of
the volume in the series.

# EVERYMAN'S LIBRARY

## BIOGRAPHY

## CLASSICAL

## ESSAYS AND BELLES-LETTRES

## FICTION

## HISTORY

# ORATORY

# PHILOSOPHY AND THEOLOGY

# POETRY AND DRAMA

# REFERENCE

The following volumes in this section are now in the special edition of
*Everyman's Reference Library*:

# ROMANCE

# SCIENCE

# TRAVEL AND TOPOGRAPHY

# FOR YOUNG PEOPLE

EVERYMAN'S LIBRARY was founded in 1906, and for all the changes and chances in the book world during its long life the series stands strong to-day as the most comprehensive, inexpensive collection of books of classic measure. It is, indeed, still what its publisher intended it to be. J. M. Dent conceived it as a library arranged to cover the whole field of English literature, including translations of the ancient classics and outstanding foreign works; a series to make widely available those great books which appeal, as he says in his Memoirs, 'to every kind of reader: the worker, the student, the cultured man, the child, the man, and the woman.' The aim and scope of the series was crystallized in the title *Everyman's Library*, a title which has justified itself by the worldwide sales, totalling in 1953 some forty millions.

There were, of course, already in being in 1906 other popular series of reprints, but none on the scale proposed for *Everyman*. 155 volumes were published in three batches in the Library's first year; they comprised a balanced selection from many branches of literature and set the standard on which the Library has been built up. By early 1915 the 733rd volume had been issued; and, in spite of the interruptions of two world wars and their aftermath, the 994th volume was published in 1953. The founder-publisher aimed at a library of a thousand volumes, and that goal will surely be achieved before the jubilee of the Library in 1956.

A rough and ready pointer to the representative character of the Library is the number of volumes in each of the broad classifications into which the Library is divided—Biography has some 80 volumes; the Greek and Latin classics, about 40; Essays and Belles-lettres, 100; Fiction, 300; History, 80; Poetry and Drama, 100; Romance, 30; Science, 25; Religion and Philosophy, 60; Travel and Topography, 45; For Young People, 65. (The reference section is now being published separately as Everyman's Reference Library.) Most of but not all these volumes are in print now; some absent ones are works which changing taste has ruled out; but the classified sections of the Library are maintained in the original proportions, and to-day there are available in the Library the works of some five hundred authors of all times and all lands, the honoured names that stand for great literature. Moreover, many 'temporarily out of print' volumes are now being reinstated.

In March 1953 a fresh development of the Library began; new volumes and all new issues of established volumes in *Everyman's Library* are now in the larger size of crown octavo (except the volumes in the Young People's Section). The larger volumes have new title-pages, bindings, and wrappers, and the text pages have generous margins. Ninety volumes in this improved format will have been issued within one year of its inauguration.

Editorially the Library is under constant survey; all volumes are re-examined and brought up to date, with new introductions, annotations, and additional matter, wherever desirable; often a completely new translation or newly edited text is substituted when transferring an old volume to the new format, such as the new editions of *Pepys's Diary*, *Caesar's War Commentaries*, and *The Anglo-Saxon Chronicle*.

The new larger volumes are in keeping with the reader's own collection in his home, for which the Library is planned, and they are also in the suitable size for the shelves of all public, institutional, university, and school libraries. Many important works in *Everyman's Library* are unobtainable in any other edition, and they are as essential to the comprehensiveness of the Library as are the masterpieces of fiction, some of which are in one *Everyman* volume of anything up to 800 or 900 pages. The new *Everyman's Library* in crown octavo is published at two prices (except in the U.S.A.), according to the length and nature of the work; volumes in red binding and wrapper are at one price and those in blue at a slightly higher price.

This development entails no break in the continuity of the Library; there are at this date nearly 600 volumes in the original format, and they will be obtainable in the old size and at the old price until they are reissued in the new. Four times a year the Publishers issue a prospectus of the volumes to be issued in the larger format during the next three months: this will be sent free to all applicants. A descriptive catalogue of all volumes is also freely available, the annotations giving the year of birth and death of the author, the date of first publication of the work, and a brief description of, or details of the contents of, the last revised *Everyman's Library* edition.

J. M. DENT & SONS LTD.

*December* 1953